BANANAS, BEACHES AND BASES

Cynthia Enloe teaches at Clark University, Massachusetts. She is the author of many books, including *Ethnic Soldiers: State Security in Divided Societies, Ethnic Conflict and Political Development, Comparative Politics of Pollution* and *Does Khaki Become You? The Militarization of Women's Lives* (also published by Pandora Press). She co-edited (with Wendy Chapkis) *Of Common Cloth: Women and the Global Textile Industry.*

W9-AOB-253

BANANAS

BEACHES

& BASES

MAKING FEMINIST SENSE
OF INTERNATIONAL POLITICS

CYNTHIA
ENLOE

University of California Press
Berkeley   Los Angeles   London

First published by Pandora Press,
an imprint of the Trade Division of Unwin Hyman in 1989

First U.S. edition published 1990'
University of California Press
Berkeley and Los Angeles, California

University of California Press, Ltd.
London, England

© Cynthia Enloe 1989

6   7   8   9

Library of Congress Cataloging-in-Publication Data

Enloe, Cynthia H., 1938–
    Bananas, beaches & bases : making feminist sense of
international politics / Cynthia Enloe. — 1st U.S. ed. —
Berkeley : University of California Press, 1990.
    xiii, 244 p. : Ill. ; 23 cm.
    Includes bibliographical references (p. 202–238) and
index.
    ISBN 0-520-06984-6 (alk. paper)
    1. Woman in politics.   2. International relations.
3. Feminist Theory.   I. Title.   II. Title: Bananas, beaches,
and bases.
HQ1236.E55   1990
327'.082—dc20   90-120472
                                            AACR 2   MARC

Printed in the United States of America

The paper used in this publication meets the minimum requirements of
American National Standard for Information Sciences—Permanence of
Paper for Printed Library Materials, ANSI Z39.48–1984. ⊗

for
Joni

CONTENTS

ILLUSTRATIONS

PREFACE

I began this book thinking about Pocahontas and ended it mulling over the life of Carmen Miranda. Pocahontas is buried in Highgate Cemetery in London and Carmen Miranda has a museum dedicated to her in Rio. Neither is the usual starting point for thoughts about contemporary international politics, but each woman made me think in new ways about just how international politics works.

Pocahontas was a Powhantan Indian, the daughter of a tribal chief who acted as an intermediary between her own people and colonizing Englishmen; she later married one of these English settlers and travelled to London, as if confirming that the colonial enterprise was indeed a civilizing mission. She never returned to her New World homeland, however, for she died of civilization's coal dust in her lungs.

Carmen Miranda lived three centuries later, but her life has remarkable parallels with her Indian foresister's. She was a Brazilian grocer's daughter who became a Hollywood star and the symbol of an American president's Latin American policy. She died prematurely of a heart attack, perhaps brought on by the frenzied pace of life in the fast lane of America's pop culture.

These women were not the sorts of international actors I had been taught to take seriously when trying to make sense of world affairs. But the more I thought about Pocahontas and Carmen Miranda, the more I began to suspect that I had been missing an entire dimension of international politics – I got an inkling of how relations between governments depend not only on capital and weaponry, but also on the control of women as symbols, consumers, workers and emotional comforters. I also began to see that brand names like Benetton and Chiquita Banana are more than merely vehicles for making international politics relevant to the already harried book-buyer. These logos, and the processes by which they have been created, marketed and assigned meaning, expose another neglected international *political* relationship. Here I consider women-as-consumers, in both industrialized and Third World countries, as global political actors. Furthermore, as tourism demonstrates, companies and their government allies are marketing things not usually thought of as 'consumer goods': tropical beaches, women's sexuality, the services of flight attendants.

The chapters that follow are just a beginning. Other feminists are also seeking a better explanation of why international politics operate in the ways they do. Some of the most exciting work is being done by Third World feminist theorists, such as Swasti Mitter, Chandra Mohanty and Peggy Antrobus. As the Notes make clear, I am especially indebted to these pioneers. Those whom Adrienne Rich has referred to as 'the women in the back rows of politics' are about to be given the serious attention they have long deserved. All of us, as a result, are likely to become much smarter, more realistic about what kinds of power have constructed the international political system as we know it. From these revelations may come fresh proposals for making relations between countries less violent, more just and ultimately more rewarding for women as well as men.

The idea for this book grew out of conversations with Philippa Brewster, friend and director of Pandora Press – conversations which ranged from feminist musings about polyester fashions and film stars to puzzling over the international politics of feminist publishing. One thing became more and more clear as this sometimes daunting project evolved: it makes a big difference to work with feminist editors. Candida Lacey, the editor for this book, has been of inestimable help in keeping it focused, never forgetting the audience, always remembering the wider world beyond the author's study or the editor's office. We have wrinkled our brows together over the stickier analytical points, and we have laughed out loud over some of the more bizarre discoveries.

It is probably a bit insane to take on the topics covered in this book. It has only been possible to make the attempt because I have had the wise and generous support of insightful friends and colleagues. First and foremost has been Joni Seager, co-author of the ground-breaking feminist atlas, *Women in the World*. There was much less chance of my slipping into parochial assumptions with her as a constant sounding-board, reading every chapter, passing on gems of information that a mere political scientist would never have seen. Others who have read chapters and given me valuable suggestions – and caveats – include Margaret Bluman, Laura Zimmerman, Serena Hilsinger, Ximena Bunster and Margaret Lazarus. Superb copy-editing has been done by Daphne Tagg. Margaret Bluman, my agent for this book, has also encouraged me to think that the questions posed were important ones for women committed to genuine social change.

A political scientist is often a bit intimidated by historians and archivists. But as I pursued my hunches about the light that Pocahontas and Carmen

Miranda might shed on international politics, I knew I had to tread on historians' ground. No one made me feel more at home in this adventure than David Doughan, librarian of the Fawcett Library, that treasure-house of surprising information about British and imperial women's history. Ann Englehart and Barbara Haber both encouraged me to make full use of the splendid resources of Radcliffe College's Schlesinger Library. Edmund Swinglehurst, of the Thomas Cook Archives in London, opened up the world of tourism history. In addition to my own digging, I was aided by the research skills of my brother, David Enloe, as well as Lauran Schultz, Shari Geistfeld and Deb Dunn.

Among the many others who shared their special knowledge with me were Beryl Smedley, Gay Murphy, Mary Ann White, Pam Moffat, Nien Ling Lieu, Susan Parsons, Saralee Hamilton, Jacqui Alexander, Georgina Ashworth, Sr. Soledad Perpinan, Raquel Tiglao, Theresa Capellan, Elizabeth Odour, Lucy Laliberte, Wendy Mishkin, Peter Armitage, Cortez Enloe, Philippe Bourgois, Lois Wasserspring, Ann Holder, Saundra Studevant, Caroline Becraft, Elaine Salo, Elaine Burns, Mary McGinn, Sandina Robbins, Nira Yuval Davis, Christine White, Sidney Mintz, Linda Richter, Rachel Kerian, Laurel Bossen, Beth Schwartz, Peg Strobel, Janice Hill, Julie Wheelwright, Antoinette Burton, Sally Davis, Patrick Miller, Anita Nesiah, Joanne Liddle and Eva Isaksson.

Over the three years during which this book has taken shape I have had my share of misgivings. Generous friends not only have put up with my occasionally odd preoccupations, but have reminded me of the point of pursuing feminist puzzles. So I am, as ever, indebted to each of them for their daily acts of friendship, especially Joni Seager, Gilda Bruckman, Judy Wachs, Serena Hilsinger and Lois Brynes.

1

GENDER MAKES THE WORLD GO ROUND

Ambassadors cabling their home ministries, legislators passing laws to restrict foreign imports, bank executives negotiating overseas loans, soldiers landing on foreign hillsides – these are some of the sites from which one can watch the international political system being made. But if we employ only the conventional, ungendered compass to chart international politics, we are likely to end up mapping a landscape peopled only by men, mostly élite men. The real landscape of international politics is less exclusively male.

A European woman decides to take her holiday in Jamaica because the weather is warm, it is cheap and safe for tourists. In choosing this form of pleasure, she is playing her part in creating the current international political system. She is helping the Jamaican government earn badly needed foreign currency to repay overseas debts. She is transforming 'chambermaid' into a major job category. And, unwittingly, if she travels on holiday with a white man, she may make some Jamaican men, seeing every day the privileges – economic and sexual – garnered by white men, feel humiliated and so nourish nationalist identities rooted in injured masculinity.

A school teacher plans a lesson around the life of Pocahontas, the brave Powhantan 'princess' who saved Captain John Smith from execution at Jamestown and so cleared the way for English colonization of America. The students come away from the lesson believing the convenient myth that local women are likely to be charmed by their own people's conquerors.

In the 1930s Hollywood moguls turned Brazilian singer Carmen Miranda into an American movie star. They were trying to aid President Franklin Roosevelt's efforts to promote friendlier relations between the US and

1

Latin America. When United Fruit executives then drew on Carmen Miranda's popular Latinized female image to create a logo for their imported bananas, they were trying to construct a new, intimate relationship between American housewives and a multinational plantation company. With her famous fruited hats and vivacious screen presence, Carmen Miranda was used by American men to reshape international relations. Carmen Miranda alerts us to the fact that it would be a mistake to confine an investigation of regional politics or international agribusiness to male foreign-policy officials, male company executives and male plantation workers. Omitting sexualized images, women as consumers and women as agribusiness workers, leaves us with a political analysis that is incomplete, even naïve.

When a British soldier on leave from duties in Belize or West Germany decides that he can't tolerate his friends' continuous razzing about being 'queer' and so finally joins them in a visit to a local brothel in order to be 'one of the boys', he is shaping power relations between the British military and the society it is supposed to be protecting. He is also reinforcing one of the crucial bulwarks – masculinity – which permits the British government to use a military force to carry out its foreign policy among its former colonies and within NATO. Military politics, which occupy such a large part of international politics today, require military bases. Bases are artificial societies created out of unequal relations between men and women of different races and classes.

The woman tourist, the Jamaican chambermaid, Carmen Miranda, the American housewife, the British soldier and Belize prostitute are all dancing an intricate international minuet.

But they aren't all in a position to call the tune. Each has been used by the makers of the international political system, but some are more complicit and better rewarded than others. A poor woman who has been deprived of literacy (especially in the language of the ruling group), bank credit or arable land is likely to find that the intrusions of foreign governments and companies in her daily life exacerbate, not relieve, those burdens. The woman tourist may not be Henry Kissinger, but she is far removed from the daily realities confronting the Jamaican woman who is changing her sheets. The American housewife who buys United Fruit bananas because the 'Chiquita' logo gives her a sense of confidence in the product may not be Margaret Thatcher, but the problems she confronts as a woman are less acute than those facing the Latin American fruit vendor making a living on the streets.

Power infuses all international relationships. Most of us, understandably, would prefer to think That our attraction to a certain food company's marketing logo is a cultural, not a political act. We would like to imagine that going on holiday to Bermuda rather than Grenada is merely a social, even aesthetic matter, not a question of politics. But in these last decades of the twentieth century, that unfortunately isn't so. Company logos are designed to nourish certain presumptions we have about different cultures; usually they reinforce global hierarchies between countries. Similarly, tourism has become a business that is maintaining dozens of governments. Power, not simply taste, is at work here. Ignoring women on the landscape of international politics perpetuates the notion that certain power relations are merely a matter of taste and culture. Paying serious attention to women can expose how *much* power it takes to maintain the international political system in its present form.

American popular culture today demands that any political idea worth its salt should fit on a bumper sticker. A feminist theory bumper sticker might say, 'Nothing is natural – well, almost nothing'. As one learns to look at this world through feminist eyes, one learns to ask whether anything that passes for inevitable, inherent, 'traditional' or biological has in fact been *made*. One begins to ask how all sorts of things have been made – a treeless landscape, a rifle-wielding police force, the 'Irishman joke', an all-women typing pool. Asking how something has been made implies that it has been made by someone. Suddenly there are clues to trace; there is also blame, credit and responsibility to apportion, not just at the start but at each point along the way.

The presumption that something that gives shape to how we live with one another is inevitable, a 'given', is hard to dislodge. It seems easier to imagine that something oozes up from an indeterminate past, that it has never been deliberately concocted, does not need to be maintained, that it's just there. But if the treeless landscape or all-women typing pool can be shown to be the result of someone's decision and has to be perpetuated, then it is possible to imagine alternatives. 'What if. . .?' can be a radical question.

Conventionally both masculinity and femininity have been treated as 'natural', not created. Today, however, there is mounting evidence that they are packages of expectations that have been created through specific decisions by specific people. We are also coming to realize that the traditional concepts of masculinity and femininity have been surprisingly hard to perpetuate: it has required the daily exercise of power – domestic power, national power, and, as we will see, international power.

So far feminist analysis has had little impact on international politics. Foreign-policy commentators and decision-makers seem particularly confident in dismissing feminist ideas. Rare is the professional commentator on international politics who takes women's experiences seriously. Women's experiences – of war, marriage, trade, travel, factory work –

are relegated to the 'human interest' column. Women's roles in creating and sustaining international politics have been treated as if they were 'natural' and thus not worthy of investigation. Consequently, how the conduct of international politics has *depended* on men's control of women has been left unexamined. This has meant that those wielding influence over foreign policy have escaped responsibility for how women have been affected by international politics.

Perhaps international politics has been impervious to feminist ideas precisely because for so many centuries in so many cultures it has been thought of as a typically 'masculine' sphere of life. Only men, not women or children, have been imagined capable of the sort of public decisiveness international politics is presumed to require. Foreign affairs are written about with a total disregard for feminist revelations about how power depends on sustaining notions about masculinity and femininity. Local housing officials, the assumption goes, may have to take women's experiences into account now and then. Social workers may have to pay some attention to feminist theorizing about poverty. Trade-union leaders and economists have to give at least a nod in the direction of feminist explanations of wage inequalities. Yet officials making international policy and their professional critics are freed from even a token consideration of women's experiences and feminist understandings of those experiences.

This book aims to cast doubt on those comfortable assumptions. By taking women's experiences of international politics seriously, I think we can acquire a more realistic understanding of how international politics actually 'works'. We may also increase women's confidence in using their own experiences and knowledge as the basis for making sense of the sprawling, abstract structure known as 'the international political economy'. Women should no longer have to disguise their feminist curiosity when they speak up on issues of international significance.

Even women who have learned how crucial it is to always ask feminist questions – about welfare, science, bus routes, police procedures – have found it hard to ask feminist questions in the midst of a discussion about the international implications of Soviet *perestroika* or Britain's trade policies in the European Economic Community. We are made to feel silly. Many women find it tempting to build up credibility in this still-masculinized area of political discussion by lowering their voices an octave, adjusting their body postures and demonstrating that they can talk 'boy's talk' as well as their male colleagues. One result of women not being able to speak out is that we may have an inaccurate understanding of how power relations between countries are created and perpetuated. Silence has made us dumb.

Relations between governments involve the workings of at least two

4

societies – sometimes twenty. Thinking about international politics is most meaningful when it derives from contact with the diverse values, anxieties and memories of people in those societies. Yet such access is itself gendered. As a British woman explained at the first meeting of the European Forum of Socialist Feminists, 'In this world it is men who do the travelling. They are so much more mobile, have so many more forums than women do – military, financial, they even have spy rings! Whereas it's rare for women to have any kind of international forum, organized by and for us.'[1]

So when women do manage to get together at their own meetings – not just in caucuses of other people's meetings – they usually become absorbed in making comparisons. In international forums women today are comparing how racism and class barriers divide women in their respective societies. We are comparing different explanations for the persistence of sexism and strategies for ending that sexism, but it is difficult to get the chance to work together to create a feminist description of the larger international frameworks that link women. For instance, when groups of women from several countries in Europe meet, do they try to hammer out a feminist analysis of 'Europe', or use their international comparisons as the basis for a fresh explanation of the political workings of NATO and the European Community? Usually they don't have an opportunity to do so. As a result, international politics remains relatively untouched by feminist thought.[2]

It's difficult to imagine just what feminist questioning would sound like in the area of international politics. Some women have come to believe that there is a fundamental difference between men and women. 'Virtually everyone at the top of the foreign-policy bureaucracies is male,' they argue, 'so how could the outcome be other than violent international conflict?' That is, men are men, and men seem almost inherently prone to violence; so violence is bound to come about if men are allowed to dominate international politics. At times this sweeping assertion has the unsettling ring of truth. There's scarcely a woman who on a dark day hasn't had a suspicion this just might be so. Yet most of the women from various cultures who have created the theories and practices which add up to feminism have not found this 'essentialist' argument convincing. Digging into the past and present has made them reluctant to accept explanations that rest on an assertion that men and women are inherently different.

Men trying to invalidate any discussion of gender in international politics tend to quote a litany of militaristic women leaders: 'Well, if you think it's men who are causing all the international violence, what about Margaret Thatcher, Indira Gandhi and Jeanne Kirkpatrick?' Most

5

women – or men – who have been treating feminist analyses seriously have little trouble in responding to this now ritualistic jibe. It's quite clear to them that a woman isn't inherently or irreversibly anti-militaristic or anti-authoritarian. It's not a matter of her chromosomes or her menstrual cycle. It's a matter of social processes and structures that have been created and sustained over the generations – sometimes coercively – to keep most women out of any political position with influence over state force. On occasion, élite men *may* let in a woman here or a woman there, but these women aren't randomly selected.

Most of the time we scarcely notice that governments look like men's clubs. We see a photo of members of the Soviet Union's Politburo, or the US Cabinet's sub-committee on national security, of negotiators at a Geneva textile bargaining session, and it's easy to miss the fact that all the people in these photographs are men. One of the most useful functions that Margaret Thatcher has served is to break through our numbness. When Margaret Thatcher stood in Venice with Mitterand, Nakasone, Reagan and the other heads of state, we suddenly noticed that everyone else was male. One woman in a photo makes it harder to ignore that the men are men.

However, when a woman is let in by the men who control the political élite it usually is precisely because that woman has learned the lessons

1   Margaret Thatcher and other heads of government meeting at the Venice Summit in September 1987. (photo: Daniel Simon/Frank Spooner Pictures, London)

of masculinized political behaviour well enough not to threaten male political privilege. Indeed she may even entrench that privilege, for when a Margaret Thatcher or Jeanne Kirkpatrick uses her state office to foment international conflict, that conflict looks less man-made, more people-made, and thus more legitimate and harder to reverse.

Still, being able to counter the 'What about Margaret Thatcher?' taunt isn't by itself a satisfactory basis for a full feminist analysis of international politics. We have to push further, open up new political terrain, listen carefully to new voices.

A fictional James Bond may have an energetic sex life, but neither sexuality nor notions of manhood nor roles of women are taken seriously by most commentators in the 'real' world of power relations between societies and their governments. What really matters, conventional international observers imply, are money, guns and the personalities of leaders – of the men who make up the political élite. The processes holding sway in most societies have been designed so that it is mainly men who have the opportunities to accumulate money, control weaponry and become public personalities. As a consequence, any investigation that treats money, guns and personalities as the key ingredients in relations between societies is almost guaranteed to obliterate women from the picture.

WHERE ARE THE WOMEN?
CLUES FROM THE IRAN/CONTRA AFFAIR

In July 1987 I turn on my television to watch the congressional hearings on the Iran/Contra affair. Senior members of the Reagan administration are accused of selling weapons to the Iranian government and funnelling the proceeds to the anti-Sandinista rebels in Nicaragua in violation of congressional policy. All of the congressional representatives sitting at their tiers of desks under the media's bright lights are men. All but one of the congressional committees' lawyers asking questions are men. All but two of the scores of witnesses subpoenaed to answer their questions are men. All of their attorneys are men. All of the men have been told that dark blue suits and red ties look best on television. Everyone wears a dark blue suit and a red tie.

The Iran/Contra hearings are heralded as the event of the decade in international politics. Now we, the ordinary folk, are going to see how foreign policy actually gets made. Some of my friends become hooked on the congressional hearings: watching or listening from morning to evening, arranging their work and social schedules so as not to miss a word. In Britain, Canada and Australia TV viewers see excerpts every evening. As much as Europe's endless drizzle, the Iran/Contra hearings seem to define the summer of 1987. Information from the hearings is woven into popular culture. There are 'instant books', songs and jokes, 'I luv Ollie' T-shirts, even Ollie North and Betsy North haircuts.

Women do appear during the hearings, though their appearances confirm rather than disturb the implied naturalness of the otherwise all-male cast. Maybe it's because all the women captured by the media's eye are so marginalized.

Ellen Garwood is one of the few women called to the witness table. She is a wealthy conservative who has donated over $2 million to the Contras after being appealed to by Colonel North and other American Contra fund raisers. Congressmen and their attorneys ask her about how her donation was solicited. They aren't interested in her views on US foreign policy. She is not a retired general or a former CIA agent. A public opinion survey comes out at about this time showing that American women are significantly less enthusiastic about US aid to the Contras than are American men, especially American white men.[3] But such revelations do not prompt any of the legislators to ask Ellen Garwood for her foreign policy ideas.

Women appear so infrequently that their very appearance in any authoritative role becomes 'news'. One day a woman assistant-attorney for the congressional committee appears on TV. She asks a minor witness questions. Feminist viewers sit up and take notice. One viewer counts seven young women sitting on the chairs arranged awkwardly just behind the congressmen. They don't speak in public. They are staff aides, ready to serve their male bosses.

Men comprise the majority of the media people assigned to tell us what each day's revelations 'mean'. The women reporters covering the hearings for radio and television do take extra care with their gender pronouns, yet shy away from posing any feminist questions. They haven't climbed this high on the news media ladder by questioning how masculinity and femininity might be shaping foreign policy. They must take care to look feminine while still sounding as though gender were irrelevant to their commentary.[4]

The one woman witness who becomes front page news is Fawn Hall. She is the 27-year-old who worked in the National Security Council as civil-service secretary to Oliver North and who admits assisting her boss in shredding important government documents. Fawn Hall is routinely described, even by the most low-key media commentators, as 'the beautiful Fawn Hall'. It's as if Fawn Hall is meant to represent the feminine side of High Politics of the 1980s: worldly, stylish, exciting, sexy. Beauty, secrecy and state power: they all enhance one another. In the élite politics of the present era, the 'beautiful secretary', the 'handsome, can-do military officer', and the bureaucratic shredding machine make an almost irresistible combination.[5]

There are at least two sorts of feminized beauty, however: the revealed and the hidden. Fawn Hall is set up as beauty revealed. She stands in stark contrast to the popularly constructed image of beauty hidden: the veiled Muslim woman. Until it began selling weapons to Iran, the Reagan administration liked to emphasize the Iranian regime's wrong-headed regressiveness by pointing to its anti-modern confinement of women. Reagan aides thought their arms sales were giving them access to a moderate 'second channel' in the Teheran political élite. Does the Iranian 'second channel' insist his secretary wear a veil? I try to imagine what Fawn Hall and the 'second channel's' secretary, if they ever had a chance to meet, would find they had in common, as government secretaries to male bosses carrying out secret operations.

Some Republicans deem Fawn Hall worthy of imitation, if not emulation. In Arkansas Republican party activists hold a gathering to celebrate Oliver North with "Ollie Dogs" on the grill, tough-talking T-shirts, water-melons and 95° heat', according to the press report. There is also a Fawn Hall look-alike contest. Women entering the contest have to perform dramatic readings of Fawn Hall's congressional testimony and act her feeding documents into a paper shredder. The winner is sixteen-year-old Renee Kumpee, who, when asked about her attitude to Oliver North, replies, 'I like him OK.'[6]

Women supply most of the clerical labor force that has made the complex communications, money transfers and arms shipments possible. They handle the procedures and technology, and more importantly, they provide many male officials with on-the-job encouragement. In today's international political system, large bureaucracies are vehicles for making, implementing and remembering decisions. Since the deliberate feminization of clerical work in the early twentieth century, every government has required women to acquire certain skills and attitudes towards their work, their superiors and themselves. Even in small states without the huge bureaucratic machines the public agencies rely on women for their smooth running. If secretaries went out on strike, foreign affairs might grind to a standstill. Without women's willingness to fill these positions in acceptably feminine ways, many men in posts of international influence might be less able to convince themselves of their own rationality, courage and seriousness.

Other Washington secretaries felt ambivalent towards Fawn Hall. They resented the media for treating Fawn Hall as the quintessential government secretary. 'I guess the media wouldn't be making such a big deal out of it if she had been fifty years old and not blond.' Still, they also saw Fawn Hall's dilemma as their own. 'You develop personal relationships when you work in a high-pressure operation like that. . . She was more than a receptionist or a typist, and she was expected to keep things confidential.' Patricia Holmes, a Black woman working as a secretary in the Department of the Interior, summed up many Washington secretaries' feelings: Fawn Hall was caught 'between a rock and a hard place'.[7]

Each woman who appears in person during the Iran/Contra proceedings is considered peripheral to the 'real' political story. None of their stories is interpreted in a way that could transform the masculinized meaning of complex international political relationships. Most of us see them as marginal characters who simply add 'color' to the all-male, blue-suited, red-tied political proceedings.

Several of the male witnesses assure their congressional interrogators that they took their state jobs so seriously that they didn't tell 'even their wives' about the secrets they were guarding. On the other hand, they expected to receive from their wives an automatic stamp of moral approval. This is the kind of marriage on which the national-security state depends.

Thousands of women today tailor their marriages to fit the peculiar demands of states operating in a trust-starved international system. Some of those women are married to men who work as national-security advisors; others have husbands who are civilian weapons-engineers working on classified contracts; still others are married to foreign-service careerists. Most of these men would not be deemed trustworthy if they were not in 'stable' marriages. Being a reliable husband and a man the state can trust with its secrets appear to be connected.

And yet it is precisely that elevation to a position of state confidence which can shake the foundations of a marriage. Patriotic marriages may serve the husbands, giving them a greater sense of public importance and less of a sense of guilt for damaging the lives of people in other countries. And they serve the national-security state. But they don't necessarily provide the women in those marriages with satisfaction or self-esteem. Typically, it is left up to the wife to cope with the tensions and disappointments. She may respond by trying to cultivate interests of her own outside her marriage, investing her relationship with her distracted husband with less importance than she once did. Or she may continue to see her relationship with her husband as her most important friendship, but adjust her notion of it so that it becomes a marriage of unequals: she will continue to confide in him all her hopes and worries, while resigning herself to hearing from him only what is 'unclassified'. In such cases some women express admiration for their husbands' patriotism, a patriotism they believe, as wives, they cannot match. This is the stance taken by Betsy North. She is praised. Her haircut becomes the new fashion.

Marriages between élite men and patriotic wives are a building block holding up the international political system. It can continue to work the way it now does, dependent on secrecy, risk-taking and state loyalty, only if men can convince women to accept the sorts of marriages that not only sustain, but also legitimize, that system. And it isn't just marriages at the pinnacles of power that must be made to fit. As we will see, marriages up and down the international pyramid can jeopardize power relations between governments if the women refuse to play their parts. They must be willing to see their husbands leave home for long periods of time – as multinational plantation workers, as migrant workers on Middle East construction projects, as soldiers posted to foreign bases. Women working as domestic servants must be willing to leave their husband and children to service other families and, in the process, their country's foreign debt. But no one asked either Betsy North or the wife of a Honduran banana-plantation worker what her analysis was of the international political system that produced the Iran/Contra affair.

One of the beliefs that informs this book is this: if we listened to women more carefully – to those trying to break out of the strait-jacket of conventional femininity *and* to those who find security and satisfaction in those very conventions – and if we made concepts such as 'wife', 'mother', 'sexy broad' central to our investigations, we might find that the Iran/Contra affair and international politics generally looked different. It's not that we would abandon our curiosity about arms dealers, presidents' men and concepts such as 'covert operations'. Rather, we would no longer find them sufficient to understand how the international political system works.

MASCULINITY AND INTERNATIONAL POLITICS

Making women invisible hides the workings of both femininity and masculinity in international politics. Some women watching the Iran/Contra hearings found it useful to speculate about how the politics of masculinity shape foreign-policy debates. They considered the verbal rituals that public men use to blunt the edges of their mutual antagonism. A congressman would, for instance, preface a devastating attack on Admiral Poindexter's rationale for destroying a document by reassuring the admiral – and his male colleagues – that he believed the admiral was 'honorable' and 'a gentleman'. Another congressman would insist that, despite his differences with Reagan officials Robert McFarlane and

Oliver North, he considered them to be 'patriots'. Would these same male members of Congress, selected for this special committee partly because they had experience of dealing with military officers and foreign-policy administrators, have used the word 'honorable' if the witness had been a woman? Would 'patriot' have been the term of respect if these men had been commending a woman? There appeared to be a platform of trust holding up these investigations of US foreign policy. It was a platform that was supported by pillars of masculinity, pillars that were never subjected to political scrutiny, but which had to be maintained by daily personal exchanges, memos and formal policy.

A theme that surfaced repeatedly during the weeks of the Iran/Contra hearings was 'We live in a dangerous world'. Critics as well as supporters of selling arms to Iran and using the profits to fund the Contras were in agreement on this view of the world in 1987. No one chimed in with, 'Well, I don't know; it doesn't feel so dangerous to me.' No one questioned this portrayal of the world as permeated by risk and violence. No one even attempted to redefine 'danger' by suggesting that the world may indeed be dangerous, but especially so for those people who are losing access to land or being subjected to unsafe contraceptives. Instead, the vision that informed these male officials' foreign-policy choices was of a world in which two super-powers were eyeball-to-eyeball, where small risks were justified in the name of staving off bigger risks – the risk of Soviet expansion, the risk of nuclear war. It was a world in which taking risks was proof of one's manliness and therefore of one's qualification to govern. Listening to these officials, I was struck by the similarity to the 'manliness' now said to be necessary for success in the international financial markets. With Britain's 'Big Bang', which deregulated its financial industry, and with the French and Japanese deregulators following close behind, financial observers began to warn that the era of gentlemanliness in banking was over. British, European and Japanese bankers and stockbrokers would now have to adopt the more robust, competitive form of manliness associated with American bankers. It wouldn't necessarily be easy. There might even be some resistance. Thus international finance and international diplomacy seem to be converging in their notions of the world and the kind of masculinity required to wield power in that world in the 1990s.[8]

At first glance, this portrayal of danger and risk is a familiar one, rooted in capitalist and Cold War ideology. But when it's a patriarchal world that is 'dangerous', masculine men and feminine women are expected to react in opposite but complementary ways. A 'real man' will become the protector in such a world. He will suppress his own fears, brace himself and step forward to defend the weak, women and children. In the same 'dangerous world' women will turn gratefully and expectantly to their fathers and husbands, real or surrogate. If a woman is a mother, then she will think first of her children, protecting them not in a manly way, but as a self-sacrificing mother. In this fashion, the 'dangerous world' evoked repeatedly in the Iran/Contra hearings is upheld by unspoken notions about masculinity. Ideas of masculinity have to be perpetuated to justify foreign-policy risk-taking. To accept the Cold War interpretation of living in a 'dangerous' world also confirms the segregation of politics into national and international. The national political arena is dominated by men but allows women some select access; the international political arena is a sphere for men only, or for those rare women who can successfully play at being men, or at least not shake masculine presumptions.

Notions of masculinity aren't necessarily identical across generations or across cultural boundaries. An Oliver North may be a peculiarly American phenomenon. He doesn't have a carbon copy in current British or Japanese politics. Even the Hollywood character 'Rambo', to whom so many likened Oliver North, may take on rather different meanings in America, Britain and Japan.[9] A Lebanese Shiite militiaman may be fulfilling an explicitly masculinist mandate, but it would be a mistake to collapse the values he represents into those of a British SAS officer or an American 'Rambo'. Introducing masculinity into a discussion of international politics, and thereby making men visible as men, should prompt us to explore differences in the politics of masculinity between countries – and between ethnic groups in the same country.

These differences have ignited nationalist movements which have challenged the existing international order, dismantling empires, ousting foreign bases, expropriating foreign mines and factories. But there have been nationalist movements which have engaged in such world challenges without upsetting patriarchal relationships within that nation. It is important, I think, to understand which kinds of nationalist movement rely on the perpetuation of patriarchal ideas of masculinity for their international political campaigns and which kinds see redefining masculinity as integral to re-establishing national sovereignty. Women do not benefit automatically every time the international system is re-ordered by a successful nationalist movement. It has taken awareness, questioning and organizing by women inside those nationalist movements to turn nationalism into something good for women.

In conventional commentaries men who wield influence in international politics are analyzed in terms of their national identities, their class origins and their paid work. Rarely are they analyzed as men who have been taught how to be manly, how to size up the trustworthiness or competence of other men in terms of their manliness. If international commentators do find masculinity interesting, it is typically when they try to make sense of 'great men' – Teddy Roosevelt, Winston Churchill, Mao Tse–t'ung – not when they seek to understand humdrum plantation workers or foreign tourists. Such men's presumptions about how to be masculine in doing their jobs, exercising influence, or seeking relief from stress are made invisible. Here are some examples:

● In 1806 executives of the Northwest Company decided it was no longer good international company politics for their trappers to take Native Canadian women as their wives; they calculated that it was more advantageous to encourage their Canadian white male employees to import European women. That was a self-conscious use of power to reshape the relationships between women and men for the sake of achieving specific international goals. The decisions of managers in London altered the way in which Canada was integrated into the British empire. It was an imperial strategy that relied on the currencies of gender and race.[10]

● When US Defense Department officials insisted that the Philippines government take responsibility for conducting physical examinations of all women working in the bars around the American military bases in the Philippines, it affected the lives of thousands of young Filipinas and sent a clear message to thousands of American sailors and Air Force pilots. The message symbolized the unequal alliance between the US and Philippines governments. Its implementation rooted that government-to-government inequality in the everyday lives of American military men and Filipino working women.[11]

The chapters that follow explore some accepted arenas of international politics: nationalist movements, diplomacy, military expansion, international debt. However, we will examine these familiar realms from unconventional vantage points. We will listen to male nationalist leaders worrying about their women abandoning traditional feminine roles. Those masculine worries and nationalist women's responses to them will be taken as seriously as male nationalists' strategies for ousting colonial rulers. We will look at diplomacy by listening to wives of foreign-service careerists. To understand how military alliances actually work, we will consider the experiences of women who live and work around military bases and women who have camped outside those bases in protest. We will explore bankers' international operations by paying attention to women who have to live on austerity budgets or work in factories, hotels and other people's kitchens in order for government debts to be serviced.

Later chapters explore areas assumed to fall outside 'international politics'. Looking at fashions in clothing and food sheds light on the

14

relationships between affluent and developing countries. The often difficult relationships between domestic servants and the middle-class women who hire them will be examined to make sense of new trends in international politics. We will take a close look at the foreign travel of Victorian women explorers and present-day businessmen to understand how power between countries is made and challenged. We will listen to women married to diplomats in order to see to what extent governments' foreign-policy machinery depends on notions of wifely duty.

BEYOND THE GLOBAL VICTIM

Some men and women active in campaigns to influence their country's foreign policy – on the right as well as the left – have called on women to become more involved in international issues, to learn more about 'what's going on in the world': 'You have to take more interest in international affairs because it affects how you live.' The gist of the argument is that women need to devote precious time and energy to learning about events outside their own country because as women they are the objects of those events. For instance, a woman working in a garment factory in Ireland should learn more about the European Economic Community because what the EEC commissioners do in Brussels is going to help determine her wages and maybe even the hazards she faces on the job. An American woman will be encouraged to learn the difference between a cruise and Pershing missile because international nuclear strategies are shaping her and her children's chances of a safe future.

Two things are striking about this line of argument. First, the activists who are trying to persuade women to 'get involved' are not inviting women to reinterpret international politics by drawing on their own experiences as women. If the explanations of how the EEC or nuclear rivalry works don't already include any concepts of femininity, masculinity or patriarchy, they are unlikely to after the women join the movement. Because organizers aren't curious about what women's experiences could lend to an understanding of international politics, many women, especially those whose energies are already stretched to the limit, are wary of becoming involved in an international campaign. It can seem like one more attempt by privileged outsiders – women and men – to dilute their political efforts. If women are asked to join an international campaign – for peace, against communism, for refugees, against apartheid, for religious evangelism, against hunger – but are not allowed to define the problem, it looks to many locally engaged women like abstract do-gooding with minimal connection to the battles for a decent life in their households and in their communities.

Second, the typical 'women-need-to-learn-more-about-foreign-affairs' approach usually portrays women as victims of the international political system. Women should learn about the EEC, the United Nations, the CIA, the IMF, NATO, the Warsaw Pact, the 'greenhouse effect' because each has an impact on them. In this world view, women are forever being acted upon; rarely are they seen to be actors.

It's true that in international politics women historically have not had access to the resources enabling them to wield influence. Today women are at the bottom of most international hierarchies: women are routinely paid less than even the lowest-paid men in multinational companies; women are two thirds of all refugees. Women activists have a harder time influencing struggling ethnic nationalist movements than do men; women get less of the ideological and job rewards from fighting in foreign wars than do men. Though a pretty dismal picture, it can tell us a lot about how the international political system has been designed and how it is maintained every day: some men at the top, most women at the bottom.

But in many arenas of power feminists have been uncovering a reality that is less simple. First, they have discovered that some women's class aspirations and their racist fears lured them into the role of controlling other women for the sake of imperial rule. British, American, Dutch, French, Spanish, Portuguese women may not have been the architects of their countries' colonial policies, but many of them took on the roles of colonial administrators' wives, missionaries, travel writers and anthropologists in ways that tightened the noose of colonial rule around the necks of African, Latin American and Asian women. To describe colonization as a process that has been carried on solely by men overlooks the ways in which male colonizers' success depended on some women's complicity. Without the willingness of 'respectable' women to see that colonization offered them an opportunity for adventure, or a new chance of financial security or moral commitment, colonization would have been even more problematic.[12]

Second, feminists who listen to women working for multinational corporations have heard these women articulate their own strategies for coping with their husbands' resentment, their foremen's sexual harassment and the paternalism of male union leaders. To depict these women merely as passive victims in the international politics of the banana or garment industries doesn't do them justice. It also produces an inaccurate picture of how these global systems operate. Corporate executives and development technocrats need some women to depend on cash wages; they need some women to see a factory or plantation job as a means of delaying marriage or fulfilling daughterly obligations. Without women's own needs, values and worries, the global assembly line would grind to a halt. But many of those needs, values and worries are defined by patriarchal structures and strictures. If fathers, brothers, husbands didn't gain some privilege, however small in global terms, from women's acquiescence to those confining notions of femininity, it might be much harder for the foreign executives and their local élite allies to recruit the cheap labor they desire. Consequently, women's capacity to challenge the men in their families, their communities or their political movements, will be a key to remaking the world.

'So what?' one may ask. A book about international politics ought to leave one with a sense that 'I can do something'. A lot of books about international politics don't. They leave one with the sense that 'it's all so complex, decided by people who don't know or care that I exist'. The spread of capitalist economics, even in countries whose officials call themselves socialists, can feel as inevitable as the tides. Governments' capacity to wound people, to destroy environments and dreams, is constantly expanding through their use of science and bureaucracy. International relationships fostered by these governments and their allies use our labor and our imaginations, but it seems beyond our reach to alter them. They have added up to a world that can dilute the liveliest of cultures, a world that can turn tacos and sushi into bland fast foods, globalize video pornography and socialize men from dozens of cultures into a common new culture of technocratic management. One closes most books on 'international political economy' with a sigh. They explain how it works, but that knowledge only makes one feel as though it is more rewarding to concentrate on problems closer to home.

Hopefully, the chapters that follow will provoke quite a different feeling. They suggest that the world is something that has been made; therefore, it can be remade. The world has been made with blunt power, but also with sleights of hand. Perhaps international policy-makers find it more 'manly' to think of themselves as dealing in guns and money rather than in notions of femininity. So they – and most of their critics as well – have tried to hide and deny their reliance on women as feminized workers, as respectable and loyal wives, as 'civilizing influences', as sex objects, as obedient daughters, as unpaid farmers, as coffee-serving campaigners, as consumers and tourists. If we can expose their dependence on feminizing women, we can show that this world system is also dependent on artificial notions of masculinity: this seemingly overwhelming world system may be more fragile and open to radical change than we have been led to imagine.

Some women have already begun the difficult process of trying to create a new international political system. Many point to the conference in Nairobi, Kenya, in 1985 to mark the end of the United Nations Decade of Women as a watershed. For eighty years Nairobi women had been trying to build new international alliances, especially to end men's exclusive right to vote in national elections and to end the exploitation of women as mothers and as prostitutes by national and imperial armies. Some of those efforts made international élites nervous. Occasionally, they wittingly or unwittingly entrenched gendered hierarchies of international power. They elevated motherhood to a political status; they made feminine respectability a criterion for political legitimacy; they proposed that white women should be the political mentors of women of color. An international feminist alliance, as we will see, doesn't automatically weaken male-run imperialist ventures. In the late 1980s there are fresh understandings, therefore, of the ways in which international feminist theorizing and organizing has to be rooted in clear explanations of how women from different, often unequal societies, are used to sustain the world patterns that feminists seek to change. Women organizing to challenge UN agencies, the International Monetary Fund or multinational corporations are developing theory and strategies simultaneously. A feminist international campaign lacking a feminist analysis of international politics is likely to subvert its own ultimate goals. Among the sectors – 'subsystems' – of the world political system that are being most affected by internationalized feminist organizing today are prostitution; population politics; development assistance; military alliances; textile and electronics production.

It takes a lot of information-gathering, a lot of thinking, a lot of trial and error and a lot of emotionally draining work to understand how notions about femininity and masculinity create and sustain global inequalities and oppressions in just one of these sectors. Yet a truly effective international feminism requires us to make sense of how patriarchal ideas and practices link all of these sectors to each other – and to other relationships whose gendered dynamics we have scarcely begun to fathom.

Thus this book is only a beginning. It draws on the theoretical and organizational work of women in 1890s Britain, 1950s Algeria, 1980s Philippines. Most of the conclusions are tentative. What readers write in the margins of these pages as they test the descriptions and explanations against their own experiences of internationalized femininity and masculinity will be at least as important in creating a different world as what appears here in deceptively solid print.

2

ON THE BEACH:
SEXISM AND TOURISM

The Portuguese woman perched on the ladder seems to be enjoying her work. Wearing a colorful dress under several layers of aprons, she is not too busy picking olives to smile at the photographer.

Selecting postcards is one of those seemingly innocent acts that has become fraught with ideological risks. Imagine for a minute that you are a British woman travelling in Portugal. You have saved for this holiday and are thoroughly enjoying the time away from stress and drizzle. But you haven't left your feminist consciousness at home. You think about the lives of the Portuguese women you see. That is one of the reasons you search the postcard racks to find pictures of Portuguese women engaged in relatively ordinary occupations – weaving, making pottery, pulling in heavy fishing nets, hoeing fields or harvesting olives. These are the images of Portuguese women you want to send your friends back home.

Still, you are a bit uneasy when you realize that in the eyes of those Portuguese women you are probably just another northern tourist able to afford leisurely travel outside her own country. They know you don't search for those less picturesque but no less real images of Portuguese women's lives today: women working in the new plastics factories around Porto, marking Portugal's entrance into the European Common Market; women working as chambermaids in hotels, representing the country's dependence on tourism. Such pictures wouldn't mesh with the holiday image you want to share with friends back in damp, chilly Britain.

No matter how good the feminist tourist's intention, the relationship between the British woman on holiday and the working women of Portugal seems to fall short of international sisterhood. But is it exploitation? As uncomfortable as we are when we look at women smiling out from foreign postcards, we might pause before leaping to the conclusion that they are merely one more group of victims under the heel of international capital. Women in many countries are being drawn into unequal relationships with each other as a result of governments' sponsorship of the international tourist industry, some because they have no choice, but others because they are making their own decisions about how to improve their lives. Many women are playing active roles in expanding and shaping the tourist industry – as travel agents, travel writers, flight attendants, craftswomen, chambermaids – even if they don't control it.

Similarly, women who travel are not merely creatures of privilege; nor today are they only from Western societies. They – or their mothers – have often had to fight against confining presumptions of feminine respectability to travel away from home on their own.

The hushed and serious tones typically reserved for discussions of nuclear escalation or spiraling international debt are rarely used in discussions of tourism. Tourism doesn't fit neatly into public preoccupations with military conflict and high finance. Although it is infused with masculine ideas about adventure, pleasure and the exotic, those are deemed 'private' and thus kept off stage in debates about international politics. Yet since World War II, planners, investors and workers in the tourist industry, and tourists themselves, have been weaving unequal patterns that are restructuring international politics. And they depend on women for their success.

By the mid-1980s, the global tourism business employed more people than the oil industry. These employees were servicing an estimated 200 million people who each year pack their bags and pocket their Berlitz phrase books to become international tourists.[1] The numbers continue to rise steadily. The United Nations World Tourism Organization forecasts that by the year 2000, tourism will have become the single most important global economic activity.[2]

The British woman's dilemma in trying to find a postcard expressing sisterhood rather than exploitation suggests that the galloping tourist industry is not necessarily making the world a more equal or harmonious place. Charter flights, time-share beach condominiums, and Himalayan trekking parties each carry with them power as well as pleasure. While tourism's supporters cite increased government revenues and modernizing influences, its critics ask whether tourism's remarkable growth is narrowing or widening the gap between the affluent and the poor. They question whether the foreign currency, new airstrips and hotels that come with the tourist industry really are adequate compensations for the exacerbation of racial tensions and other problems that so often accompany tourism.[3]

FOOT-LOOSE AND GENDERED

Tourism has its own political history, reaching back to the Roman empire. It overlaps with other forms of travel that appear to be less dedicated to pleasure. Government missions, military tours of duty, business trips, scientific explorations, forced migrations – women and men have experienced them differently, in ways that have helped construct today's global tourism industry and the international political system it sustains.

In many societies being feminine has been defined as sticking close to home. Masculinity, by contrast, has been the passport for travel. Feminist geographers and ethnographers have been amassing evidence revealing that a principal difference between women and men in countless societies has been the licence to travel away from a place thought of as 'home'.

A woman who travels away from the ideological protection of 'home' and without the protection of an acceptable male escort is likely to be tarred with the brush of 'unrespectability'. She risks losing her honor or being blamed for any harm that befalls her on her travels. One need only think of the lack of sympathy accorded a woman who has been assaulted when trying to hitchhike on her own: 'What does she expect, after all?' Some women may unwittingly reinforce the patriarchal link between respectable womanhood and geographical confinement with their own gestures of defiance. A bumper sticker has begun to appear on women's well-travelled vans: 'Good girls go to Heaven. Bad girls go everywhere.'

By contrast a man is deemed less than manly until he breaks away from home and strikes out on his own. Some men leave the farm and travel to the city or mining town looking for work. Other men set off hitchhiking with only a knapsack and a good pair of boots. Still others answer the call to 'Join the Navy and see the world'.

'I cut off my hair and dressed me in a suit of my husband's having had the precaution to quilt the waistcoat to preserve my breasts from hurt which were not large enough to betray my sex and putting on the wig and hat I had prepared I went out and brought me a silver hilted sword and some Holland shirts.'[4] So Christian Davies set off in the 1690s to enlist in the British army. If she couldn't travel as a woman, she would disguise herself as a man. The stories of Christian and women like her are not unmixed tales of feminist rebellion, however. While some of the women ran away to sea or enlisted as drummer boys to escape suffocating village life, others claimed they were simply acting as a loyal wife or sweetheart, following their man.

21

If a woman was exposed – while being treated for a battle wound or giving birth – the punishment she received frequently depended on which of these two interpretations was believed by the men who pulled away her disguise.

Vita Sackville-West came from a privileged background but she emulated her working-class sisters and resorted to male disguise. After World War I demobilized veterans were a common sight in Europe. In 1920 Vita dressed as a man and ran away to Paris impulsively with her woman lover. In this masculine camouflage she felt liberated:

> the evenings were ours. I have never told a soul of what I did. I hesitate to write it here, but I must. . .I dressed as a boy. It was easy, because I could put a khaki bandage round my head, which in those days was so common that it attracted no attention at all. I browned my face and hands. It must have been successful, because no one looked at me at all curiously or suspiciously. . .I looked like a rather untidy young man, a sort of undergraduate, of about nineteen. I shall never forget the evenings when we walked back slowly to our flat through the streets of Paris. I, personally, had never felt so free in my life.[5]

More recently, women have been lured into joining the military – without a disguise – by thoughts of leaving home. Getting away from home, not killing Russians or Vietnamese, is what Peggy Perri, just out of nursing school, had in mind when she and her best friend decided to enlist in the US Army nursing corps in 1967. 'Pat and I were both living at home and we were both miserable. I was living at my mother's house. I was unhappy, really unhappy,' Peggy recalls. 'Pat and I had become nurses with the expectation that we could go anywhere and work. We wanted to go somewhere, and we wanted to do something really different.' Peggy wasn't a classic 'good girl'. She chewed gum and liked parties. But she didn't want to surrender her status as a respectable young woman. 'We needed to know that there was going to be some kind of structure to hold us up. The military sure promised that. . .I was infatuated by the idea of going to Vietnam. . .I really didn't know where I wanted to go. I wanted to go everywhere in the world.' She soon got her wish. 'I remember we got our orders; my mother took me shopping in every major department store. Pat and I both bought new sets of luggage, Pat's was hot pink!. . .It was January and we would go to all the "cruise" shops looking for light-weight clothing. I wanted everyone to think I was going on a cruise.'[6]

The most famous of the women who set out to travel further than convention allowed without disguise are now referred to as the 'Victorian lady travellers'. Most of them came from the white middle classes of North

America and Europe. They set out upon travels that were supposed to be the preserve of men. They defied the strictures of femininity by choosing parts of the world which whites in the late nineteenth and early twentieth century considered 'uncharted', 'uncivilized'. Not for them the chic tourist meccas of Italy and Greece. These Victorian lady travellers wanted *adventure*. That meant going to lands just being opened up by imperial armies and capitalist traders.

In their own day these women were viewed with suspicion because they dared to travel such long distances with so little proper male protection. Even if their husbands accompanied them as missionaries or scientists, these women insisted upon the separateness of their own experiences. The fact that most of them were white and chose to travel in continents whose populations were not, added to the 'exotic' aura surrounding their journeys. Space and race, when combined, have different implications for women and men, even of the same social class.[7]

Mary Kingsley, Isabella Bird, Alexandra David-Neel, Nina Mazuchelli, Annie Bullock Workman, Nina Benson Hubbard – these women in the nineteenth and early twentieth centuries took for themselves the identities of 'adventurer' and 'explorer'. Both labels were thoroughly masculinized. Masculinity and exploration had been as tightly woven together as masculinity and soldiering. These audacious women challenged that ideological assumption, but they have left us with a bundle of contradictions. While they defied, apparently self-consciously, the ban on far-flung travel by 'respectable' women, in some respects they seem quite conventional. Some of them rejected female suffrage. Some refused to acknowledge fully how far their own insistence on the right to adventure undermined not only Victorian notions of femininity, but the bond being forged between Western masculinity and Western imperialism.

Mary Kingsley is one of the most intriguing lady travellers. Mary's father was an explorer, her brother an adventurer. Mary was born in 1862 and grew up as the twin movements of women's domestication of women and imperial expansion were flowering in Victoria's England. She seemed destined to nurse her invalid mother and to keep the homefires burning for her globe-trotting brother. But Mary had other ideas. In 1892 she set out on the first of several expeditions to Africa. She traveled without male escort and headed for the West African interior. For it was in the continent's interior where 'real' adventures were thought to happen. In subsequent years she befriended European male traders plying their business along the coasts and up the rivers of Africa. Her detailed knowledge of African societies' ritual fetishes was even acknowledged by the men of the British Museum.[8]

Mary Kingsley also became one of the most popular speakers on the lively lecture circuit. She drew enthusiastic audiences from all over England to hear about her travels to Africa and her descriptions of lives lived in the newly penetrated areas of Victoria's empire. Many women travellers helped finance their travels by giving public lectures. The lecture circuit may have provided a crucial setting in which the women who stayed at home could become engaged in the British empire. They could take part vicariously in British officials' debates over how best to incorporate African and Asian peoples into that empire by listening to Mary Kingsley describe colonial policies and their consequences for local peoples.

The women lecture-goers are as politically interesting as Mary Kingsley herself. Together, lecturer and audience helped to fashion a British culture of imperialism. The stay-at-home listeners would develop a sense of imperial pride as they heard another woman describe her travels among their empire's more 'exotic' peoples. And they could expand their knowledge of the world without risking loss of that feminine respectability which enabled them to feel superior to colonized women. Their imperial curiosity, in turn, helped Mary Kingsley finance her breaking of gendered convention.

A century later librarians at the American Museum of Natural History in New York mounted an exhibition honoring some of the American women who had made contributions to scientific exploration. 'Ladies of the Field: The Museum's Unsung Explorers' was designed to make visible Delia Akeley, Dina Brodsky and other women explorers whose contributions to science had been neglected because they were dismissed as amateurs or as mere wives-of-explorers. The exhibition consisted of just three small glass cases in the ante-room of the Rare Book Library. As two women visitors peered through the glass to read faded diaries and letters, they could hear the shouts of schoolchildren racing through millennia of dinosaurs not far away. But here there were no curious crowds. They were the only visitors. Something about finding themselves before this modest exhibit prompted the strangers to exchange a few words. As they looked at a photo of Delia Akeley standing proudly between giant tusks she had just collected for the museum, one woman said, 'A friend of mine had wanted to be an explorer, but she resigned herself to being a librarian.'

Some of these contributors to the museum were the first white women to travel to a particular region. That seemed to give their travels greater significance. Historians often think it worth noting when the 'first white woman' arrived, as if that profoundly transformed a place. A white woman's arrival destined it to be sucked into the international system.

2   Delia Akeley on an expedition in Africa for the American Museum of Natural History (photo: Carl Akeley/American Museum of Natural History, New York)

If a white woman traveler reached such a place, could the white wife or white tourist be far behind?[9]

FEMININITY IN A WORLD OF PROGRESS

The idea that the world is out there for the taking by ordinary citizens as well as adventurers emerged alongside the growth of tourism as an industry. World's fairs, together with museums and travel lectures, nourished this idea.

Without leaving her own country, the fair-goer could experience remote corners of the world, choosing to 'visit' the Philippines, Alaska, Japan or Hawaii. It is estimated that in the United States alone, close to one million people visited world's fairs between 1876 and 1916.[10] World's fairs were designed to be more than popular entertainments; they were intended by their planners to help the public imagine an industrializing, colonizing global enterprise.

At the hub of all the world's fairs was the idea of progress, global progress. It could be best celebrated, fair investors believed, by graphically comparing 'uncivilized' with 'civilized' cultures. Between the two extremes fair designers placed Afro-American and Native American cultures – those apparently already on the track to civilization. They constructed elaborate scenes that they imagined visitors would find exotic. They imported women and men from as far away as Samoa and the Philippines to demonstrate their point. They called on the budding profession of anthropology to order their ideas and ensure authenticity. In the end fair designers created living postcards, clichés of cultures apparently at opposite ends of the modernity scale.

The natives in their exotic environment were as crucial to the celebration of progress as were exhibits of the latest feats of technological invention. Walking between a simple Samoan village and a powerful, shiny locomotive gave fair-goers an exhilarating sense of inevitable progress. By implication, it was America – or France or Britain – which was leading the way in the march of globalized progress. For the cultures most deeply afffected by the colonial experience were furthest along the fair's scale of progress. Eventually, so the fair scenario suggested, the primitive peoples of the world would be led into the light of civilization by imperial trusteeship. The world's fair expressed an elaborate international political cosmology.

It was a gendered America, a gendered Britain, however, that was leading the procession and formulating the heartening comparisons. A reporter for the *Omaha Bee* captured this spirit when describing the 1898 Trans-Mississippi and International Exposition:

> To see these ever formidable and hereditary enemies of the white man encamped together in a frame of architectural splendor erected by courage, manhood, and sterling integrity, will impress upon the growing sons and daughters a lesson which will bear fruit in years hence when the yet unsettled and uncultured possessions of the United States shall have become jewels upon the Star Spangled Banner.[11]

The year was 1898. The US government was extending its imperial reach. American men were exerting their manliness in defeating Spanish, Cuban and Filipino troops. They were proving in the process that industrialization and the rise of urban middle-class lifestyles were not,

26

as some had feared, weakening white American manhood. Within several decades Americans would no longer have to be satisfied with fair exhibits of Cuban dancers or Philippines villages. Those countries would have built tourist hotels, beach resorts and casinos to lure American pleasure-seekers – all due to world-wide progress generated by a civilizing sort of American masculinity.

The world's fairs of this era preached that white men's manliness fueled the civilizing imperial mission and in turn, that pursuing the imperial mission revitalized the nation's masculinity. At the same time, world's fairs were designed to show that women's domestication was proof of the manly mission's worthiness.

Thus femininity as well as masculinity structured the comparisons and the lessons visitors were to derive from the world's fairs. Women became the viewers and the viewed. White women were meant to come away from the fair feeling grateful for the benefits of civilization they enjoyed. They were not expected to measure progress from savagery to civilization in terms of voting rights or economic independence; they were to adopt a scale that had domesticated respectability at one end and hard manual labor at the other. White men were to look at 'savage' men's treatment of their over-worked women and congratulate themselves on their own civilized roles as protectors and breadwinners. Without the Samoan, Filipino and other colonized women, neither male nor female fair-goers would have been able to feel so confident about their own places in this emergent world.

Some American women saw the world's fair as a perfect venue for showing women's special contributions to the nation's progress. America's Centennial Exhibition in 1876 featured a Women's Pavilion, which celebrated the new concept of domestic science, as well as arts and crafts by women from around the world. Progress, technology and feminine domestic space were combined in a revised version of gendered civilization. In 1893 there was to be a great fair at Chicago to commemorate the four-hundredth anniversary of Columbus's discovery of America. Susan B. Anthony, the suffragist, led a drive to ensure that women wouldn't be excluded from the planning as they had been in 1876. The US Congress responded by mandating the appointment of a Board of Lady Managers to participate in the design of the 1893 Columbian Exposition. The Board commissioned a Women's Building. It was among the fair's largest and most impressive, designed by a woman architect, 23-year-old Sophia Hayden. But the Women's Building and its exhibits did not challenge the underlying message of the fair. The white women who took charge of this ambitious project still believed their mission was to demonstrate that American women were leading the world in improving the domestic condition of women. The Women's Building was filled with exhibits of the latest household technology that would lighten women's load. Nor did they challenge the racial hierarchy that was implicitly condoned by the fair. The Board of Lady Managers, chaired by a wealthy Chicago socialite, rejected the proposal that a Black woman be appointed to any influential post.[12]

PACKAGE TOURS FOR THE RESPECTABLE WOMAN

Tourism is as much ideology as physical movement. It is a package of ideas about industrial, bureaucratic life.[13] It is a set of presumptions about manhood, education and pleasure.[14]

Tourism has depended on presumptions about masculinity and femininity. Often women have been set up as the quintessence of the exotic. To many men, women are something to be experienced. Women don't have experiences of their own. If the women are of a different culture, the male tourist feels he has entered a region where he can shed civilization's constraints, where he is freed from standards of behavior imposed by respectable women back home.

Thomas Cook perhaps deserves credit for making the world safe for the respectable woman tourist. On an English summer's day in 1841, walking to a temperance meeting, Thomas Cook had the idea of chartering a train for the next meeting so that participants could board a single train, pay a reduced rate, and while traveling to their meeting be treated to 'hams, loaves and tea' interspersed with exhortations against the evils of drink. Some 570 people signed up for that first trip.[15]

Initially, Thomas Cook was concerned primarily with working men like himself. He wanted to provide them with a diversion that didn't involve liquor. In 1851 he urged men to join his tour to the London Exhibition:

> There are a number of you who ask, 'of what use and benefit would be a visit to us?' . . . I ask, of what use was your apprenticeship? Did it make you more useful members of society? . . . Such will be the difference betwixt the man who visits the Exhibition and he that does not – the one will be blind with his eyes open, and the other will enjoy the sight, and admire the skill and labour of his fellow-workmen of different parts of the globe.[16]

Only later did Cook come to realize that package tours might attract working men and their wives and children and eventually women traveling without a male member of the family By the 1850s Britain's more adventurous middle-class women were beginning to earn their own income and to think about traveling for pleasure, if not to West Africa, at least to Germany. They still needed to safeguard their respectability in order to stay marriageable and so were looking for a chaperoned tour led by an honorable man. Thomas Cook, temperance advocate, offered precisely such a service. He only realized the business potential of respectable travel for women in 1855, after receiving a letter from four sisters – Matilda, Elizabeth, Lucilla and Marion Lincolne of Suffolk. The Lincolne sisters came from a large middle-class temperance family. Each of them had worked for wages when they were in their twenties and had income to spend on pleasure.[17] They had read about the beauties of the Rhine and the cities of the Continent, but how could they go?

How could ladies alone and unprotected, go 600 or 700 miles away from home? However, after many pros and cons, the idea gradually grew on us and we found ourselves consulting guides, hunting in guide-books, reading descriptions, making notes, and corresponding with Mr. Cook . . . Tis true, we encountered some opposition – one friend declaring that it was improper for ladies to go alone – the gentleman thinking we were far too independent . . . But somehow or other one interview with Mr. Cook removed all our hesitation, and we forthwith placed ourselves under his care . . .

Many of our friends thought us too independent and adventurous to leave the shores of old England, and thus plunge into foreign lands not beneath Victoria's sway with no protecting relative, but we can only say that we hope this will not be our last Excursion of the kind. We would venture anywhere with such a guide and guardian as Mr. Cook.[18]

Cook was so struck by Matilda and her sisters' letter that he began to run excerpts in his advertisements, making appeals directly to women. By 1907, the company's magazine, *Traveller's Gazette*, featured on its cover a vigorous young woman bestriding the globe.

Today the package tour holiday is a profitable commodity for some of the international economy's most successful companies. In Britain 40 per cent of the population cannot afford an annual holiday, but one third of the upper-middle class take two or more holidays a year. There are now 700 tour operators in Britain selling more than 12.5 million package holidays annually, worth £3.1 billion. While most of their customers pick

Vol. LVII. Established 1841 FEBRUARY, 1907. GRATUITOUS COPY

THE TRAVELLER'S GAZETTE.

An Illustrated Journal Devoted to Travel

Published Monthly by
THOS. COOK & SON
CHIEF OFFICE
LUDGATE CIRCUS, LONDON. E.C.

NOTICE TO TRAVELLERS.—Cook's Interpreters in Uniform meet the Principal Trains and Steamers at the chief cities and ports of Europe and the East, to render assistance to all holders of Cook's Tickets.

3   Cover of one of Thomas Cook's early holiday brochures, 1907 (Thomas Cook Archives, London)

the Mediterranean, British and continental tour companies are nudging clients to travel further afield – to North Africa, North America and the Caribbean.[19]

Japanese government officials are predicting that foreign travel will be one of that country's major growth industries in the 1990s. Although only 5 per cent of Japanese took holidays abroad in 1987, large tourist companies like JTB and Kinki Nippon Tourist Agency have already turned foreign travel into a $16 billion business. One third of Japanese overseas tourists today travel as part of a package tour. Most notorious are groups of businessmen traveling to South Korea, the Philippines and Thailand on sex tours. But the country's second largest tourist market is single working women: 18 per cent of all Japanese tourists. Their favored destinations are the shops and beaches of Hong Kong, Hawaii and California.[20]

THE TOURISM FORMULA FOR DEVELOPMENT

From its beginnings, tourism has been a powerful motor for global integration. Even more than other forms of investment, it has symbolized a country's entrance into the world community. Foreign-owned mines, military outposts and museum explorations have drawn previously 'remote' societies into the international system, usually on unequal terms. Tourism entails a more politically potent kind of intimacy. For a tourist isn't expected to be very adventurous or daring, to learn a foreign language or adapt to local custom. Making sense of the strange local currency is about all that is demanded. Perhaps it is for this reason that international technocrats express such satisfaction when a government announces that it plans to promote tourism as one of its major industries. For such a policy implies a willingness to meet the expectations of those foreigners who want political stability, safety and congeniality when they travel. A government which decides to rely on money from tourism for its development is a government which has decided to be internationally compliant enough that even a woman traveling on her own will be made to feel at home there.

When mass tourism began to overtake élite travel following World War II, most travel occurred within and between North America and Western Europe. By the mid-1970s, 8 per cent of all tourists were North Americans and Europeans traveling on holiday to Third World countries. A decade later 17 per cent were.[21] Middle-class Canadians who a decade ago thought of going across the border to Cape Cod or Florida in search of holiday warmth are now as likely to head for the Bahamas. Their French counterparts are as apt to make Tunisia or Morocco rather than Nice their holiday destination. Scandinavians are choosing Sri Lanka or Goa instead of the Costa del Sol.

Third World officials and their European, American and Japanese bankers have become avid tourism boosters. Tourism is promoted today as an industry that can turn poor countries' very poverty into a magnet for sorely needed foreign currency. For to be a poor society in the late twentieth century is to be 'unspoilt'. Tourism is being touted as an alternative to the one-commodity dependency inherited from colonial rule. Foreign sun-seekers replace bananas. Hiltons replace sugar mills. Multinational corporations such as Gulf and Western or Castle and Cook convert their large landholdings into resorts or sell them off to developers. By the mid-1980s tourism had replaced sugar as the Dominican Republic's top foreign-exchange earner. In Jamaica, tourism had outstripped bauxite as the leading earner of foreign exchange. Caribbean development officials are happily reporting that, with more than 10 million visitors a year, the region is outstripping its main tourism rivals, Hawaii and Mexico. But, they add reassuringly, all the new hotel construction isn't turning Caribbean islands into concrete jungles: 'Many of the islands are mainly wild and underpopulated, with room for many more hotels and resorts before their appeal is threatened.'[22]

In reality, tourism may be creating a new kind of dependency for poor nations. Today tourism represents 40,000 jobs for Tunisia and is the country's biggest foreign-currency earner. Countries such as Puerto Rico, Haiti, Nepal, Gambia and Mexico have put their development eggs in the tourism basket, spending millions of dollars from public funds to build the sorts of facilities that foreign tourists demand. Officials in these countries hope above all that tourism will get their countries out of debt. The international politics of debt and the international pursuit of pleasure have become tightly knotted together as we enter the 1990s.[23]

The indebted governments that have begun to rely on tourism include those which previously were most dubious about this as a route to genuine development, especially if 'development' is to include preservation of national sovereignty. Cuba, Tanzania, North Korea, Vietnam and Nicaragua all are being governed today by officials who have adopted a friendlier attitude toward tourism. They are being complimented and called 'pragmatic' by mainstream international observers because they are putting the reduction of international debt and the earning of foreign currency on the top of their political agenda.[24]

This belief in the logic of fueling development and economic growth with tourism underlies the full-page color advertisements in the Sunday supplements. Many of those ads luring travelers to sunny beaches and romantic ruins are designed and paid for by government tourist offices. Most of those bureaucratic agencies depend on femininity, masculinity and heterosexuality to make their appeals and achieve their goals. Local men in police or military uniforms and local women in colorful peasant dresses – or in very little dress at all – are the preferred images. The local men are militarized in their manliness; the local women are welcoming and available in their femininity. The Cayman Islands Department of Tourism ran an expensive advertisement in the *New York Times* 'Sophisticated Traveller' supplement in October 1987. It pictured a white couple on an expanse of sandy beach. Underneath were smaller snapshots of local life and tourist activities – the tourists were portrayed as white couples shopping, swimming, dining; the local people were uniformed men on parade and a single black woman smiling out at the reader. Over her head ran the caption, 'Those who know us, love us.'

FLIGHT ATTENDANTS AND CHAMBERMAIDS

Singapore Airlines, a government company, runs a center-fold advertisement that shows an Asian woman of somewhat vague ethnicity. She could be Chinese, Indian or Malay. She stands in a misty, impressionistic setting, looking out at the reader demurely, holding a single water lily. There is no information about the airline's rates or safety record, just this message in delicate print: 'Singapore Girl . . . You're a great way to fly.'

On the oceans and in the skies: the international business travelers are men, the service workers are women. Flight attendants in the United States began organizing in the 1970s and won the right not to dress in uniforms that they believed turned them into airborne Playboy bunnies. But most women working today as flight attendants do not yet have the backing of strong trade unions. They are subject to their employers' desire for flight attendants to represent not only the airline company that employs them, but the feminine essence of their nation. For that distinctive femininity is a major attraction in the eyes of the flight attendant's employer and her government. 'When your business is business . . . our business is pleasure,' runs a Sri Lankan airline's advertisement.[25]

The airlines have taken their cues from the longer established ocean-liner companies. It was they who first used a racial and gendered division of labor to maximize profits while constructing a notion of leisure. Initially, ocean-liner crews were male, ranked by class and race. The white officers were to exude both competence and romance for passengers. The Indonesian, Filipino and other men of color serving in the dining rooms and below deck reflected a comforting global hierarchy while permitting the company to pay lower wages. Women crew members multiplied when company executives began to realize that their women passengers preferred to be waited on by women. Elaine Lang and Evelyn Huston were among the handful of British women who signed up to work on the *Empress of Scotland* in the 1930s, a time when shore jobs were hard to find. They worked as stewardesses, rising gradually in rank, but finding it impossible to break into the ship's all-male officer corps. Their best hope was to service first-class rather than steerage-class passengers: 'work and bed, work and bed, that's all it was.' Today hundreds of women are hired to work as service personnel in the burgeoning cruise-ship industry. 'Love Boat' is still kept afloat by a sexual division of labor.[26]

When people go on holiday they expect to be freed from humdrum domestic tasks. To be a tourist means to have someone else make your bed.

Thus chambermaids, waitresses and cooks are as crucial to the international tourism industry – and the official hopes that underpin it – as sugar workers and miners were to colonial industries. Still, a chambermaid seems different. Even a low-paid, over-worked male employee on a banana or sugar plantation has a machete, a sense of strength, a perception of his work as manly. Many nationalist movements have rallied around the image of the exploited male plantation worker; he has represented the denial of national sovereignty.

Nationalist leaders who have become alarmed at the tourism-dependent policies imposed by foreign bankers and their own governments have been reluctant to rally around the symbol of the oppressed chambermaid. Men in nationalist movements may find it easier to be roused to anger by the vision of a machete-swinging man transformed into a tray-carrying waiter in a white resort – he is a man who has had his masculine pride stolen from him. Caribbean nationalists have complained that their government's pro-tourism policies have turned their society into a 'nation of busboys'. 'Nation of chambermaids' doesn't seem to have the same mobilizing ring in their ears. After all, a woman who has traded work as an unpaid agricultural worker for work as a hotel cleaner hasn't lost any of her femininity.

In reality, tourism is not dependent on busboys. Tourism is what economists call a 'labor-intensive' industry. It requires construction crews, airplanes, gallons of frozen orange juice, and above all a high ratio of employees to paying customers; people who come as tourists need and expect a lot of service. As in other labor-intensive industries – garments, health and childcare, food processing and electronics assembly – owners make money and governments earn tax revenues to the extent that they can keep down the cost of wages and benefits of the relatively large numbers of workers they must hire.

Since the eighteenth century, employers have tried to minimize the cost of employing workers in labor-intensive industries by defining most jobs as 'unskilled' or 'low-skilled' – jobs, in other words, that workers naturally know how to do. Women in most societies are presumed to be naturally capable at cleaning, washing, cooking, serving. Since tourism companies need precisely those jobs done, they can keep their labor costs low if they can define those jobs as women's work. In the Caribbean in the early 1980s, 75 per cent of tourism workers were women.[27]

Hawaiians refer to the large hotels owned by Americans and Japanese as 'the new plantations': Caucasian men are the hotel managers, Hawaiian men and women the entertainers, Hawaiian men the coach drivers and Filipino women the chambermaids. In China, post-Mao officials, eager to attract foreign industry and foreign exchange, are approving the construction of new hotels within coastal zones set aside for electronics, textile and other export factories, and are helping managers hire workers. Shenzhen's new Bamboo Garden Hotel employs 360 employees; 80 per cent are women.[28]

In the Philippines, where tourism under both the Marcos and Aquino regimes has been relied on to earn badly needed foreign exchange, the Manila Garden Hotel employs 500 workers; 300 are women. But there is something different here. Workers are represented by an independent union, the Philippines National Union of Workers in Hotels, Restaurants and Allied Industries, and equal numbers of women and men are union representatives. In the wake of the widespread political mobilization of women that helped to bring down the Marcos regime in 1986, women in the union created a Working Women's Council. Beth Valenzuela, a single mother working in the hotel's food department, is one of the Manila Garden Hotel's active women unionists. She told a Filipino reporter that she hoped to make the Women's Council a place where issues of particular importance to women hotel workers could be studied and discussed. It would also train women union members in public speaking and decision-making, skills that in the past 'have been jealously guarded by the men as their exclusive preserve'.[29]

In Britain, too, the Conservative government has been trumpeting tourism as a growth industry. In the late 1980s and early 1990s, tourist companies are creating 45,000 new jobs per year, especially in the depressed industrial areas of the North. A new museum is opening every two weeks: deserted steel mills are becoming part of the 'heritage industry'. But most tourism jobs are part-time, seasonal and provide little chance for advancement. This means that they are also likely to be filled by women. Nevertheless, some British critics of the tourism formula for economic revival seem less upset at the prospect of a British woman struggling on a part-time wage than at the idea of a former steel worker compromising his masculinity by taking a 'candy-floss job' at a theme park.[30]

SEX TOURISM IN INTERNATIONAL POLITICS

Pat Bong is a neighborhood of Bangkok that caters to foreign men. There are 400,000 more women than men living in Bangkok, but male tourists outnumber female tourists by three to one. Pat Bong's urban landscape makes the census figures come alive. Although the government passed a Prostitution Prohibition Act in 1960, six years later it undercut that ban by passing an Entertainment Places Act, which had enough loopholes to encourage coffee shops and restaurants to add prostitution to their menus. Thus today Pat Bong is crowded with discos, bars and massage parlors. In the early 1980s, it was estimated that Bangkok had 119 massage parlors, 119 barbershop-cum-massage parlors and teahouses, 97 nightclubs, 248 disguised brothels and 394 disco-restaurants, all of which sold sexual companionship to male customers. Some of the women who work here as prostitutes have migrated from the countryside where agricultural development projects have left them on the margins; other women are second, even third generation prostitutes increasingly cut off from the rest of Thai society. A woman working in a Bangkok massage parlor can earn an average of 5,000 baht per month; wages in non-entertainment jobs open to women average a paltry 840 baht per month. Marriage to a foreigner frequently appears to be the only avenue out of Pat Bong, but it too can prove illusory:

> [She] had lived with an English man working as a technician on an oil rig. But he left her and went back to England. She said she was not working when she was with him, but returned to her job after some months since he failed to send her money and it was impossible for her to keep such an expensive flat. 'What else can I do? After all, these men are good business.'[31]

Sex tourism is not an anomaly; it is one strand of the gendered tourism industry. While economists in industrialized societies presume that the 'service economy', with its explosion of feminized job categories, follows a decline in manufacturing, policy-makers in many Third World countries have been encouraged by international advisers to develop service sectors *before* manufacturing industries mature. Bar hostesses before automobile workers, not after.[32]

A network of local and foreign companies encourages men – especially from North America, Western Europe, Japan, the Middle East and Australia – to travel to Third World countries specifically to purchase the sexual services of local women. The countries that have been developed as the destinations for sex tourists include those which have served as 'rest and recreation' sites for the American military: Thailand, South Korea, the Philippines. Nearby Indonesia and Sri Lanka also have received sex tourists. Goa, a coastal state of India, is among the newest regions to be targeted by sex tourism's promoters. Local laws explicitly prohibiting prostitution are often ignored, not only by pimps and bar owners, but by India's police and tourism officials as well.[33]

To succeed, sex tourism requires Third World women to be economically desperate enough to enter prostitution; having done so it is made difficult to leave. The other side of the equation requires men from affluent societies to imagine certain women, usually women of color, to be more available and submissive than the women in their own countries. Finally, the industry depends on an alliance between local governments in search of foreign currency and local and foreign businessmen willing to invest in sexualized travel.

> Thailand is a world full of extremes and the possibilities are unlimited. Anything goes in this exotic country, especially when it comes to girls. Still it appears to be a problem for visitors to Thailand to find the right places where they can indulge in unknown pleasures . . . Rosie [Rosie Reisen, a West German travel company] has done something about this. For the first time in history you can book a trip to Thailand with exotic pleasures included in the price.[34]

In 1986 Thailand earned more foreign currency from tourism – $1.5 billion – than it did from any other economic activity including its traditional export leader, rice. The Thai government's Sixth National Economic and Social Development Plan for 1978–1991 makes 'tourism and exports' its top priority. In pursuing this goal Thai officials want to increase the numbers of tourists (2.7 million came in 1986), but also to alter the mix, especially to get Japanese men, who now stay an average of only four days, to stay longer.[35]

Sex tourism is part of the domestic and international political system. And changes are now occurring both within and between countries that could radically alter the sex tourism industry: AIDS; official nationalism; Asian and African feminist movements; and international alliances between feminist organizations.

By October 1987 Thai tourism officials had become alarmed at the sharp drop in the numbers of single male visitors to the beach resort of Pattaya. After Bangkok, Pattaya was the favored destination for foreign male tourists. The number of Middle Eastern men had declined to such an extent that Pattaya's VD clinics, which advertise in Arabic as well as English, had begun to see a fall in clients. Initially, the Thai government was reluctant to talk about AIDS. Like other governments dependent on tourism and on sex tourism in particular, public admission of AIDS was seen as damaging to the economy and national pride. Then, once acknowledged, officials set about compelling women working in bars and massage parlors in Pattaya and Bangkok to take tests for the HIV virus. Government health officials were pressed by government tourism officials to co-operate. By mid-1987 only six people, five Thais and one foreigner, had died of AIDS according to official statistics. Most of the other twenty-five people reported by the government as having been infected with the virus and developing AIDS-related symptoms were categorized by the government as homosexual men and drug addicts. Female prostitutes are the group that most worried Thai officials. Bureaucrats began talking of building more golf courses. If foreign men began to avoid Thai women there had to be an alternative attraction. But little was said of the poor women who have taken jobs in the sex industry because they have had to leave the Thai countryside for lack of land and decently paid waged work.[36]

Empower and Friends of Women are two of the Thai women's organizations formed in the 1980s to fill the gaps left by uninterested policy-makers and investors. Each group works directly with women in the sex-tourism industry, providing English lessons so that the women can deal on a more equal footing with their clients. They publish and distribute cartoon brochures informing women about AIDS. Most recently they have begun efforts to work with Thai women who have traveled to Europe to work as entertainers or to marry as mail-order brides.[37]

Feminist groups in the Philippines have had a better political opening for making sex tourism a national political issue. The overthrow of the authoritarian and export-oriented regime of Ferdinand Marcos in 1986 made the government's entire development formula vulnerable to popular scrutiny. Marcos and his advisors, with encouragement from foreign banks and technical consultants, had viewed tourism as a primary building block of development. The regime had used the reputed beauty and generosity of Filipino women as 'natural resources' to compete in the international tourism market. The result was that by the mid-1980s, 85 per cent of tourists visiting the country were men, and sex tourism had become crucial to the government's economic survival. While many outside observers focussed their attention on the prostitution that had grown up around the large American bases in the Philippines, some Filipino feminists noted that there were many more women working as prostitutes in Manila's tourist establishments.

Another evening is starting in the history of the international political system:

> Rows of taxis, cars and minibuses pull up behind a number of Manila hotels. Long lines of women pass the guards and enter a private door, sign a book, hand over their identification cards and take a private elevator to one of the special floors designated for prostitution. . .
>
> The woman goes to her assigned room; if the man is out she waits in the corridor . . . [A prostitute] may not be taken to any public area of the hotel, all food and drink orders must be by room service. Hotels charge a $10 'joiners fee' for the privilege of taking a woman to a room . . .
>
> Before breakfast the next day the women collect their IDs and leave.[38]

When Corazon Aquino replaced Ferdinand Marcos as president, Filipino women activists pressed the new regime to give up sex tourism as a development strategy. Aquino herself was not a feminist, but she had made restoration of the nation's dignity a central theme in her political campaign. As president, she took steps to change the Tourism Ministry's leadership and policies. The new minister brought a tour of Japanese women to the Philippines in order to demonstrate that the government was making the country a more wholesome tourist destination. But when Aquino authorized police to make raids on establishments in Ermita, Manila's infamous entertainment district, feminists were alarmed. The policy was not devised in consultation with women's groups such as Gabriela. Women working in the industry were not asked about the causes or likely consequences of such a heavy-handed approach. No steps were taken by the government to provide alternative livelihoods for the women working as dancers, hostesses and masseurs. In the name of cleaning up the city, washing away the degeneracy of the Marcos years, police arrested hundreds of women. Virtually no pimps, businessmen or male clients were jailed.[39]

Several Filipino feminist groups have created drop-in centers in those areas where prostitution is concentrated. They acknowledge that there are class barriers to be overcome in these new relationships between women in prostitution and women in political organizations. Filipino women activists, including a number of feminist nuns, have tried to avoid moralism. To provide a place to meet other prostitutes outside of the bars, to allow women to sort out together the conditions that pull Filipino women into prostitution, to provide practical information on AIDS, VD and contraception – these are feminists' first objectives. Yet the lack of the substantial resources it takes to offer prostitutes realistic job alternatives has been frustrating. Learning handicrafts may provide a woman working in Ermita or on the fringes of an American military base with a new sense of confidence or self-worth, but it doesn't pay the rent or support a child. 'When it comes to income-generating alternatives, we don't think we offer anything because we are up against so much. Economically we cannot give them anything.'[40]

Filipino feminists refuse to discuss prostitution or sex tourism in a vacuum. They insist that all analyses and organizational strategies should tie sex tourism to the issues of Philippines nationalism, land reform and demilitarization. Nowadays, they argue, sex tourism must also be understood in relation to Filipinas' migration overseas.

Migration as entertainers and as brides to foreign men has been the latest step in making world travel different for men than for women. Men in Scandinavia, West Germany, Australia, Britain, the United States and Japan now want to have access to Third World women not just in Third

World tourism centers; they want to enjoy their services at home. Thus feminist organizations in Thailand, South Korea and the Philippines are having to make alliances with women in Europe, North America and Japan in order to protect women in the international tourism/entertainment/marriage industry. Thai feminist social workers go to West Germany to investigate the conditions Thai women encounter there; Filipino feminists travel to Japan to take part in meetings organized by Japanese feminists concerned about Filipinas recruited to work in discos and bars, women now referred to as 'japayukisan'; South Korean feminists fly to New York to attend a conference on international prostitution to urge American women activists to think and organize internationally.[41]

CONCLUSION

Tourism is not just about escaping work and drizzle; it is about power, increasingly internationalized power. That tourism is not discussed as seriously by conventional political commentators as oil or weaponry may tell us more about the ideological construction of 'seriousness' than about the politics of tourism.

Government and corporate officials have come to depend on international travel for pleasure in several ways. First, over the last forty years they have come to see tourism as an industry that can help diversify local economies suffering from reliance on one or two products for export. Tourism is embedded in the inequalities of international trade, but is often tied to the politics of particular products such as sugar, bananas, tea and copper. Second, officials have looked to tourism to provide them with foreign currency, a necessity in the ever more globalized economies of both poor and rich countries. Third, tourism development has been looked upon as a spur to more general social development; the 'trickle down' of modern skills, new technology and improved public services is imagined to follow in the wake of foreign tourists. Fourth, many government officials have used the expansion of tourism to secure the political loyalty of local élites. For instance, certain hotel licences may win a politician more strategic allies today than a mere civil-service appointment. Finally, many officials have hoped that tourism would raise their nations' international visibility and even prestige.

Many of these hopes have been dashed. Yet tourism continues to be promoted by bankers and development planners as a means of making the international system less unequal, more financially sound and more politically stable. A lot is riding on sun, surf and souvenirs.

From the Roman empire to the eighteenth century European grand tour, the rise of Cooks Tours and Club Med, travel for pleasure and adventure has been profoundly gendered. Without ideas about masculinity and femininity – and the enforcement of both – in the societies of departure and the societies of destination, it would be impossible to sustain the tourism industry and its political agenda in their current form. It is not simply that ideas about pleasure, travel, escape, bed-making and sexuality have affected women in rich and poor countries. The very structure of international tourism *needs* patriarchy to survive. Men's capacity to control women's sense of their security and self-worth has been central to the evolution of tourism politics. It is for this reason that actions by feminists – as airline stewardesses, hotel workers, prostitutes, wives of businessmen and organizers of alternative tours for women – should be seen as political, internationally political.

Movements which upset any of the patterns in today's international tourist industry are likely to upset one of the principal pillars of contemporary world power. Such a realization forces one to take a second look at the Portuguese woman on her ladder picking olives, smiling for the postcard photographer. She has the potential for reshaping the international political order. What is behind her smile?

3

NATIONALISM
AND MASCULINITY

Women haven't had an easy relationship with nationalism. Even when they have suffered abuse at the hands of colonialists and racists, they have often been treated more as symbols than as active participants by nationalist movements organized to end colonialism and racism.

Colonialism was good for the postcard business. Colonial administrators, soldiers, settlers and tourists were looking for ways to send home images of the societies they were ruling, images that were appealing and yet made it clear that these alien societies needed the civilizing government only whites could bestow. The colonial postcard images were frequently eroticized and surprisingly standardized – a Zulu woman from southern Africa and a Maori woman from New Zealand were asked to assume similar poses for the British imperialists' photographer.

French colonialists also sent home postcard pictures of Arab women in their North African colonies. Some were veiled, others were not. Some were obviously posed in a photographer's studio, others apparently caught on film unawares.[1] Many of these postcards convey a sexual message. 'Aicha and Zorah' is the caption for a photo of two young Algerian women, unveiled and looking straight at the photographer – and thus at the buyer and eventual recipient of the postcard. The two women are sitting on a window ledge behind an ornate iron grille. Another card, captioned 'Moorish woman' – as if representing all Arab women – shows a woman wearing neither a veil nor a robe to cover her breasts. She too is leaning against a window grille, looking through it from the inside, available, though almost beyond reach.

Malek Alloula is the collector of these French colonial postcards. He is an Algerian nationalist. The ephemera of colonialist culture, these postcards capture for him the concepts of masculine adventure and the

4 'The Beauty of the Kraal, Zululand': a Zulu woman pictured on a British colonial postcard from South Africa, taken in the early 1900s

5 'Kia-Ora: Greetings from Maoriland': A Maori woman pictured on a British colonial postcard from New Zealand, c. 1930

'exotic' that were as crucial to French colonial domination as the Foreign Legion. European 'Orientalism' nurtured an appreciative fascination with these cultures while justifying European rule in the name of 'civilization'. The image of the tantalizingly veiled Muslim woman was a cornerstone of this Orientalist ideology and of the imperial structure it supported.[2]

Malek Alloula uses these images to explore his own identity as a male nationalist: for a man, to be conquered is to have his women turned into fodder for imperialist postcards. Becoming a nationalist requires a man to resist the foreigner's use and abuse of his women.

But what of the women themselves? Aicha and Zora must have had their own thoughts about being posed unveiled and behind bars. Maybe they later saw the postcard on sale near a hotel. Maybe they were flattered; maybe they were humiliated. How were they persuaded to sit for the photographer in the first place? Were they paid? Who got the money? Malek Alloula and other male nationalists seem remarkably *un*curious about the abused women's own thoughts – about the meaning they might have assigned to foreign conquest.

Colonized women have served as sex objects for foreign men. Some have married foreign men and thus facilitated alliances between foreign governments and companies and conquered peoples.[3] Others have worked as cooks and nannies for the wives of those foreign men. They have bolstered white women's sense of moral superiority by accepting their religious and social instruction. They have sustained men in their communities when their masculine self-respect has been battered by colonists' contempt and condescension. Women have planted maize, yams and rice in small plots to support families so that their husbands could be recruited to work miles away in foreign-owned mines or plantations. Women as symbols, women as workers and women as nurturers have been crucial to the entire colonial undertaking.[4]

Yet nationalist movements have rarely taken women's experiences as the starting point for an understanding of how a people becomes colonized or how it throws off the shackles of that material and psychological domination. Rather, nationalism typically has sprung from masculinized memory, masculinized humiliation and masculinized hope. Anger at being 'emasculated' – or turned into a 'nation of busboys' – has been presumed to be the natural fuel for igniting a nationalist movement.

> Not only are we prevented from speaking for women but also [not allowed] to think, and even to dream about a different fate. We are deprived of our dreams, because we are made to believe that leading the life we lead is the only way to be a good Algerian . . .[5]

The speaker, Algerian feminist Marie-Aimée Hélie-Lucas, is describing the conditions under which her nationalist government could rationalize new legislation to restrict women's social and political participation, despite women's active part in their country's anti-colonial war. She is quick, however, to warn her feminist listeners gathered at an international meeting:

> Probably most of the women present at this Symposium take for granted that they belong to a country, a nation, which does not have to prove its existence; it allows for transcending the concept of nation, and criticizing it. It has not been allowed for us . . . it is not for so many people in still colonized countries, or countries facing imperialism at war . . . [Under these conditions it is] much more difficult to come to criticize the nation, and even the State which pretends it represents the Nation.[6]

A 'nation' is a collection of people who have come to believe that they have been shaped by a common past and are destined to share a common future. That belief is usually nurtured by a common language and a sense of otherness from groups around them. Nationalism is a commitment to fostering those beliefs and promoting policies which permit the nation to control its own destiny. Colonialism is especially fertile ground for nationalist ideas because it gives an otherwise divided people such a potent shared experience of foreign domination. But not all nationalists respect other communities' need for feelings of self-worth and control. Some nationalists have been the victims of racism and colonialism; others have been the perpetrators of racism and colonialism.

Today nationalism still thrives, despite the waning of classic colonialism, because foreign influence works in new ways to give peoples a sense that they do not control their own fates. Where once the British, Dutch, French or American colonial administration was a rallying point for nationalists, today the interventions of foreign corporations, bankers and armies mobilize nationalist energies. Nationalism also remains a powerful political force because so many of the countries which won independence from colonial rule in fact include within their borders more than one national community. Thus while nationalism is alive and well among those Canadians who feel as though their very identities are on the verge of being blotted out by the behemoth to the south, it is also shaping relations *between* Canadians; since the 1960s French-Canadians have tried to develop nationalist strategies to stave off absorption by dominant Anglo-Canada. Nationalist ideas, therefore, are informing people's relationships with their neighbors – and the larger world – in industrialized as well as agrarian societies. It is a driving force in the political lives of men and women in countries as different as Ethiopia, South Africa, South Korea, Britain, Ireland and the Soviet Union.

Nationalist movements have transformed the landscape of international politics. If a state is a vertical creature of authority, a nation is a horizontal creature of identity. The most stable political system, it is now thought, is one in which state power rests on a bed of national identity: a 'nation-state'. Most governments nowadays assert that they rule in nation-states. The reality is less simple. State officials frequently lay claim to nationally rooted legitimacy because those who cannot stand on wobbly political ground. Without a national foundation to legitimize their power, officials' demands lack credibility in the eyes of their counterparts around the international bargaining table.[7]

One becomes a nationalist when one begins to recognize shared public pasts and futures. But most women's past experiences and strategies for the future are not made the basis of the nationalism they are urged to support. Yet, as Algerian feminists warn, it is a very risky enterprise for women to criticize a movement claiming to represent their own nation or the regime that exercises authority in the name of that nation. Living as a nationalist feminist is one of the most difficult political projects in today's world. Developing nationalist feminist politics is not made easier by the fact that, as we will see below, so many women in colonizing countries supported the policies nationalist movements have organized to reverse. The seriousness of patriarchal discrimination can seem diluted when women as well as men have participated in the outsiders' conquest.

GENDERED COLONIALISM

Many women from imperial countries have served their own governments by teaching in state and mission schools. An American white woman recalls the thrill she felt when she sailed to Manila as one of the first teachers to help establish American rule over the Philippines in 1901. Pattie Paxton was recruited by the US army. As she sailed out of San Francisco Bay, American soldiers were still engaged in a campaign to quash Filipino anti-colonial insurgents who had fought their former Spanish rulers in the name of nationalism.

Pattie Paxton hardly fits the conventional picture of an imperialist. She had just graduated from college, a rare achievement for a young American woman at the turn of the century. A classmate had told her of 'the interesting flora in the Philippine Islands, of orchids, of pleasant Nipa houses, and the best behaved children he had ever seen', while assuring Pattie that the army would never send teachers to 'dangerous spots'. Pattie

Paxton recalled later that she saw herself 'playing my small part in this great adventure' and seeing 'the world at the expense of Uncle Sam'. Her mind was made up when she learned that her college friend, Stella, was going as well and that they could make the voyage together. Aboard ship they met other unmarried women teachers, as well as men just out of the University of California. The women met in one of the staterooms 'to read and gossip' and joined the young men to 'spend pleasant evenings on deck singing, chiefly college songs'.[8]

Few American women raised their voices to protest at the sailing. Susan B. Anthony, despite her leadership of the emergent American suffrage movement, found she had few followers when she protested to President McKinley in 1900 that annexation of Hawaii and colonial expansion in the Caribbean and the Pacific did little more than extend American-style subjugation of women. Indeed, some suffragists in the United States and Europe argued that their *service* to the empire was proof of their reliability as voters.[9]

After several weeks in Manila and Iloila, during which they lived like tourists and provided a seemingly innocent change for the American soldiers, Pattie and Stella were sent to the provincial town of Bacolod, headquarters of the American Sixth Infantry. In Bacolod prominent Filipino families were trying to accommodate the country's newest foreign occupiers. Sabina, the landowner with whom Pattie and Stella were lodged, did her best to introduce the two young women to her relatives and friends. Then, at last, the two American women received their first teaching assignments. They were sent to a village in the Negros mountains where *insurrectos* were still active. Pattie and Stella didn't seem perturbed; this was the adventure they had longed for. They wasted no time in setting about transforming the village's two existing schools, one for boys and one for girls. Each reflected the earlier Spanish colonists' approach to learning: religious texts and recitation in unison. 'Upon such a foundation,' Pattie Paxton recalls, 'we were to build American schools, and in that foundation we recognized at least three strong blocks: a disciplined group, an eagerness to learn, a desire to excel. In addition,' she remembers gratefully, 'we found the teachers keen to learn our language and our methods of teaching.'

She spent four years teaching in the Philippines. Some of her most frustrating moments came when she could not persuade local Filipino officials to encourage little girls to attend school. She was plagued, too, by a lack of proper materials. But she made do, taught vocabulary and numbers, learned local songs, and helped her students make handicrafts. And life wasn't all work. There were picnics and holiday celebrations to attend with the American soldiers.

Pattie Paxton wasn't overtly racist. She was disgusted by an American colonel's 'white man's burden' dinner speech and by his wife's arrogance. None the less, Pattie Paxton and the other young women who came to the Philippines to teach in those heady days of American colonial rule helped to establish the values and institutions that would become the objects of intense Filipino nationalist controversy eight decades later. Corazon Aquino became president of the Philippines on a wave of nationalism, but she herself is a graduate of an American college. Like many other Filipinos today, she remains torn between nationalist pride and an admiration for American values, the legacy of Pattie, Stella and other women who saw adventure in working in the service of colonialism.

European and American women taught not only letters and numbers in their governments' colonies; they taught notions of respectability. They traveled to colonized societies as settlers, explorers, and missionaries. They served colonial administrations without pay as the wives of soldiers, planters, missionaries and administrators. European and American women volunteered to work as nurses, governesses and teachers. The colonial governments expected women in all of these roles to set standards of ladylike behavior. The Victorian code of feminine respectability would set a positive example for the colonized women. Colonial administrators hoped, too, that such a code would maintain the proper distance between the small numbers of white women and the large numbers of local men. Sexual liaisons between colonial men and local women usually were winked at; affairs between colonial women and local men were threats to imperial order.

Ladylike behavior was a mainstay of imperialist civilization. Like sanitation and Christianity, feminine respectability was meant to convince both the colonizing and the colonized peoples that foreign conquest was right and necessary.[10] Ladylike behavior would also have an uplifting effect on the colonizing men: it would encourage them to act according to those Victorian standards of manliness thought crucial for colonial order. Part of that empire-building masculinity was protection of the respectable lady. She stood for the civilizing mission which, in turn, justified the colonization of benighted peoples.

'Among rude people the women are generally degraded, among civilized people they are exalted,' wrote James Mill, one of the most popular promoters of British colonialism in the nineteenth century.[11] British colonial officers blamed the existing ideologies of masculinity in the colonized societies for women's degradation; if men's sense of manliness was such that it didn't include reverence toward women, then they couldn't expect to be allowed to govern their own societies. Thus, for instance, in India British commentators created the idea of the 'effeminate' Bengali male,

6   Area set aside for European women at the marriage of a Maharajah's daughter in colonial India, 1932. (photo: Harald Lechenperg/Acme Cards, London)

only to berate him because he wasn't manly enough to recognize his obligation to protect and revere women.[12] British officials passed legislation in India improving women's inheritance rights (1874, 1929, 1937), prohibiting widow-burning (1829) and allowing widow remarriage (1856), all in the name of advancing civilization. At the same time, Victorian values allowed these British officials to enact laws which imposed prison sentences on wives who refused to fulfill their sexual obligations to their husbands and imposed a system of prostitution that provided Indian women to sexually service British soldiers stationed in India. The riddle of two such contradictory sets of colonial policies comes unravelled if one sees British masculinized imperialism not as a crusade to abolish male domination of women but as a crusade to establish European male rule over the men in Asian and African societies.[13]

At the turn of the century masculinity – its importance to the nation and the threats to its healthy survival – was a topic of a lively, if nervous, political debate in several imperial countries. The Boer War, following in the wake of the Crimean War, shook Britons' confidence that their men were masculine enough to maintain the empire. Robert Baden-Powell founded the Boy Scouts in 1908 because venereal disease, intermarriage of the races

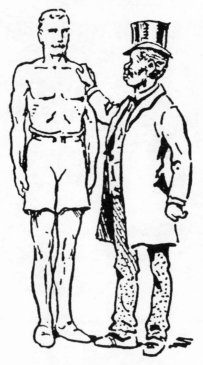

A WHITE MAN AND A MAN.

7   Illustration drawn by the author in *Rovering to Success: A Book of Life-Sport for Young Men* by Robert Baden-Powell (Herbert Jenkins Limited, London, 1922)

and declining birthrates were allegedly endangering the maintenance of Britain's international power. Baden-Powell and other British imperialists saw sportsmanship combined with respect for the respectable woman as the bedrock of British imperial success. Although Boy Scout branches were eventually established throughout the world, Baden-Powell's original intention was to restore manly self-control in white boys: in their hands lay the future of the empire. To make certain that his followers didn't mistake his intentions, Baden-Powell contrasted the images of 'a white man' and 'a man'. The latter was pictured in Baden-Powell's guides as short and black, wearing a top hat and a rumpled coat. This was not what a Boy Scout aspired to become. He wanted to emulate the 'white man' standing next to this figure: tall, muscular, eyes straight ahead, body at attention.[14]

The 'white man' towered over the black man not only because he had learned how to fight tooth decay, walk without slouching and properly carry his rucksack, but also because he had learned the importance of revering women, especially mothers and 'the right girl'. The surest way for a young man to find the 'right girl' was to marry a Girl Guide. All of this required the same kind of skillful maneuvering that a Boy Scout learned to employ when paddling his canoe through the rapids:

> You will, I hope, have gathered from what I have said about this Rock, 'Woman', that it has its dangers for the woman as well as for the man. But it has also its very bright side if you only maneuver your canoe aright.
>
> The paddle to use for this job is CHIVALRY. . .
>
> A man without chivalry is no man. A man who has this chivalry and respect for women could never lower himself to behave like a beast, nor would he allow a woman to ruin herself with him by losing her own self-respect and the respect of others. It is up to him to give the lead – and that a right one; and not be led astray.[15]

HOLLYWOOD AND COLONIAL NOSTALGIA

In recent years there has been a flood of cinematic nostalgia for European imperialism. The stars are white women. Larger-than-life portrayals of European women have lured us to re-imagine the colonization of Africa and Asia. Through the romanticized lives of Isak Dinesen (Karen Blixen) and Beryl Markham, Hollywood has invited us to picture colonies as places where white women had passionate affairs, flew planes, tamed the wilderness. The fashion industry has fed the nostalgia. Shops throughout Britain, Continental Europe and North America (the most famous chain being 'Banana Republic') now market clothes described as 'safari wear', encouraging women to adopt the colonial look of Isak Dinesen à la Meryl Streep. These white women's lives, as portrayed by Hollywood, were a nose-thumbing not only at stuffy Victorian England, but at those white women settlers in Kenya who tried so desperately to preserve Victorian propriety far away from home. Karen Blixen and Beryl Markham didn't care if the silver was set correctly; they wanted to have adventures.

'It was said that the best people went out to Kenya. In the hierarchy of Africa snobberies, Kenya got the titles, and the ordinary people went to Uganda or Rhodesia or South Africa.'[16] In her early novels Doris Lessing, herself a daughter of a white settler family, captures the more sordid dailiness of lower-middle-class white women's lives in Rhodesia. For her white women characters, social humiliation poses a greater danger than lions.[17]

Even when, as in the film *White Mischief*, the later decades of white rule in Kenya are stripped of their romantic glow to reveal moral decay, the cinematic message is that colonies allowed white women to escape the suffocating confines of patriarchal conventions back home, though breaking down these confines altogether could jeopardize the imperial order: 'In the colonial imagination, Africa was a dangerous country which inspired violence. At the furthest end of the scale was the subconscious fear that someone might break ranks, betray his country and his class by "going native". From the romantic *Out of Africa* to *White Mischief*, African women and men remain cinematically either part of the movie backdrop or are totally invisible. They appear as reminders of the need to keep up the very Victorian conventions that the white heroines came to Africa to escape.[18]

As African nationalist movements slip further back into history – it is already thirty years since the Mau Mau uprising in Kenya – these Hollywood creations are gaining in ideological potency, making white women and their white male lovers the 'real' people of Africa for thousands of European and North American film viewers. The perpetuation of such myths doesn't make it easier for women in nationalist movements to find reliable allies among women in the formerly imperialist societies. It also opens nationalist feminists' attempts at such alliances to criticism from male nationalists already resistant to feminist ideas.

NATIONALISM AND THE VEIL

No practice has been more heatedly debated among nationalists than the veil: should a Muslim woman demonstrate her commitment to the nationalist cause by wearing a veil – or by throwing off the veil? Men and women in Algeria, Egypt, Iran, Turkey, and Malaysia have lined up on both sides of this controversy. Colonial officials and men and women from the colonizing societies have also exercised moral and coercive pressure to tilt the argument one way or the other, usually toward rejecting the veil. The more colonialists have promoted the anti-veil movement in the name of Western civilization, the harder it has been for Muslim women in the colonized (or neo-colonized) country to control the argument. For if colonial male administrators and progressive European women take prominent public stances against the veil, and if they do so without a genuine alliance with local women, as is usually the case, they ensure that rejection of the veil will be taken as compliance with colonial rule. In Algeria, French administrators saw removing the veil as part of France's 'civilizing mission'. Egyptian feminists in the 1920s and 1930s had more success in controlling the debate, but they too risked being tarred with the anti-nationalist brush when they stepped out in public unveiled. Those anti-veil women who came from the local upper classes, as many did, were only partly protected from ridicule by their privileged status.[19]

European women in Egypt usually expressed strong opinions about the veil. They saw it as emblematic of Muslim women's seclusion, and linked it to the harem. Many of the European women who wrote about the veil did so not primarily out of genuine curiosity about the lives and thoughts of Egyptian women, but because it allowed them to feel sanguine about their own condition as European women: 'By thinking of themselves as all powerful and free vis-à-vis Egyptian women, Western women could avoid confronting their own powerlessness and gender oppression at home.'[20] All too often, European women who traveled to Egypt and stayed on as teachers, governesses and sometimes wives of Egyptian men were notably reluctant to explain why it was that they felt so much freer in the 'Orient'.

For their part, Egyptian women organizing and writing as feminists in the early twentieth century were frequently more exercised by European women's stereotypical attitudes than they were by Egyptian men's protection of male privilege. They felt compelled to defend Islam in the face of racist Orientalism. They objected to portrayals of Islamic society as incapable of dynamism and reform and to writings that pictured all Arab women as mindless members of the harem, preoccupied with petty domestic rivalries rather than with the artistic and political affairs of their times. They were pressed into this defensive position not only by European women's myopia, but by their need to preserve their alliances with Egyptian nationalist men. Under British colonial rule, some Egyptian men reached positions of considerable influence, positions not open to Egyptian women. In order to protect Egyptian women from some of the most oppressive consequences of British policy, Egyptian feminists needed élite Egyptian men to intervene on their behalf. 'Because men were faithful allies during the early phases of the struggle for women's rights, paternalist strategies for change acquired a certain degree of legitimacy.'[21] Focussing on European women's misrepresentations and being pressed into defending Islam in response not only kept these practical alliances between local men and women alive; it also allowed male privilege to seep deep into the Egyptian nationalist movement.

What is striking about these past and present arguments over whether a veiled woman is strengthening her nation or betraying it is that they are so important to men in their communities. One is hard pressed to think of an equally heated debate in any national community about men's attire – or diet or linguistic style – in which women have had so predominant a role to play. Sikh men's wearing of the customary turban is important to Sikh communal solidarity; Sikh men in India and Britain have had to fight for the right to wear their turbans (for instance, as bus conductors in Britain). Yet one doesn't see Sikh women acting as the chief proponents or enforcers of this male ethnic practice. Rather, men in many communities appear to assign such ideological weight to the outward attire and sexual purity of women in the community because they see women as 1) the community's – or the nation's – most valuable *possessions*; 2) the principal *vehicles* for transmitting the whole nation's values from one generation to the next; 3) *bearers* of the community's future generations – crudely, nationalist wombs; 4) the members of the community most *vulnerable* to defilement and exploitation by oppressive alien rulers; and 5) most susceptible to *assimilation* and cooption by insidious outsiders. All of these presumptions have made women's behavior important in the eyes of nationalist men. But these ideas have not necessarily ensured that women themselves would be taken seriously as active creators of the nation's newly assertive politics. Nor have these ideas guaranteed that male privilege would be effectively challenged in the new state derived from that nation.[22]

PATRIARCHY INSIDE THE MOVEMENT

Arguments about the proper role of women in the nationalist struggle and in the future nation-state have occurred in virtually every nationalist movement since the eighteenth century precisely because these five assumptions have had such potency for people trying to redraw political boundaries.

The American revolution against British colonial rule should stand as a warning. So should the French revolution, fought against an indigenous monarchy in the name of the newly self-conscious nation. During and after both nationalist revolutions the concept of 'citizenship' provided the terrain on which gendered struggles were fought between nationalist women and nationalist men. French and American women lost those post-revolutionary contests. Changes in relations between women and men necessitated by the exigencies of nationalist warfare did not survive once the new nation-state was established.[23]

Women within the oppressed national communities have often been split over how to connect their emerging sense of national identity and participation with their emerging political identities as women. For instance, women in Jaffna, Sri Lanka, formed a study group in the late 1980s, in the midst of a civil war, in order to work out together how their oppression as women is related to their oppression as Tamils in a Singhalese-dominated state. Some women had become politically conscious because the Tamil nationalist movement made them aware that their status as Tamils affected their chances of educational and economic opportunities in Sri Lanka.

It was only after this initial politicization through nationalism that they became aware that women and men were being made to play quite different roles in the escalating violence between Tamil guerillas, the government's military and the occupying Indian army. The changes wrought by ethnic mobilization and spiraling violence prompted these Tamil women to come together in a study group. There is no guarantee that their examination of women's conditions in Tamil and Sri Lankan societies will make them feel more comfortable with the nationalist movement as it is currently structured and directed. Participation in the women's study group could make them less willing to be the stalwarts of refugee camps or the symbols of outsiders' victimization. Their discussions might even prompt some of the women to see feminists in the Singhalese community as potential allies.[24]

Yet it isn't always obvious that surrendering the role of cultural transmitter or rejecting male protection will enhance a woman's daily security, reduce her burdens. Women in many communities trying to assert their sense of national identity find that coming into an emergent nationalist movement *through* the accepted feminine roles of bearer of the community's memory and children is empowering. Being praised by men in the nationalist movement for bearing more children and raising them well doesn't always feel like being patronized or marginalized.

But a woman who begins to go out of her home in the evening to attend nationalist meetings in the name of securing a better future for her children may meet strong resistance from her husband. Her husband may accuse her of neglecting her home duties, having a sexual liaison, making him look a fool in the eyes of other men, who may taunt him for not being able to control his wife. He never imagined that supporting the nationalist movement would entail losing control of his family. He may even beat her to stop her from attending such meetings.

Such experiences have raised wife battering to the status of a political issue for women in some nationalist movements. When they became involved in nationalist activities they may not have imagined that critiques of foreign rule, foreign bases or foreign investment would lead to critiques of relations between husbands and wives. In fact, many women became involved *as* good wives and good mothers. It was only later that they concluded that they would have to overcome male resistance in their homes and neighborhoods if they were to be able to participate fully in the movement. A Filipino nationalist active in resisting her government's alliances with foreign bankers, corporations and militaries describes a new step in nationalist organizing:

> We have a forum, we call it the women's soirée, where we invite women who are involved in the movement and also encourage them

to bring their husbands . . . One evening our topic was 'Feminism and Marriage – Do They Mix?' We went into a discussion of the family and some even questioned the value of the family because of the oppression of females that emanates from the family. Then some of the men started airing their grievances, such as that since their wives joined this movement they are no longer attending to the needs of the children . . . It was a very healthy exchange, and it was a very different kind of dialog because it was a group dialog, not just between husbands and wives.[25]

Women active in nationalist movements in the Philippines, Ireland, South Africa, Canada, Sri Lanka, Mexico and Nicaragua have begun to analyze how the 'home' and the 'international system' are integrally tied to one another. In doing so they are far ahead of those women in industrialized countries who have scarcely glimpsed those political connections. The process that ties them together is not just globalized consumer advertising, it is domestic relations between women and men. If women, they argue, are kept in marginalized roles by men as lovers, fathers or husbands, the chances of halting foreign-financed invasion, ending an unfair military bases treaty or holding accountable a multinational employer will be slim. In this sense foreign base commanders and entrepreneurs may depend on domestic violence as much as they do on alliances with men in the local élite.[26]

On the other hand, it can be very difficult for women to raise these sorts of issues inside a nationalist movement that is under siege. The more imminent and coercive the threat posed by an outside power – a foreign force or the local government's police – the more successful men in the community are likely to be in persuading women to keep quiet, to swallow their grievances and their analyses. When a nationalist movement becomes militarized, either on its leaders' initiative or in reaction to external intimidation, male privilege in the community usually becomes more entrenched.

When, on top of this, foreign governments become involved to defend an ethnic group from attack by an alien-backed power and thereby legitimize their involvement, male privilege gains a foreign ally. This appears to be what happened in Afghanistan. The United States government and its allies cast the war in Afghanistan in classic Cold War terms: the Soviet Union invaded a neighboring country, propping up a puppet regime which lacked a popular base; the anti-regime insurgents represented the real nation, and their brave resistance deserved the Free World's moral and military support. This picture becomes murky, however, when one looks at the situation from the vantage point of Afghan women. The cause for which the insurgent muhjahidin fought was a traditional rural clan way of life that is unambiguously patriarchal. One of the policies the Soviet-backed government in Kabul pursued that so alienated male clan leaders was expanding economic and educational opportunities for Afghanistan's women. While there is little evidence that the Soviet-backed Kabul regime enjoyed wide public legitimacy, outside observers report that its tenure proved beneficial to those mainly urban women who have been able to take advantage of the government's policy. In its hostile foreign policy toward the Khomeini regime in Iran, the US government had been eager to use that regime's harsh repression of women to justify its opposition; but this concern for women conveniently slipped off the policy stage when US officials designed their response to the civil war in Afghanistan.[27]

The militarization of Afghanistan has proved disastrous for women in the rural clan communities waging war. They have been subjected to bombing and exile. The refugee camps over the border in Pakistan had radically different meanings for women and men. For young men the refugee camp was a staging area for guerrilla campaigns across the border; they came to the camps to recoup from battle, to see their wives and children. For the women, 'camp life is so sad . . . they cry from morning to night', according to Sadia Ansari, one of the few Afghan women fortunate enough to have a teaching job in the United Nations-run schools. The women's husbands and fathers enforced the seclusion of their women far more strictly in the camps than they did in Afghanistan itself. Here they believed the risk was greater that their women would be seen by men outside the safe boundaries of the family. Whereas back in their villages women had field work, cooking and housework to do, in the camps they have no legitimate reason to leave their mud huts. Girls are kept out of the UN schools by protective fathers. In March 1988 the total enrollment in UN schools stood at 104,600 boys and 7,800 girls. 'The women are like birds in a cage,' admitted one guerrilla commander.[28] This civil war has been fought in a way that has militarized purdah. It has threatened men's control over women and so intensified men's determination to police the behavior of women.

Military mobilization, it is true, may make it necessary for men to permit women to acquire new skills and take on new responsibilities. This has been one of the motivations for the Kabul government to increase opportunities of paid work for women citizens. Journalists visiting rebel camps in the Southern Sahara and Eritrea also report that the women in those nationalist movements have used wartime's premium on their contributions to substantially widen women's sphere of public and private participation.[29] But simultaneously, militarization puts a premium on communal unity in the name of national survival, a priority which can silence women critical of patriarchal practices and attitudes; in so doing, nationalist militarization can privilege men.

If both pressures occur at the same time, a gendered tension will develop within the national community. This could produce a radically new definition of 'the nation'. Still, it is not assured. In the Palestinian communities in Lebanon and the occupied territories of Israel there is evidence of such two-sided pressures emanating from escalating militarization. On the one hand, militarization is providing young Palestinian men with new opportunities to prove their manhood, often in defiance not only of Israeli men's authority but also of what many perceive as their fathers' outworn authority. On the other hand, 'women are bearing the brunt of the *intifadah*', as one Palestinian told a reporter in 1988. The Israeli government's use of soldiers to enforce strict curfews and to arrest an estimated 6,000 Palestinian men has raised women's household chores to the stature of national imperatives: 'They have to watch the money, make all the family chores, bake their own bread, grow vegetables, take care of chickens and goats. These traditional roles are more important now.' Najwa Jardali, a Palestinian woman long active in a movement to provide day care and health clinics for women in the occupied territories, warned Western women not to imagine that day care is simply a women's issue. With militarization, it has become a national concern: 'Most Western feminists wouldn't regard kindergarten as important . . . but for us it's very important. The military government doesn't allow us kindergartens in schools, and day care enables women to get involved in other activities.' Proof of day care centers' national importance is the Israeli military's efforts to harass the women teachers and close them down.[30]

The popular image of the Palestinian nation until now has been the young male street-fighter of the Palestine Liberation Organization. With his checkered scarf, rock in hand, defiant and alert, he has stood for an entire nation. Palestinian women remained in the shadows. They were the protected, or the unprotected. But in 1988 Palestinian women began holding their own marches in the occupied territories to protest against the Israeli government's 'Iron Fist' policy. They defied heavily armed soldiers with chants of 'We are people, we are women. Never are we subdued. Never do we feel self-pity'. The community's leadership committee, the Unified National Command of the Intifadah, began addressing women's as well as men's concerns in its bulletins. The nature of Israeli military policy compelled Palestinians to develop a new way of organizing, one reliant less on outside help and more on small neighborhood committees, less susceptible to police and military disruption. In this type of organization, especially with so many men and boys jailed after the more visible stone–throwing confrontations, women began to come into their own as political actors. Women on the neighborhood committees went from house to house recruiting more members – 'collecting money and food for the besieged, asking people knowledgeable about health care to provide health services, urging participation in demonstrations'.[31] Will such militarizing pressures lead to an enduring reordering of femininity and masculinity within the Palestinian nation?

THE OTHER NOSTALGIA

Whereas Hollywood has been making colonial white women larger than life, some nationalist historians have been denying the centrality of relations between women and men that shaped nationalist movements and the states they created. This common practice of sweeping nationalist debates about women's relations with men under the nation's historical rug has bestowed inordinate power on future nationalist male leaders: they can claim that they are inheritors of an unambiguous legacy of communal solidarity. In reality, they may be inheritors of a patriarchal victory within the community a generation ago. The history of a nationalist movement is almost always a history filled with gendered debate. If a decade or a century later it looks as if there was no confusion, no argument about women's relations to men in the ruling community and to men in their own ethnic community, that is probably evidence only that the nostalgic patriarchal interpretation of nationalism has won, for the time being.

And the impact of winning – or being defeated – can be tricky to calculate at the time if the nation is fragile and outside threats are formidable. For example, Hue-Tam Ho-Tai, a contemporary Vietnamese feminist historian, describes one of those seemingly minor incidences in which the patriarchal side of the nationalist debate inched a step further toward victory.[32] In the 1920s there was a vital women's movement in French-ruled Vietnam. It raised issues of literacy, marriage conditions and public participation, challenging some of the most entrenched ideas of Viet- namese Confucian culture. Male intellectuals within the early nationalist movement also began speaking out against patriarchal values and practices which, they said, deprived the Vietnamese nation of talents and energies needed to throw off French colonialism.[33] Vietnamese women were encouraged by male and female nationalists to learn to read and write. The Trung Sisters, who had led the Vietnamese against Chinese colonialists in the past, were heralded as models for contemporary Vietnamese. Women began to join the Indochinese Communist Party and other nationalist groups. In the process, earlier women's groups became overshadowed by mixed nationalist organizations. Fighting for women's rights increasingly came to be seen as part of creating a Vietnamese sense of nationhood vital enough to challenge French colonial rule, a rule that grew harsher as the nationalist movement spread. During the 1930s there seemed little tension between advocating women's rights and joining the struggle for national rights: each served to bolster the other; both questioned the capacity of Vietnam's traditional Confucian culture to protect the nation from foreign domination.

Then some women began to examine relations between men and women in the nationalist movement. At a Communist Party conference women delegates were told by nationalist leaders to omit mention of problems between husbands and wives in their public report. Raising such questions on the floor, they were warned, would only generate hostile feelings within the nationalist movement at a time when it was already threatened by French police arrests. The women excised those sections from their report. Problems were legitimate if they were obstacles to nationalist unity; they were illegitimate if they made men in the nation anxious.

To make sense of the 'decline of the French empire', we have to understand how women saw the choices they faced at each precarious step in the creation of an effective Vietnamese nationalist movement. For many Vietnamese women did find strength and meaning through participation in the nationalist struggles for the next four decades of war.[34]

Later women may not have been able to see the same choices. But every time women succumb to the pressures to hold their tongues about problems they are having with men in a nationalist organization, nationalism becomes that much more masculinized. Today Vietnamese women are almost invisible in the senior ranks of the party and government: in 1979, five years after the expulsion of American troops, women comprised a mere 17 per cent of the Vietnamese Communist Party's membership; a decade after the nationalist victory the Politburo of the party, the most powerful decision-making body, was an all-male enclave; women have even lost some of the influence they had acquired in village and collective farm councils during the war.[35] Women in contemporary Vietnam are beginning to challenge this masculinization of public life, but it could prove rough going if they cannot retrace the steps of the nationalist movement back to the points at which women's relations with men were pushed off the nationalist agenda.

Nationalism places a high value on anything indigenous. Thus Sri Lankan feminist scholar Kumari Jayawardena explains that 'those who want to continue to keep the women of our countries in a position of subordination find it convenient to dismiss feminism as a foreign ideology . . .'[36] Sometimes this dismissal is combined with a homophobic attack. Feminists pressing their own nationalist movements to rethink the roles of women in politics, to reassess the effects of militant violence on women and men in the community, have been labeled 'lesbians' by critics. The label is designed to dismiss the feminists as tainted by alien ideas, as if heterosexuality were the sole indigenous practice in the local community, and to marginalize feminist ideas as stemming from degenerate women.[37]

Coming face to face with a Vietnamese feminist of the 1920s not only makes it less possible for British or American women to imagine that *their* foremothers were the creators of feminist ideas; it also subverts nervous local men's attempts to write off Third World feminists in the 1980s as nothing more than unwitting dupes of foreign imperialism.

In addition, nationalist feminists' critiques raise new questions about the relationships between pre-colonial and colonial culture. If their nation was free of patriarchy prior to the imposition of foreign colonial rule, then the task is relatively simple: by joining with men to roll back foreign domination and to restore pre-colonial values, they can restore equality between women and men inside the community. *If*, however, women discover that patriarchal values and practices predated colonial rule, and subsequently were exploited and exacerbated by colonialists, then regaining control of that society will not liberate women. In Quebec, the Philippines and Afro-America nationalist women have become wary of nationalist spokespeople who glorify the pre-colonial past. They have become uncomfortable when women warriors and queens are offered as proof that women had genuine influence over land and sexuality in the past. And yet they have to conduct these historical explorations carefully, knowing that outsiders might use their findings to discredit the nationalism they want to reform.[38]

CONCLUSION

Nationalism has provided millions of women with a space to be international actors. To learn that one's culture is full of riches, to learn that outsiders depend on coercion not innate superiority to wield their influence, to recognize bonds of community where before there were only barriers of class and party – this has been empowering. National consciousness has induced many women to feel confident enough to take part in public organizing and public debate for the first time in their lives. Furthermore, nationalism, more than many other ideologies, has a vision that includes women, for no nation can survive without culture being transmitted and children being born and nurtured.

Nationalism, by definition, is a set of ideas that sharpens distinctions between 'us' and 'them'. It is, moreover, a tool for explaining how inequities have been created between 'us' and 'them'. A woman who becomes politicized through nationalism is more likely to see a man from her community as sharing a common destiny than women from another community, especially if those women, no matter what their politics, come from a community that has treated her with derision.

But many of the nationalisms that have rearranged the pattern of world politics over the last two centuries have been patriarchal nationalisms. They have presumed that all the forces marginalizing or oppressing women have been generated by the dynamics of colonialism or neo-colonialism, and hence that the pre-colonial society was one in which women enjoyed security and autonomy. Thus simply restoring the nation's independence will ensure women's liberation. Many nationalists have assumed, too, that the significance of the community's women being raped or vulgarly photographed by foreign men is that the honor of the community's men has been assaulted. And frequently they have urged women to take active roles in nationalist movements, but confined them to the roles of ego-stroking girlfriend, stoic wife or nurturing mother. Repeatedly male nationalist organizers have elevated unity of the community to such political primacy that any questioning of relations between women and men inside the movement could be labeled as divisive, even traitorous. Women who have called for more genuine equality between the sexes – in the movement, in the home – have been told that now is not the time, the nation is too fragile, the enemy is too near. Women must be patient, they must wait until the nationalist goal is achieved; *then* relations between women and men can be addressed. 'Not now, later', is the advice that rings in the ears of many nationalist women.

'Not now, later', is weighted with implications. It is advice predicated on the belief that the most dire problems facing the nascent national community are problems which can be explained and solved without reference to power relations between women and men. That is, the causes and effects of foreign investments and indebtedness can be understood without taking women's experiences seriously; foreign military bases and agribusiness-induced landlessness can be challenged without coming to grips with how each has relied on women's labor and silence; the subtle allure of cultural imperialism can be dissected without reference to masculine pride and desire. Each of these presumptions seems politically shallow.

In addition, the 'not now, later' advice implies that what happens during the nationalist campaign will not make it harder in the future to transform the conditions that marginalize women and privilege men. It also rests on the prediction that political institutions born out of a nationalist victory will be at least as open to women's analysis and demands as the institutions of a nationalist movement. Both of these assumptions are questionable.

The very experiences of a nationalist campaign – whether at the polls in Quebec, or in the streets of Armenia, or in the hills of Algeria – frequently harden masculine political privilege. If men are allowed to take most of the policy-making roles in the movement, they are more likely to be arrested, gain the status of heroes in jail, learn public skills, all of which will enable them to claim positions of authority after the campaign is won. If women are confined to playing the nationalist wife, girlfriend or mother – albeit making crucial contributions to a successful nationalist campaign – they are unlikely to have either the skills or the communal prestige to gain community-wide authority at a later time. The notion of what 'the nation' was in its finest hour – when it was most unified, most altruistic – will be of a community in which women sacrificed their desires for the sake of the male-led collective. Risky though it might indeed be for a nationalist movement to confront current inequities between its women and men, it is more likely to produce lasting change than waiting until the mythical 'later'.

There is a long history of nationalist women challenging masculine privilege in the midst of popular mobilization. Erasing those women's efforts from the nationalist chronicles makes it harder for contemporary women to claim that their critical attitudes are indigenous and hence legitimate. Thus nationalist feminists in countries such as Vietnam, Sri Lanka and Jamaica have invested energy in recapturing local women's nationalist history. As Honor Ford Smith of the Jamaican feminist theater group Sistren recalls,

> What we knew was that a spate of tongue-in-cheek newspaper and television reports had projected white feminists in Europe and North America as 'women's libbers', hysterical perverts . . .
> We did not know of the struggles of women for education and political rights between 1898 and 1944. We did not know the names of the early black feminists . . .[39]

Challenges have been hardest to mount when women within a movement have lacked the chance to talk with each other in confidence about their own experiences and how they shape their priorities. Women in an oppressed or colonized national community are usually not from a single social class, and thus they have not experienced relations with the foreign power or the coopted ruling élite in the same ways. Nor do all women within a national community have identical sexual experiences with men – or with other women. Women who haven't had the space to discuss their differences and anxieties together have been less able to withstand men's charges of being lesbians or aliens.

Women's efforts to redefine the nation in the midst of a nationalist campaign have been especially difficult when potentially supportive women outside the community have failed to understand how important it is to women within the community not to be forced to choose between their nationalist and their feminist aspirations. As stressful as it is to live as a feminist nationalist, to surrender one's national identity may mean absorption into an international women's movement led by middle-class women from affluent societies. This is the caveat issued by Delia Aguilar, a Filipino nationalist feminist:

> when feminist solidarity networks are today proposed and extended globally, without a firm sense of identity – national, racial and class – we are likely to yield to feminist models designed by and for white, middle-class women in the industrial West and uncritically adopt these as our own.[40]

Given the scores of nationalist movements which have managed to topple empires and create new states, it is surprising that the international political system hasn't been more radically altered than it has. But a nationalist movement informed by masculinist pride and holding a patriarchal vision of the new nation-state is likely to produce just one more actor in the international arena. A dozen new patriarchal nation-states may make the international bargaining table a bit more crowded, but it won't change the international game being played at that table.

It is worth imagining, therefore, what would happen to international politics if more nationalist movements were informed by women's experiences of oppression. If more nation-states grew out of feminist nationalists' ideas and experiences, community identities within the international political system might be tempered by cross-national identities. Resolutions of inter-state conflicts would last longer because the significance of women to those conflicts would be considered directly, not dismissed as too trivial to be the topic of serious state-to-state negotiation.

4

BASE WOMEN

American bases in Britain are the objects of intense controversy among the British, while most Americans are scarcely aware of their government's airfields and submarine installations around the globe. British journalists, Members of Parliament and peace activists highlight the US bases as launching pads for deadly weapons over which the British have no control. There is little discussion, on the other hand, about the dating practices of American soldiers.

One occasionally hears rumors of 'barracks girls', young British girls who leave home and in time become resident sexual partners of American male soldiers. The debates that make the headlines, however, are about the capacity of the British government to protect British sovereignty: do elected officials have any say in the deployment of American bombers stationed in Britain? Could the American government launch nuclear missiles from Greenham or Molesworth with little heed to British opinion? Nationalist pride, ignited by Britain's war against Argentina for the Falklands in 1983, was wounded when the Americans used bases in East Anglia to launch their 1986 punitive bombing raid against Libya in 1986 without consulting Parliament.

Most of this controversy over US bases has taken place as if only strategic doctrine and democratic accountability were involved. British critics have chastised the Labour and Conservative governments for waxing nostalgic over the 'special relationship' between Washington and London, while failing to notice that the 'gentlemanly period is over; the United States is attempting to flex its political muscles'.[1]

Public discussions in Britain have brushed aside questions of American male soldiers' sexuality or British women's sexual availability. These issues may be pertinent to American bases in the Philippines or Honduras, but not in Britain. So goes conventional reasoning. Except when the bases raise questions about international strategic doctrine or blatant infringements of national sovereignty, they seem to fade into the backdrop of ordinary life. This sort of nationalist approach to American bases – or any foreign military bases – makes women invisible except occasionally as symbols. It thus serves to hide the strategic character of sexual politics; in so doing it misreads the actual character of military-bases agreements.

RACE AND SEX ON
THE UNSINKABLE AIRCRAFT CARRIER

There are literally thousands of military bases around the world. Some of them are the bases of the local armed forces; others service foreign militaries. By the mid-1980s there were 3,000 bases controlled by one country but situated in another country. Today there are British bases in West Germany, Cyprus, the Falklands and Belize. To many local residents and soldiers alike, Britain's bases in Northern Ireland feel like foreign bases. The Indian government stationed 45,000 of its soldiers on counter-insurgency duty in Sri Lanka. There have been 50,000 Cuban soldiers stationed in Angola. The Soviet Union maintains bases in Vietnam and Eastern Europe. Vietnamese troops only now are withdrawing from Kampuchea. The French military bases 8,000 of its soldiers in Chad, the Central African Republic, Gabon, Senegal, the Ivory Coast and Djibouti, as well as others in its remaining Pacific and Caribbean colonies. Canada sends troops to its bases in West Germany. Finnish, Fijian, Irish and other men serve overseas as part of United Nations peace-keeping forces. The United States government maintains that it needs all of its 1,500 military installations outside its borders to support 354,000 soldiers in Europe, 144,000 in the Pacific and Asia and thousands more on land and sea in the Caribbean, the Middle East, Africa and Latin America.[2]

Most bases have managed to slip into the daily lives of the nearby community. A military base, even one controlled by soldiers of another country, can become politically invisible if its ways of doing business and seeing the world insinuate themselves into a community's schools, consumer tastes, housing patterns, children's games, adults' friendships, jobs and gossip.

On any given day, therefore, only a handful of these scores of bases scattered around the world are the objects of dispute. Most have draped themselves with the camouflage of normalcy. Real-estate agents, town officials, charity volunteers, barmaids, local police, business owners – all accept the base, its soldiers and their families as givens. They may even see them as valuable, as good for their own well-being. Rumors of a base closing can send shivers of economic alarm through a civilian community that has come to depend on base jobs and soldiers' spending.

Military alliances between governments need this daily acceptance. NATO and the Warsaw Pact would be far more fragile than they already are if local women and men didn't find reasons for accepting foreign military bases in their midst. American, British, French, Soviet governments – those with the most soldiers stationed outside their own borders – would find it more difficult to sustain their sense of world influence if they couldn't maintain military bases in other people's backyards.

Understanding how a military base acquires its local camouflage – or perhaps loses it – is critical to making sense of how international military alliances are perpetuated, or undone.

The normalcy that sustains a military base in a local community rests on ideas about masculinity and femininity. A foreign base requires especially delicate adjustment of relations between men and women, for if the fit between local and foreign men and local and foreign women breaks down, the base may lose its protective cover. It may become the target of nationalist resentment that could subvert the very structure of a military alliance.

'A friendly, unquestioning, geographically convenient but expendable launching point for the projections of US military power' is what many British people believe their country has become.[3] They feel as though their country is less a sovereign nation than an aircraft-carrier for the American armed forces. Between 1948, when American forces returned to post-war Britain, and 1986 the US military created some 130 bases and facilities in England, Scotland, Wales and Northern Ireland. They did this with the British government's – often secret – acquiescence.[4] Some of these installations are mere offices, hardly noticeable to the casual passer-by. Others, like those at Greenham Common, Molesworth, Mildenhall and Holy Loch, are full-fledged communities with elaborate facilities and large workforces.

Most of the larger bases have their roots in the American installations which were established during World War II. These were easier to re-establish during the Cold War precisely because they had become a familiar part of British life in the early 1940s. But even during World War II local acceptance could not be taken for granted. Policy-makers had to fashion policies that would make the introduction of thousands of foreign soldiers palatable to local civilians, without offending the people back home. In Britain this meant ensuring that British and American men could work together as allies, not sexual rivals.

One of the most explosive topics of policy debate among British and American officers during World War II was relations between Black American male soldiers and white British women.[5] During the course of the war 130,000 Black American soldiers were stationed in Britain. Though they represented only a fraction of all the American troops based there, they became the topic of intense controversy – in village pubs, the press, Parliament and war rooms. When the first soldiers arrived in 1942, the American military was a segregated institution. However, Blacks had become a political force to be reckoned with in America; the Democratic administration of Franklin Roosevelt had entered office indebted to thousands of Black voters in northern cities who had transferred their electoral support from the Republican to the Democratic party.

British society in 1942 was overwhelmingly white, imbued with a sense of imperial superiority over the Asian and African peoples it still ruled. The British armed forces had fought World War I, and were fighting World War II, with regiments mobilized in India and the West Indies.[6] Both the British and American governments were ready with racial formulas when they sat down to talk about how to ensure that Black American men stationed in Britain would relate to white British women in ways that would enhance the joint war effort.

When white British women dated Black American soldiers, they made comparisons between American and British manhood. Comparing Black and white American men, they often found the former more polite, better company and perhaps more 'exotic'. By 1943, some white British women were giving birth to children fathered by Black GIs. Some were choosing to marry their Black American boyfriends. Certain members of Winston Churchill's cabinet became alarmed at what they considered a dangerous trend.

Top-level discussions had already begun in 1942. Three possible solutions were suggested in Cabinet sessions: 1) stop the Americans sending any Black male soldiers to Britain; 2) if that proved impossible, confine Black soldiers to certain coastal bases in Britain; 3) if all else failed, press the American armed forces to send more Black women soldiers and Red Cross volunteers to Britain so that Black male soldiers wouldn't have to look to white British women for companionship.[7]

None of these proposals proved feasible. The Allies' war effort depended too much on optimum use of human resources to keep over 100,000 American troops out of Britain or holed up in coastal towns. Furthermore, experience of World War I, when British whites turned against West Indian Black men who had served as maritime workers in the port of Liverpool, suggested that coastal quarantining was no insurance against racial hostility. Finally, the American government refused to send thousands of Black women to Britain. NAACP (National Association for the Advancement of Colored People) leaders made it clear to the Roosevelt administration that they did not see such a plan as respectful

8 and 9   Black American soldiers and their dates in one of London's
'colored' clubs, probably The Bouillabaisse in New Compton Street, July
1943. (The Hulton Picture Company, London)

of Black womanhood: Black women were volunteering for the US army
to be soldiers, not sexual companions. Furthermore, some of the British
didn't think that the plan was wise; white British men might start dating
the Black American women. In the end, only 800 Black military women
were sent to Britain, and not until 1945; they were members of the 6888th
Central Postal Battalion.[8]

As a result attempts to keep white British women from dating Black soldiers took the more diffuse forms of official and unofficial warnings directed at local women. To some observers this amounted to a campaign. British women who went out with Black men stationed at nearby bases were warned that they were more likely to get VD. Women who dated Black soldiers were branded as 'loose' or even traitorous to Britain. Whenever some infraction of disciplinary rules involved a Black soldier, the press was likely to specify his race. Parents who allowed their daughters to date Black GIs were portrayed by local papers as irresponsible.

During the early years of the war, there was a widespread suspicion, expressed in British newspapers and by Members of Parliament, that Black American soldiers were more likely than white GIs to be charged for sexual offences such as rape and to receive harsher sentences if convicted. By 1945, while Blacks (the great majority of them male) constituted only 8 per cent of all US troops stationed in Europe, they represented 21 per cent of all American servicemen convicted of crimes. When the criminal convictions are broken down by category, the discrepancies are even more startling: Black soldiers were 42 per cent of those convicted of sex crimes.[9] None the less, in August 1942 Parliament passed the United States of America (Visiting Forces) Act, which gave the American authorities the right to try American soldiers for offences committed on British soil. It was one step towards permitting the Americans to maintain their kind of racial/sexual system despite the unusual circumstances of wartime. Many white Americans were afraid that if sexual relations between Black men and white women were allowed in wartime Britain, sexual segregation would be harder to maintain in post-war America. Governmental and press persuasion was hardly overwhelming in its success, however. A Mass Observation survey conducted in August 1943 revealed that only one in seven British people questioned disapproved of marriages between Blacks and whites; 25 per cent told interviewers that they had become more friendly toward Black people partly because of meeting Black American soldiers.[10] Yet by the end of the war, and especially after the first babies had been born of white British women and Black soldiers, it took considerable social courage for a young white British woman to go out to a local pub with a Black soldier.

American military commanders weren't passive in these debates. General Dwight Eisenhower, senior US commander in Europe, tolerated white-Black dating because he believed that the US–British alliance would be harmed if Americans tried to impose segregationist 'Jim Crow' conventions on the British. Other American officers, however, thought that clashes between white and Black soldiers in Bristol and Leicester were due to white soldiers' justifiable resentment of Black troops 'using up' the limited pool of local white women. Some were also firmly opposed to 'mixed' marriages and used their authority to prohibit men under their command from marrying British women. By the end of the war at least 60,000 British women had filed applications with US officials to emigrate to America as war brides.[11] Very few of those whose prospective husbands were Black were accepted. There appeared to be a 'gentleman's agreement' between British and American middle-level officials to forbid marriages between Black GIs and white British women. The Black soldier intent on marriage would be transferred and given a serious talking-to by a superior; the woman was counseled by an American military officer or a British welfare officer.[12]

LIVING WITH THE BASE

By the late 1960s the American military base at Effingham had become an integral part of the social and economic life of nearby Long Crendon, a modest English village in Essex. The expansion of the base in the 1950s had wrought subtle but fundamental changes in townspeople's lives. The Americans started to hire local men and women and soon became one of the region's principal employers. More American soldiers arrived, bringing with them more wives and children. And with the families came American-style consumption: 'air transports began to fly in to Effingham laden with deep-freezers, washing machines, pressure- and microwave cookers, hi-fi equipment, Hoovers, electric organs and even Persian carpets.'[13] Some of the appliances made their way on to the now flourishing local second-hand market. Still, the ideological overspill from the American model of family life was contained by the married soldiers' preference for staying on the base, where the US Defense Department provided everything to make them feel as though they had never left home.

Keeping soldiers happy on a foreign base requires keeping soldiers' wives happy. For a century both British and American military commanders had been weighing up the advantages and disadvantages of allowing their soldiers to marry. Would marriage raise the moral tenor of the troops and cut down on drunkenness and VD? Or would marriage divide a soldier's loyalty, make him slower to mobilize, while burdening the armed forces with responsibilities for maintaining housing, health care, family harmony? The debate remains unsettled today.[14]

Despite commanders' ambivalence, the inclusion of wives and their children in the armed forces has altered the nature of a military base. No longer can a soldier's wife be easily marginalized as a camp-follower, on the edge of military operations, cooking her husband food and doing his laundry in return for rations. There are too many of them. And for the British, Canadian and American armed forces, which today have to recruit – and *keep* – large numbers of expensively trained male soldiers without the aid of compulsory male conscription, wives' dissatisfaction with military life can produce worrisome manpower shortages. The Hoovers, washing machines and electric organs flown into the US base at Effingham are evidence of the American army's attempt to satisfy not only male soldiers, but also their wives, while serving abroad.

Many women are quite content with these privileges. They find life on a base secure and comfortable. They adopt the military's way of viewing the world: the military's adversary is their adversary; their husband's rank is their rank. While serving overseas – and, though technically civilians, military wives refer to themselves as 'serving' – women become the backbone of social services on most bases. The armed forces depend on their largely unpaid work to transform an overseas base into a 'community'. For commanders responsible for bases on foreign soil the community works best if home-grown gender conventions are kept in place. Those conventions lower wives' expectations of paid work and careers of their own, encourage them to derive their own sense of self-worth from their husbands' accomplishments, and suppress wives' stories of depression and physical abuse for fear that they might damage their husbands' chances of promotion. Base commanders also need beliefs about femininity that encourage wives to take charge of family affairs when their husbands are away on maneuvers yet gladly relinquish any authority that comes from such responsibilities when the husband returns. They count on presumptions about both femininity and masculinity that will make military wives raise their daughters to look up to their fathers and their sons to emulate their fathers by choosing a military career themselves. A well-run military base not only serves today's military priorities, but also ensures a cohesive military a generation later. Any country's armed forces are more impervious to outside political control if they can reproduce themselves. Without military wives' active cooperation, a military cannot achieve this political goal.[15]

Relationships are changing between women and men on foreign and domestic bases, however, for several reasons. First, many armed forces are having to recruit substantial numbers of women in order to compensate for falling birthrates and to obtain the well-educated recruits a technology-laden military now requires. These women have begun to organize and acquire political lobbying skills. They are making alliances with legislators and civilian women to press for a wider selection of postings and for an end to sexual harassment and other obstacles barring their military advancement. They are less likely than women mobilized during World War II to maintain a stiff upper lip in the face of discrimination intended to keep women soldiers in their place. American servicewomen complain that pornographic magazines are still sold routinely in base stores, but many military bases are not quite the monolithic patriarchal enclaves they were a generation ago. Despite the problems of joint deployment, thousands of American servicemen are marrying servicewomen to form two-career military marriages. Despite their continuing illegality, lesbian relationships are being formed on military bases. Despite fears of 'fraternization', women soldiers are being stationed with male partners in underground nuclear missile silos. Nascent alliances are even being forged between women soldiers and military wives.

Second, since the early 1980s military wives have become more aware of the services they render. Divorce settlements, in particular, have focussed the issue. In reaction to a series of what they perceived to be unfair alimony settlements, American military wives formed their own organizations and effectively lobbied the US Congress. Their political aim was to ensure that women who have been married to servicemen are compensated for all they have contributed not only to their husbands' careers but also to the military itself if, as so often happens, their husbands divorce them on retiring from the military.

Third, Canadian, American and British military wives have begun to object publicly to the conventional assumption that they will surrender their paid jobs when their husbands reach senior rank in order to devote themselves exclusively to volunteer work on the base. In 1988 American women appeared before congressional committees to decry this practice. They wanted to be recognized as private citizens with financial and career aspirations and needs of their own. So, too, do Canadian military wives who discovered while petitioning for family dental insurance that, though legally civilians, they were prohibited from carrying on what a base commander deemed 'political' activity. American women told legislators that they didn't want their husbands' chances of promotion to be jeopardized by their decisions to keep their paid jobs. The result: the Pentagon was compelled to issue formal statements affirming wives' autonomy. For instance, the Air Force Secretary told his base commanders in March 1988, 'no commander, supervisor or other Air Force official will directly or indirectly impede or otherwise interfere with' the decision by a military spouse to work outside the home. Furthermore, 'neither the decision of the spouse in this matter, nor the marital status of the military member, will be a factor used to affect the evaluation, promotion or assignment of the military member.'[16]

Finally, defense officials around the world are being pressed to slash expenditure on military personnel so that weapons procurement doesn't take the brunt of budgetary cuts. This has thrown into doubt the wisdom of sending soldiers' wives and children overseas. British, Canadian and American officials are considering new schemes to send soldiers abroad on shorter duties, to rationalize wives and children staying at home. The US Defense Department spends some $2 billion annually on dependent housing and services just in Europe.[17] If wives could be kept in the US, a lot of money could be saved, which could be spent on costly weapons projects like the new Stealth bomber. But this maneuver would not be easy. It would entail shifting more family and emotional burdens on to military wives. It would also mean that thousands more male soldiers would be living far from home without their wives, a fact likely to foster complicated relationships between married American men and single British, Italian and West German women. Even without such a policy, many West German women have found themselves raising children fathered by American soldiers on their own when those men have ended relationships abruptly at the end of their tours.[18]

Young single soldiers stationed at Effingham were always more likely than married soldiers to form relationships with women off the base. They didn't have the wives and daughters and sons to help them create a sense of secure American domesticity in a foreign country; they also had more money to spend.

Some of the American men who go into town are in search of no more than a bit of off-base companionship. Others are far more ambivalent about women as a direct result of their militarized sexuality. Women can seem as much a threat as a comfort to the modern warrior. A woman is to be destroyed just as the enemy is to be destroyed. At the Upper Heyford US Air Force Base, not far from Effingham, pilots of the 77th Tactical Fighter Squadron recently published their own songbook. The lyrics written by the pilots suggest the sexualization of military life as well as the militarization of male soldiers' sexuality. For the squadron's 'Victor Alert Song', they sing these lyrics to the tune of Rogers and Hammerstein's once-innocent 'My Favorite Things':

> *Reading our porno and picking our asses*
> *Checking our forms out and passing our gasses*
> *Silver sleek b-61s slung below*
> *Nuclear war and we're ready to go.*[19]

A few pages later, a pilot contributes lyrics that weave his dreams of sex with death:

I fucked a dead whore by the side of the road,
I knew right away she was dead
The skin was all gone from her tummy
The hair was all gone from her head.
And as I lay down beside her,
I knew right away I had sinned . . .[20]

Young British women, like their mothers before them, make comparisons. They aren't always privy to the American soldiers' secret dreams when they weigh up the American and British varieties of masculinity. To the young women of the quiet villages around Effingham, the American soldiers 'were a godsend.' According to one local resident, 'The Essex girls found the Americans more polite, considerate and enthusiastic than the English boys.'[21] The American's aura was enhanced by the social resources of the base, which easily outstripped the local pub or Saturday-night disco. 'A girl escorted to one by a local lad had to resign herself to a loutish rather than romantic experience. By contrast the weekend dances at the base offered a model of propriety and good order.'[22] Still, parents worried about their daughters' reputations. Dating foreign soldiers wasn't the path to ladylike respectability. The daughters, for their part, chose to go out

10 US Air Force pilot and the squadron's 'mascot' at US Air Force Base, Upper Hayeford, Oxfordshire. (photo: Monique Cabral, 1988)

for their part, chose to go out with Americans as a way of asserting their autonomy. The more defiant dated Black American soldiers.

And although local young men have to compete against the American soldiers for the women of Essex, they, too, seem to gain something from the base. More of them began to get jobs on the base, to acquire cars sold by the Americans and to modify the deferential attitudes traditional among working men in rural England.

Thus the coming of an American base had to be negotiated at the ideological level of masculinity and femininity. But this occurred locally, out of the media's limelight. For their part, cabinet ministers and defense officials were content to let the crucial sexual politics of military-bases agreements take place beyond their accepted area of responsibility.

GREENHAM AND SEXUALITY

The British Ministry of Defence requisitioned Greenham Common for the war effort in 1941. The arrangement was to be 'temporary'. For five years after the war the airfield was unused; nearby Newbury's Chamber of Commerce called for its return to the town. But in 1952 the Labour government gave the US Strategic Air Command permission to use Greenham Common as a base and to expand its facilities. The people of Newbury weren't unaccustomed to military bases in the area. The entire region southwest of London had become home for military facilities: RAF Welford, one of the world's largest ammunition stores, was a few miles away; the Atomic Weapons Research Establishment was at Aldermaston; the Royal Ordnance Factory helped build atomic bombs at Burghfield; the army depot at Thatcham was a main supplier of uniforms; and the School of Military Survey was at Hermitage. Each employed residents from the Newbury area. Moreover, Newbury was solidly Conservative. All this helped make the presence of a foreign military base if not normal, at least digestible. Helping the digestive process was the British government's legal stipulation that Greenham Common would remain nominally, if not practically, under RAF control and that the Ministry of Defence would pay the local authority £100,000 a year instead of paying local taxes.[23]

When the government announced in 1981 that the Americans would be deploying nuclear warheaded cruise missiles at Greenham, the mostly middle-class, home-owning residents felt reassured because the new installations necessary to house the missiles were to be designed so that they were inconspicuous, thus not affecting house prices. Indeed, the *Newbury Weekly News* reported in 1983 that within two years the base would have 5,900 American Air Force staff and their wives and children, plus an additional 100 RAF personnel.[24] For a variety of reasons – perhaps because so many of the American soldiers stationed at Greenham were married, the base was designed so that most of the Americans were content to do their socializing and shopping within its confines, most of the personnel were white, the local commander made a special effort to discourage sexual relations between his personnel and local residents – there appears to have been little sexualized politics around Greenham Common Air Force base, until 1981.

That autumn a small group of women walked from Wales to Greenham and decided to establish a permanent encampment outside the base fence to protest against plans to deploy cruise missiles there.[25] It wasn't the American military men's sexuality or the sexuality of the civilian British men or civilian British women which became the object of controversy. It was the sexuality of the women protesters. The national press and local residents took the lead in describing the Greenham women – at times a small number of full-time campers, at times several thousand day-long demonstrators – as irresponsible mothers, unwashed women, lesbians, hysterical political naïfs.[26]

Whereas a military base is designed to keep the soldiers' wives domestic, respectable and politically quiescent, the peace camp, withstanding mud, rain and bulldozers, inevitably brought women face to face with each other and with soldiers and policemen. Conventionally feminine respectability was largely irrelevant to an anti-nuclear peace camp. As a result, the women at Greenham appeared to threaten not just defense policies and house prices, but the very meaning of being female.

For some British women, however, the Greenham peace-campers' formulation of womanhood struck a chord. It provided a way to rethink the divisions between private and public life. Even some Conservative women, when Conservative ministers were instructing authorities to bulldoze the camp, became more admiring than frightened of the women who pitched their make-shift tents or 'benders' outside the missile base. Journalist Beatrix Campbell interviewed one Tory woman who had cut her hair short to make it clear to her husband and sons that she identified with the Greenham women:

'Before Greenham I didn't realise that the Americans had got their missiles here. Then I realised. What a cheek! It was the fuss the Greenham Common women made that made me realise.' The peace camp became the source of endless attrition over the kitchen table: 'The men in this house [her husband and two sons] think they're butch, queers.' Did she? She thought for a moment. 'No.' Would it have bothered her if they were butch or if they were lesbians? She

11 Women peace campaigners dance on a cruise missile silo inside the US Air Force base at Greenham Common, 1 January 1983. (photo: Raissa Page/Format)

thought again. 'No.' Women irritated her men anyway, she said, not without affection. 'They never stop talking about Land Rovers and bikes, and they've not finished their dinner before they're asking for their tea.'[27]

Women who have taken part in the peace camps have found that sustaining a peace encampment in the shadow of a masculinized base demands humor and ingenuity. It also requires a continuing reassessment by each woman of what it means to be feminine in a militarized world. At peace camps at Greenham, Comiso in Sicily, Saskatchewan in Canada, Seneca and Seattle in America, women have tackled questions about mothering, autonomy, safety, heterosexuality, fear and racial divisions between women.[28] They began to chart the connections between violence and hierarchy on the one hand, and femininity and feminism on the other. What were the relationships between women who could climb over the base fence and those who could not? When soldiers from Greenham took cruise missiles out to the countryside on maneuvers, their wives and girlfriends stood at the fence to cheer them on. What were the connections between peace-camp women and women living and working on the base? How should peace-camp women relate to policemen and soldiers guarding the base? Some women peace activists believed that they could accomplish more if they joined peace camps organized by men and women. What did they risk in giving up the autonomy of a women-only camp?

> Okay, who wants tea? Coffee? One, two. Barleycup? Three, . . .
> Humble equipment, limited space, a caravan outing multiplied by
> 365 days, divided by a dozen different opinions. I don't like cigarette
> smoke. He doesn't like garlic. Someone doesn't speak to someone
> else, and if I don't find that book I'm going to scream. Could you
> turn the radio down *please*.
> Peace . . . Anyone who goes to a peace camp thinking peace is a
> commodity dished out like lentil stew will have second thoughts.[29]

Women who spent any time at Greenham began to sort out with each other what kinds of ideas about manhood seemed necessary to sustain a military base. They looked through the wire at the British policemen who were assigned to keep them out. They watched the American Air Force men who were kept at a distance, instructed by their superiors to keep a low profile. They talked about the civilian men from surrounding towns who came out to taunt campers and the government men sent to physically remove them again and again.

> I've been quite badly bruised by the police, but they are accessible
> . . . just looking at them and saying, 'This is my body. I'm protecting
> my life with my body because I don't feel protected by you and these
> weapons . . . Aren't you more threatened by cruise missiles?' I've not
> found a policeman able to use violence after that.[30]

Any military base is designed to be secure. By cutting the fences, dancing on the missile silos, challenging charges of trespassing in court, the Greenham women managed to transform the very meaning of a base, and of public security. A military base easily penetrated by a group of non-violent women was no longer a military base.

In 1988 the United States and Soviet governments ratified the Inter-mediate Range Nuclear Force Treaty, a bilateral agreement to dismantle ground-launched SS-20, cruise and Pershing II missiles. Reporters were eager to know what the Greenham women would do. Women at peace camps in North America and Western Europe expressed doubt that the INF treaty by itself would bring an end to the base mentality. It seemed likely that bases at Greenham, Comiso and elsewhere would be used for alternative American-controlled NATO weapons once the missiles were removed. Furthermore, air- and sea-launched nuclear warheaded missiles are still permitted under the INF treaty, encouraging NATO strategists to expand their Air Force and naval installations. Thus in October

1988 British women began adapting principles from Greenham to a women's peace action at Portsmouth, port of call for American missile-carrying submarines: 'The protest is non-violent; the group is a network of small groups organized autonomously; women's groups and mixed groups will cooperate without compromising women-only groups; land protest is an integral part of any sea action; swimming and sea-skills training will be undertaken on a voluntary basis; safety is a prime consideration.' They began offering swimming lessons while the cruise missiles were still in their silos underneath Greenham Common.[31]

At the same time, other Greenham women created a new all-women's peace camp outside the nuclear weapons facility at nearby Aldermaston to draw attention to the role Britain itself was playing in the continued nuclear arms build-up. Aldermaston, though a weapons factory, not a base, was similar to a military base in that it nurtured a false sense of security behind a public façade of masculinized strength.[32]

WHEN BASES MOVE

NATO in the 1990s will not be the NATO of the 1960s. The United States cannot be so sure of its political dominance over the alliance as it once was. Canadian and European governments now have to pay at least some attention to sophisticated grassroots peace movements, movements fueled in large part by women's activism.

In 1988 Spain's Socialist government was compelled to renegotiate its military bases agreement with the US because of a popular movement against the bases. While it stopped far short of ousting the American bases altogether, it did insist that the Americans transfer their F-16 fighter bombers, capable of carrying nuclear as well as conventional bombs. But where could the F-16s and their 3,800 personnel and families go? The search for a new base had implications for women in Greece and Italy, many of whom had already spoken out against the foreign military personnel in their midst. Ultimately, the Italian government, eager to prove its reliability as an ally, offered the Americans Calabria as a new home for the F-16s. In a region suffering from economic depression, Calabria's residents were assured that the bases would bring needed jobs. There was no public discussion of what the arrival of the pilots would do to local women's sexual relationships or their sense of safety.[33]

In the eyes of military bases negotiators the world is a single 'market'. If a base is forced to close in one place, it will have to be relocated somewhere else. The alternative, to radically rethink the very nature of national security, is rarely considered. This single-market outlook ties women in current base towns and potential base towns together, though they have few resources for sharing information and tactics. It also means that a victory for women in one country can exacerbate the militarization of daily life for women in another country. Their region will be selected as a replacement site precisely because they do not have the resources to mount an effective political obstacle to a new base.

Nowhere has this been more clear than in Goose Bay, Labrador. This northern Canadian region has been chosen by the Canadian government and its NATO allies as a perfect spot for an air force training base. Its remoteness from heavily populated centers allows pilots to practice low-level flying without kicking up embarrassing political dust. Canadian, British, Dutch, American and West German pilots are already sent there to develop their special skills. Now it appears likely that more West German pilots will be sent. West German civilians living near the huge air force base at Ramstein have successfully lobbied officials in Bonn to cut back the low-level flying and its deafening noise pollution. Bonn has announced that it will accede to its citizens' demands and send more of its pilots to train in Labrador.

But Labrador isn't an empty land. It is the home of native Canadians of the Innu community. Innu leaders and their white supporters have been monitoring the sexual ramifications of having NATO pilots stationed nearby. They describe how pilots, their cars well stocked with beer, drive from Goose Bay to the villages in search of young Innu women. Some of the girls, often teenagers, have been made pregnant by British, West German and American pilots. It then has been left to the Innu community to raise these children. Needless to say, the lives of Innu teenage girls have not been a topic of consideration in Ramstein or Bonn.[34]

FOREIGN BASES IN THE THIRD WORLD: IS PROSTITUTION THE ISSUE?

Military bases and prostitution have been assumed to 'go together'. But it has taken calculated policies to sustain that fit: policies to shape men's sexuality, to ensure battle readiness, to determine the location of businesses, to structure women's economic opportunities, to affect wives, entertainment and public health. It is striking that these policies have been so successfully made invisible around bases – local and foreign – in North America and Western and Eastern Europe, whereas they have attracted so much notoriety around bases in the poorer countries of the Third World.

It is worth thinking about why military prostitution is so politically invisible in some places and so notorious in others. Which facets of foreign and domestic military base life have been deemed to be 'political' and so to warrant public action? In North America, Europe, New Zealand

and Australia, local military bases only rarely become issues (often when threatened with closure), while foreign military bases have become politicized when local citizens have begun to see them as jeopardizing their own security and sovereignty. Prostitution and its attendant threats to public health and morality have been scarcely mentioned. By contrast, groups protesting against foreign bases in Third World countries have made prostitution a central issue.*

By the late nineteenth century the British government had its troops spread throughout the globe sustaining its empire. These troops were not so likely to seek sexual liaisons with working-class white women as with colonized women of color – Chinese women in Hong Kong, Indian women in India, Egyptian women in Egypt. British officials had been thwarted in their efforts to control white working-class women in Britain by the Anti-Contagious Diseases Acts Campaign led by feminists of the Ladies National League. They were determined not to lose control over colonial women. First, they refashioned marriage policies for soldiers, considering whether allowing British soldiers to marry Indian women would harm or enhance military readiness and white settler morale. Some officials believed that if British soldiers were allowed to marry Indian women, they might be less likely to frequent prostitutes and thus, presumably, be less likely to pick up venereal diseases. But on the other hand, such a policy of encouraging inter-racial marriage might have jeopardized British men's sense of their racial superiority. Second, they continued enforcing the Contagious Diseases Acts outside Britain after they had been repealed at home in the 1880s. These laws, called the Cantonment Acts overseas, permitted colonial police authorities to conduct compulsory genital examinations on women around imperial military bases for the sake of allowing British soldiers overseas to have sexual relations with colonial women without fear of venereal disease.

In 1888 Josephine Butler, founder of Britain's Ladies National League, launched an international campaign calling for the abolition of the Cantonment Acts. Her new journal, *The Dawn*, criticized British authorities'

---

* Soviet bases in Third World countries do not appear to provoke public debate about prostitution. Two of the Soviet Union's largest overseas bases are Cam Ranh Bay, in Vietnam, and, until mid-1988, Kabul in Afghanistan. Prostitution, while it may exist, has not attracted sufficient attention to make it politically salient. One well-researched description of personnel problems experienced by the Soviet military during its engagement in Afghanistan does not mention prostitution or VD at all. The report – written under contract for the US army and thus with every incentive to reveal any warts on the Soviet army – cites drug abuse, inter-rank bullying and ethnic hostility between Slavic and Muslim Soviet soldiers as the problems of most concern to Soviet officers.[35]

double standard: controlling of women's sexual behavior for the sake of protecting soldiers' sexual pleasures. Butler's movement was feminist in its analysis, but not in its organization. Her chief abolitionist allies appear to have been British men and educated men in the colonized societies. Colonial women – a study in 1891 found that 90 per cent of military prostitutes were widows – were seen by abolitionists as the victims but rarely as organizational allies with political ideas and resources of their own.[36]

Anti-Cantonment Acts campaigners saw these policies in imperial perspective: if such regulations were allowed to persist in India, they would provide lessons for military authorities in other British colonies and even in the colonies of rival imperial powers, such as the Netherlands, who also needed to station soldiers abroad, provide them with sexual access to colonial women, and yet ensure that the soldiers were physically fit enough to carry out their military duties for the empire. A letter written in 1888 by one of Butler's Dutch correspondents charts the flow of military lessons:

If you should succeed in your next great attack upon India, it will be an immense lever for us.

We have dreadful accounts of this evil in our barracks in Batavia [Netherlands East Indies, now Indonesia] . . .

One of the official gentlemen quietly remarked that they thought of introducing the Anglo-Indian system of having separate tents inhabited by the licensed women in the camps. At present at a fixed hour in the evening the doors of the Barracks are opened in order to admit a certain number of these poor victims. I can scarcely record all that we have learned. Life in the Barracks is *morally horrible* . . .

The fact stated here shows that the bad example set by the English government in India is infecting Java, and no doubt other Colonies of other nations, thus doubling and trebling our motives for urging the Abolition of the hideous Indian Ordinances and Cantonment Acts . . . [37]

By 1895 Butler and her campaigners had persuaded the British government to repeal the Cantonment Acts. Nevertheless, her informants in the colonies, who continued to monitor barracks and police practices, found that forced examinations of local women continued despite the repeal. *The Dawn* published letters from British military officers who articulated the widespread official view that such practices remained necessary. They were allegedly necessary for individual British soldiers (not for Indian soldiers; they seemed to have a strikingly lower incidence of VD, which puzzled their British commanders), but also for the very well-being of the British empire. To this argument Josephine Butler's editorial retorted: 'We had not realized that the women of a conquered race, in the character of official prostitutes, constituted one of the bulwarks of our great Empire!'[38]

Thus the connection between bases and prostitution has not been confined to colonies and poor countries. Governments in France, the United States and Canada all attempted to create military and civil law to control women for the sake of ensuring soldiers' morale and health.[39] When they were not able to carry out those laws at home they tried to put them into effect abroad. Yet today it is mainly in poor countries that prostitution is used politically by opponents of bases to question whether military alliances are in the interests of the local population, as their governments argue they are.

It may be that prostitution really doesn't exist around US bases in Britain or British bases in West Germany or Soviet bases in East Germany and Poland. Or it may be that prostitution – as distinct from white American servicemen having white British 'girlfriends' – is politically visible only when most of the foreign soldiers and the local women they date are from different racial groups. It would be surprising if a military base in Massachusetts, Belfast, Ramstein or Berlin were any less sexually constructed than bases in Belize, Honduras or Guam. The crucial difference, therefore, may be in the ways issues are politically constructed.

It may be that West and East German, British, Italian, Spanish, Polish and Greek women have access to other forms of livelihood so they aren't pressed into taking jobs at dance halls and massage parlors. Or it may be that Western peace activists have assumed that security and sovereignty are their most serious grounds for anti-bases campaigns and so haven't looked closely to see whether, in reality, sexual politics defines the role that those bases play in their communities as much as weapons politics.

AIDS, BASES AND THE 'PACIFIC RIM'

Mon. [November] 4 – Rained all day.
Tues. 5 – Rained all day
Wed. 6 – Rained part of day. Got pay check.
Thurs. 7 – Rained all day.[40]

Thus wrote Jessie Anglum, wife of an American army officer, in her diary. She did not enjoy her stay in the Philippines. The year was 1901. The American army had been sent by President McKinley to quash a Filipino insurgency which first fought the islands' Spanish colonizers and then resisted American plans for colonization. Jessie Anglum was one of the first American military wives to join her husband in the Philippines. She was put up in a Manila hotel. As the monsoon rains poured steadily outside the shutters, she was bored. Her husband spent most of his days on maneuvers against the insurgents. She went for occasional carriage rides and had tea with the few other American women then in Manila. But she didn't want to be in the Philippines. She only sailed to Asia out of wifely duty. She counted the days until her husband's tour was over. And she was happy when she could repack her trunks and sail back home.

There were no elaborate American bases when Jessie Anglum endured her damp hotel stay. But in the ninety years since her arrival the US government has made up for that deficiency. Today the now independent Philippines hosts a score of US military facilities. Subic Bay Naval Base and Clark Air Force Base, both situated on the main island of Luzon, are deemed by Pentagon strategists to be among the most crucial for American global defense.

When American military planners look at the world these days they imagine the territories encircling the Pacific ocean as part of a single security – or insecurity – chain. To be secure, this 'Pacific Rim' must be strung with a necklace of American-controlled military bases: from Anchorage to San Diego, Hawaii, Vladivostok, Seoul, Yokahama, Cam Ranh Bay, Subic Bay and Clark, Wellington, Belau and Kwajalein. Having created this mental map, this assumption of militarized interconnectedness, the American strategist is on the look-out for gaps and disturbances. The Soviet Union's Pacific coastline catches the strategist's eye; so now does Cam Ranh Bay, a large naval base built by the Americans during the Vietnam War, but since 1975 given over by the Vietnamese government to the Soviet military for its use. Less tinged with outright hostility, but still worrying for the strategists are the political changes that make American ships, planes and personnel less welcome in New Zealand, South Korea, Belau and the Philippines.

The American–Philippines bases agreement comes to an end in 1991. The American government must persuade the post-Marcos government of President Corazon Aquino, under pressure from both anti-base nationalists on the left and anti-communist army officers on the right, to renew the bases agreement. Failure would mean radically redesigning the necklace meant to secure the Pacific Rim. This would entail finding another country willing to accept some of the world's largest military bases and the social problems they bring with them.

The social problem that has attracted most Filipino attention is prostitution. Filipinos, like South Koreans, Okinawans, Guameans, Thais and Belauans, have held foreign military bases responsible for creating or exacerbating conditions which promote prostitution. Consequently, as the American bases have become the objects of nationalist ideas and campaigns, so prostitution has to become an issue defined in terms of nationalist anger and nationalist hopes. The arrival of AIDS in the Philippines in 1987 only served to escalate nationalists' sense that the current American-Philippines bases agreement violates not just Filipino women's rights but ('more fundamentally' some might say) the sovereignty and integrity of the Filipino nation as a whole.

Filipino feminists took up militarization as a women's issue. During the 1970s and early 1980s they began analyzing how the Marcos regime's growing reliance on coercion undermined women's already fragile support systems. Since the fall of Marcos in 1986, Filipino women activists have charted with dismay the Aquino regime's continuation of militarization as a strategy for resolving the country's deepening social crises. Integrating anti-militarism into their analysis and practice has made it easier for women active in Gabriela and other feminist organizations to find common cause with other nationalist, anti-militarist political groups, even if those groups did not accord women's concerns top priority in their own work.

Subic Bay Naval Base overshadows the town of Olongapo. The Navy base is home for many of the 15,000 American military personnel and their families stationed in the Philippines. When an aircraft-carrier docks, another 18,000 men pour into town. The Subic Bay base relies on civilian Filipino labor to keep it running. Workers are paid at lower rates than workers on American bases in South Korea or Japan, but for many Filipino men and women these base jobs provide a livelihood. By 1985 the US military had become the second largest employer in the Philippines, hiring over 40,000 Filipinos: 20,581 full-time workers, 14,249 contract workers, 5,064 domestics and 1,746 concessionaries. The sum of their salaries amounted to almost $83 million a year. By 1987 the American bases were employing over 68,000 Filipinos, who enjoyed medical insurance as well as other benefits not commonly offered by most Filipino employers. Many were women. Many more women were married to or mothers of male workers. On the other hand, some Filipino analysts warned against letting this figure weigh too heavily, for those employees amounted to a mere 5 per cent of the 1.18 million people employed by the Philippines government itself.[41]

As the price of sugar has declined on the international market and as large landowners have pushed more and more Filipinos into landless poverty, more young women have come to make a living by servicing the social and sexual needs of American military men. In 1987 the Aquino government estimated that there were between 6,000 and 9,000 women entertainment workers registered and licensed in Olongapo City.

Independent researchers, taking account of unlicensed as well as licensed women, put the figure as high as 20,000. Another 5,000 women often come to Olongapo City from Pampanga province and Manila when one of the American aircraft-carriers comes into port.[42]

In addition, in recent years rising numbers of children have been recruited into the prostitution trade. Of the approximately 30,000 children born each year of Filipino mothers and American fathers, some 10,000 are thought to become street children, many of them working as prostitutes servicing American pedophiles. Some of the Amer-Asian children who avoid the streets have been sold. An insider described the racialized market to Filipino researchers: 'Those Caucasian-looking children are each allegedly sold for $50–200 (around P1,000–4,000), whereas the Negro-fathered ones fetch only $25–30 (around P500–600).'[43]

There are more Filipino women working as prostitutes in the tourist industry than around US bases. Filipino feminists have drawn the links between the two, revealing how distorted investment, patriarchal conventions and short-sighted government priorities have together forced thousands of poor women off the land and out of exploitative jobs to service civilian as well as military men. It has been militarized prostitution, however, that has been made the most prominent symbol of compromised sovereignty by the male-led nationalist movement. Without feminist prompting, these anti-bases organizations rarely delve into the patriarchal causes for women coming to Olongapo.[44]

Two quite disparate worries have made American officials somewhat less complacent about prostitution around their Philippines bases in the late 1980s: Defense Department women's advocates' claim that prostitution is lowering *American* women's morale; and the spread of AIDS.

The US Defense Advisory Committee on the Status of Women in the Services (DACOWITS) is a group of civilian men and women appointed by the Secretary of Defense to monitor the conditions under which women in the US military serve. It has become an in-house advocate for equal promotions, for attacking sexual harassment, for redefining 'combat'. DACOWITS members traveled to Asia in 1987 to inspect the conditions under which American women soldiers and sailors were serving overseas. For the first time in its history, DACOWITS members began to make a connection between the treatment of local women around the American bases and the treatment of American women on the bases. They blamed American Navy women's low morale on the sexist environment created by the 'availability of inexpensive female companionship from the local population and its adverse consequences for legitimate social opportunities of Service women'.[45]

Still, the American DACOWITS members fell far short of allying with Filipino women. They confined their brief to the well-being of American servicewomen. They were concerned with the impact housing was having on Navy women's heterosexual relationships. Women serving on Okinawa and at Subic Bay told them that the command's policy of placing women personnel in barracks separated from the male sailors' barracks, when combined with the condoning of local prostitution, was fostering a base-wide impression that American servicewomen were merely 'second team' members. 'More serious', according to DACOWITS members, such policies were contributing to 'conditions in which extremist behavior [lesbianism] is fostered . . . For example, one barracks at Camp Butler is widely referred to as Lessy Land.'[46]

But it has been AIDS that has sparked alarm – and confusion – among the military and local policy-makers responsible for managing a system of sexual relations that supports the American Pacific Rim security strategy.

By January 1987 doctors had recorded twenty-five HIV-positive cases in the Philippines. All twenty-five carriers were women. Twenty-two of them worked as entertainers in bars around Clark, Subic and Wallace US military bases. Six of the twenty-five showed signs of AIDS. Women in Gabriela, the umbrella feminist organization active in the anti-bases campaign, helped open Olongapo's first Women's Center and started to make the information known. Women criticized the Manila government for not giving HIV-positive women any counseling or medical care and for blaming the women themselves for AIDS, pointing to them as a threat not only to American men but to other Filipinos.

> Who are the producers of AIDS in the Philippines? Why does prostitution exist and proliferate in the military bases and our tourist spots? *The danger and damage of AIDS to women and the existence of prostitution are, in fact, crimes against women.* We are the products, the commodities in the transaction . . . Who, then, we ask, are the real criminals of AIDS and prostitution? Indict them, not us.[47]

Filipino women activists called for a reversal of the century-old formula for safeguarding the morale and physical health of soldiers serving on overseas bases. Specifically, Gabriela members called on the Philippines government to insist that the American government institute a policy that all servicemen or base employees showing any signs of AIDS not be allowed 'on Philippine soil':

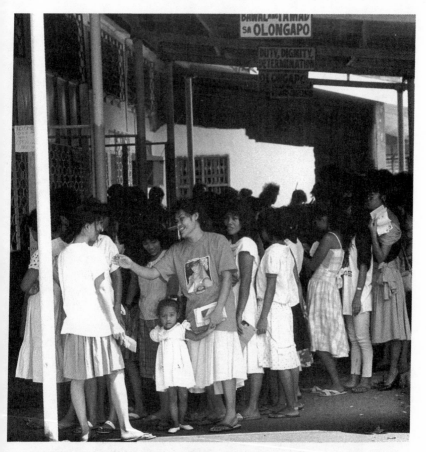

12 Twice a month Filipino women who are working as prostitutes around the US Navy base in Olongapo have to wait in line for their compulsory VD and AIDS tests. (photo: Saundra Sturdevant, 1988)

In the same way that American servicemen demand V D clearo from the women, the Filipinos have the right to demand AI. and V D clearance from the servicemen.[48]

A year later the Philippines Immigration Commissioner declared that henceforth US military personnel and all foreign sailors arriving in the Philippines would be required to present certificates showing that they are free of AIDS.[49] If this policy is actually implemented, it will make it far harder for American military planners to maintain their Pacific Rim strategy. Either they will have to fundamentally alter servicemen's assumptions about what rewards they deserve in return for months away

13 US sailor with a Filipino prostitute in Olongapo. (photo: Saundra Sturdevant, 1988)

from home and weeks cooped up on board ship. Or they will have to modify their global security doctrine in order to rely on fewer and more modest bases abroad.

CONCLUSION

Belizean women (and, some say, imported Guatemalan women) have a lot to tell us about how the British armed forces use sexuality to conduct their foreign policy.[50] Northern Irish and West German women who date British troops have important insights to share with the women in Belize. British women married to British soldiers could help round out the picture, as could British women peace activists and those in uniform. All together, these women's seemingly different experiences add up to a gendered government bases policy.

But it is the very divisions between these women that provide a military base with its security. The armed forces need women to maintain their bases, but they need those women to imagine that they belong to mutually exclusive categories. Women from different countries are separated by distance, and often race and inequalities of political influence. Prostitutes, girlfriends, wives, peace activists and women soldiers have learned to view each other as sexual or ideological rivals. An anti-bases movement uninformed by feminist questioning leaves these divisions in place. In this sense, an anti-bases movement that ignores the armed forces' dependence on the complex relations between women leaves the structure of military bases in tact even if it manages to close down a particular base.

A woman living on a military base as a wife wants to feel secure. And her own advancement depends on her husband performing successfully enough to win promotion. Thus she sees women peace activists camped outside her gates as the enemy, not an ally. The woman in uniform is trying to challenge the military's masculinist conventions; she sees herself as a war-making partner, not a sexually available object for her male team-mates. So it is not surprising that she deeply resents the women who work as prostitutes outside (and sometimes inside) the base gates, eroticizing, she thinks, her workplace. Girlfriends of soldiers are never quite sure whether the soldier they are dating may have a wife back home, whether the promises of marriage will be realized when a superior warns against marrying a foreign women or when the tour of duty is over and the need for local companionship comes to an abrupt end.

Thus when Kenyan and Filipino women met in Nairobi in 1985 and launched the Campaign Against Military Prostitution (CAMP) to create a network of women in all countries hosting American bases, they were taking a step towards dismantling the global gender structure on which each individual base depends.[51] So, too, are Filipino anti-bases activists who try to imagine what their actions might mean for the already politically conscious women in the small Pacific nation of Belau, the US military's favored back-up site for its giant Subic Bay naval base.[52] When a base is successfully ousted from one place it is likely to be moved somewhere else. If women active in anti-bases movements see developing contacts with women in alternative countries as integral to their work, there is a better chance of the removal of a military base producing a fundamental reassessment of global strategy, not simply a transfer of equipment and personnel. If military wives and women soldiers begin to explore the ways that prostitution pollutes not only their on-base lives but the life of the country off which they are living, the respect they seek for themselves is likely to have deeper roots. Such an exploration might also prompt them to broaden their political horizons, to focus less exclusively on benefits and ask more questions about the consequences of militarization.

5

DIPLOMATIC WIVES

As children, we are encouraged to memorize kings and queens. Who married whom was the stuff of courtiers' intrigues and wars between monarchs. Empires rose and fell according to which marriage schemes succeeded and which failed. As we grow older we are taught that tracking royal marriages is a naïve way to understand politics. We shift our attention to more sophisticated political topics: the technology of warfare, the patterns of trade, the fashions in art and philosophy.

But we may have to take new stock of our early understanding. Marriage has in fact been treated as serious business by the makers of foreign policy. And it hasn't been just kings and queens who have preoccupied government officials when they have tried to promote their country in the international system. It has been humbler folk: diplomats, settlers, traders and soldiers. Should they marry? If so, whom should they marry? What kind of marriage should it be? These questions are of great interest to governments. Colonization and military bases policies have depended on these calculations.

IMPERIAL DIPLOMACY

Men and women have not been assigned equal weight in these governmental efforts to assert control. Men are seen as having the skills and resources that the government needs if its international status is to be enhanced. They are presumed to be the diplomats, they are the traders, the planters, the soldiers. Women loom up as objects of worry for the makers of foreign policy chiefly as 'wives'. Reduced to wives, women are not thought to possess the political acumen of a Queen Elizabeth I or a Catherine the Great. They are faceless, but a cause for anxiety. If managed correctly, women as wives can help a government achieve its international objectives. If they aren't controlled effectively, however, they can do serious damage to a government's global interests.

It is a lamentable fact that almost every difficulty we have had with Indians throughout the Country may be traced to our interference with their Women or their Intrigues with the Women of the Forts in short 9 Murders out of 10 Committed on Whites by Indians have arisen through Women.[1]

This statement marked a U-turn in the marriage policy of the Northwest Company, which, with the Hudson's Bay Company, was Britain's principal vehicle for colonizing Canada. Until the early 1800s, the British and French fur trading companies had encouraged marriages between their white male fur traders and local Indian women. Such marriages, officially encouraged by the Northwest Company's officers and unofficially sanctioned by managers of the Hudson's Bay Company, were considered strategically and politically important. Trapper-Indian marriages became a means of cementing alliances on a frontier that still eluded secure imperial control. Indian women were expected by British and French policy-makers to lead the men of their tribes into cordial relations with the companies. The trappers gained the chance to create a family despite the hardships of life on the northern frontier. Moreover, marriage to an Indian woman gave a white man a sense that he was superior, that he was saving a woman from the deplorable condition of savagery. This belief bolstered white men's sense of the moral rightness of their role in the lucrative international beaver-pelt trade.

Though they were treated merely as a strategic resource by the French and British companies and governments in the eighteenth and nineteenth centuries, the Indian women were making their own decisions. They were not passive in the face of imperial rivalries in Canada. They had their own reasons for promoting marriages with white men. Some Indian women valued the objects, such as metal kettles, that they gained through the fur trade and thus did what they could to ensure that the trade continued. Others preferred life inside the forts, where food was more plentiful than was often the case in their villages. A few Indian women accumulated considerable influence through liaising between their tribal communities and the trading companies.[2] Nevertheless, in 1806 when the British policy changed and officials began to encourage the trappers to seek European wives, the Indian women could do little to resist. Their control over the international politics of marriage was severely constrained. After the companies decided that trappers' relations with Indian women were fomenting as many hostilities as alliances and that the costs of maintaining so many women and children outweighed the commercial advantages, the ideological rationale for the marriages was transformed as well.

Previously the London-based officials of the fur-trading companies had judged that the dangers and hardships of Canadian fort life made them no place to bring a white women, certainly not a 'lady'; white women would be a costly burden and a nuisance for the company. In 1686 the Hudson's Bay Company managers passed a resolution forbidding their men in Canada from importing white wives. A few European women managed to join their trader husbands, but only by deception. Among the most renowned was Isabel Gunn, who arrived at a fort in 1806 from the Orkney Islands, where many of the Hudson's Bay Company's men came from. She had skirted the company's ban on white women by disguising herself as a man.[3] But by the middle of the nineteenth century white men in the companies were praising the contributions that white women, 'the delicate flowers of civilization', were making to fort life. Their graces were compared to the 'deficiencies' of Indian wives. In reality, white women lacked the skills that Indian women possessed to assist their fur-trading husbands. They followed their husbands to Canada out of what they imagined to be wifely loyalty and duty, but, once there, many endured boredom and isolation.[4]

In colony after colony governments tried to fashion a marriage strategy suited to their political ends, but their policies had to be flexible. There were too many variables to consider – and reconsider: white men's presumed sexual needs; white women's presumed frailty; the vulnerability or security of the colonial administration; the availability and assets of local women; the threats posed by local men; the desirability of establishing a full-fledged white community (not just forts and plantations) in the colony (see also chapter 3).

Governments never have been as effective in controlling the foreign policy of marriage as they would have liked. But they haven't given up. Today many governments are being challenged by women who for the past century have been thought to be among the most compliant: diplomatic wives.

THE DOMESTICATION OF DIPLOMACY

Women who are married to Swedish, Canadian, British and American diplomats are creating new organizations and revitalizing existing organizations. They are demanding recognition for the contributions they make as diplomatic wives to their countries' foreign-policy operations. Some want more than recognition: they are making public demands for services, jobs, alimony, even salaries. Diplomatic wives, furthermore, have been joined in their political lobbying by military wives. Their organizing has revealed how reliant governments continue to be on their control of marriage in order to conduct international relations in a 'comfortable' manner.[5]

For a government to extend its influence in the world, it must send abroad at least some of its own citizens. Diplomatic influence requires foreign-service officers, not just telex machines and embassy residences. Military power relies on sailors and soldiers, not simply ships and artillery. Commercial influence depends on company employees as well as bank accounts and beaver pelts. The citizens scattered around the world are presumed to be male and policies toward marriage are designed to encourage them to help achieve the government's political and economic goals. Women are important because they are thought to threaten or enhance a diplomat's, businessman's or soldier's ability to serve *his* government effectively.

Today the diplomatic wife seems a fixture of international politics. It wasn't always so. According to Beryl Smedley's research, the first British woman to accompany her husband as an ambassador's wife – not simply as the wife of a colonial official – was Lady Mary Wortley Montagu. She went with her husband to Constantinople in 1716. Today she is more famous for her letters and her critiques of women's second-class status than for her diplomatic significance. But in accompanying her diplomat husband on assignment to Turkey, Lady Mary Wortley Montagu marked a turning point in the way diplomacy has been conducted between governments.[6]

Her breakthrough initially went unnoticed because governments hadn't yet realized the uses to which they could put ambassadors' wives. For the next century and a half women married to senior British diplomats only occasionally joined their husbands in foreign embassies. They, like their husbands, came from the nobility and supplied their own staff and paid their own way.[7] While many of these women were well educated and skilled reporters, little was expected of them by their governments. And it was still mainly senior diplomats whose wives accompanied them. Men of junior rank were expected either to remain single or to leave their wives at home.

By the end of the nineteenth century, however, diplomacy and hostessing had become tightly intertwined. It became harder for women married to diplomats to pursue their own interests. They were not on the official payroll, but they were on their government's minds. For many of these women hostessing was what they had been raised to do. After 1900 the British Foreign Office began to open its ranks to men outside the nobility, although serving abroad still required one to have independent means. This encouraged the sons of industrialists who joined the Foreign Office to look upon daughters of the aristocracy as appropriate wives.

Not all of these successors to Lady Mary Wortley Montagu were eager to serve as hostesses for their governments. 'I don't like diplomacy, though I like Persia,' wrote a disgruntled Vita Sackville-West in 1926. She had gone out to Teheran to join her diplomat husband, Harold Nicolson. Despite her forceful resistance to playing the dutiful wife in either private or public, by the 1920s Vita had encountered role expectations she couldn't avoid: 'She paid calls, attended and gave luncheons and dinners . . . she even gave away hockey prizes.'[8] Yet her heart wasn't in it. She was writing intense letters from Persia to her new friend, Virginia Woolf, and within a few months was heading back to England, leaving Harold to cope with diplomatic rituals on his own.

Any woman considering marriage to a man set upon a career in the diplomatic corps should think hard about 'the itinerant life and the poor pay'. This is the advice of one of Britain's most seasoned diplomatic wives, Beryl Smedley. After having served with her husband – like military wives, foreign-service wives refer to themselves as 'serving' abroad – for thirty years in posts as varied as Sri Lanka, Laos and Rhodesia, she has no regrets. 'Most of us who married in the forties and fifties felt that we were partners in diplomacy; some of us had careers, but we had no hesitation in giving them up to work alongside our husbands.'[9] Having given up a civil-service job in her native country of New Zealand, she learned to take satisfaction in contributing to her husband's diplomatic mission by doing volunteer work wherever they were posted, representing her adopted country by her very presence abroad and by being her husband's 'eyes and ears' at public functions. Some diplomatic wives also act as a safe sounding-board, one of the few people on whom their husbands can try out ideas. Jane Ewart-Biggs, now a Labour Life Peer and party spokesperson on Home Affairs in the House of Lords, believes that the kind of work she did as a volunteer while serving overseas, as well as her experience as a single mother since her husband was assassinated while ambassador to Ireland, helped prepare her for her current public role.[10]

Diplomacy runs smoothly when there is trust and confidence between officials representing governments which usually have different, if not conflicting interests. That trust and confidence has to be created in a congenial environment; it doesn't sprout naturally. Most men find that congenial environment outside their offices. The home – the ambassador's official residence, or the homes of lower-ranking diplomats – is seen as the place where this trust between men can best be cultivated. The home is the domain of the wife. The domestic duties of foreign-service wives include creating an atmosphere where men from different states can get to know one another 'man to man'.

The more male diplomats rely on informal relationships to accomplish their political tasks, the more formal the expectations are that their wives will come to the government's aid.

Quite frankly, it is only by meeting people socially that you get the sort of relationship that you are seeking. You'll never establish it just going to visit people in their offices.

There is a great deal of diplomatic life which is irksome . . . I do find the social side of the thing tedious and so does my wife: not, I hasten to say, the concept of entertaining in itself, which is a valuable – indeed essential – part of the business . . . actually off-the-record conversations are the stuff of diplomacy.[11]

Men often feel, they say, as though they are judged by their male colleagues in the embassy according to how much they 'pull their own weight' in being seen, socially showing the flag. They depend on their wives to be considered a worthy member of the embassy team, for without a wife's active cooperation, a male diplomat can't perform these tasks well. The higher the male foreign-service officer climbs on the career ladder, the more time he will have to devote to these social duties and thus the more he will rely on the participation of a wife. The wife of the British ambassador to India, where Britain has one of its largest embassies, described a typical day in her life:

On Monday morning we already had Mr and Mrs Norman Tebbit staying with us [Norman Tebbit was then a senior minister in the Conservative government], so the day began with a briefing meeting here for the minister with members of the high commission. Quite often when we have briefing meetings here in the house we invite the wives of our own members of staff to come and meet the wife of the visitor who is being briefed. It is very valuable for everybody and great fun for the girls to be included. In the evening we had the Director of the Washington National Gallery and his wife . . . He had come to look at things to borrow, and was a great friend of friends. Then we went out to an official dinner being given for Mr Tebbit . . . So on that day there was the morning meeting, people to lunch, people to drinks, dinner out. Tuesday morning at 11 o'clock I went to call on the wife of a colleague to talk about the Delhi Flower Show, which is run by the YWCA to make money for their village projects. The Delhi Flower Show is quite old and traditionally diplomats, particularly British diplomats, have been involved in running it.[12]

The expectations that foreign-service wives must try to meet vary. They may be different to those of the wife of a British ambassador posted to the capital of a country once part of the British empire. Some women say that they prefer assignments to countries where their governments are not the leaders of the diplomatic pack or where their government's interests are not vital. This gives even women married to ambassadors more leeway; they are less visible and the expectations of them less rigid. Such a posting may not suit their husbands. They are in the foreign service to pursue a career and need to carve a path to more prestigious postings on the foreign service pyramid. Some women share their husbands' ambitions and take pride in acquiring the skills required to run the American ambassador's home in Tokyo or the British ambassador's home in Washington.

The British ambassador's wife described her house in Washington as 'my tool of the trade'. It is used for more than just entertaining. With a staff of 300, Britain's Washington embassy is one of its largest, reflecting the closeness – some might say dependency – that Britain has developed with the United States in international affairs since 1945. That intimacy shows up in sales figures. One of the priorities of the British embassy in Washington is to sell British goods, especially British military equipment, to American buyers. So the ambassador's wife, supervising a domestic staff of twenty, uses her home to promote sales, as her husband, the ambassador, explained to a BBC reporter:

> Our houses are a part of that and one doesn't entertain simply to have a good scoff and a booze-up. One entertains because it does in fact facilitate the transaction of business. People are in a better temper when they know each other and have had a meal together.[13]

The ambassador's wife has learned her trade well if she can plan the progress from drinks to formal dinner to coffee so that a maximum amount of business can be conducted 'with a minimum of artificiality'.[14]

Her wardrobe may itself advance her country's economic interests. This is the rationale behind many ambassadors' wives, especially those from affluent countries posted in major capitals, wearing expensive gowns from *haute couture* designers. The US ambassador's wife makes a point of wearing Bill Blass and Oscar de la Renta. The wife of the French ambassador wears Chanel creations. Her Italian counterpart wears Valentino. To show off the designer's clothes to advantage the ambassador's wife should be svelt and attractive. Her physique becomes more politically significant as her government's efforts to export designer clothes become more aggressive. Lady Fretwell, wife of Britain's former ambassador to France, kept a photograph of the chic Mme Giscard d'Estaing greeting the 'lumpy, unkempt' wives of Brezhnev and Gromyko on her study bulletin board 'as a reminder of what can happen if you let yourself go'.[15]

An ambassador's wife's finely honed skills promote not only the evening-gown trade, but also sales of technology, weapons and financial services. A diplomat's wife has become part of an international strategy to reduce trade imbalances. By playing that part well, diplomatic wives also oil the wheels of the international arms trade.

'DON'T AGONIZE, ORGANIZE'

However, a successful diplomatic wife may have a gnawing sense that her work isn't valued. It is expected by governments, but it's not truly respected. In Beryl Smedley's small study, stuffed with books on diplomatic history and notes from her research at the British Museum, there is one file she thinks sums up this gap between expectation and respect. It is her obituary file. She opens it with annoyance. When men who have been diplomats die, they are accorded long obituaries describing their careers, their various postings abroad. When their wives die, they receive nothing more than a cursory death notice. That doesn't add up to the full partnership that diplomatic wives devote themselves to and that governments have come to depend on in the twentieth century for the sake of smooth international relations. Yet complaining, Beryl Smedley reminds us, has never been acceptable behavior for the model diplomatic wife. Today that model is being challenged.

The Diplomatic Service Wives Association (DSWA) is housed in a large room in the Foreign Office in London, a stone's throw away from Westminster. Two secretaries paid by the Foreign Office work away at desks, Constable posters decorate the walls, a tea kettle is steaming and tables are cluttered with work in progress. Gay Murphy, a diplomatic wife finishing her term as chair of the DSWA, is in the office for one of her two days a week of unpaid organizational work. As the DSWA has adopted a more activist role, the job of chair has become increasingly demanding.[16]

'We're always about fifteen years behind.' Gay Murphy was explaining why it wasn't until the early 1980s that women married to men in the British diplomatic corps began to speak out on some of the subjects that fueled Britain's women's movement in the 1970s. The reasons for this time lag include the fact that diplomatic wives are constantly moving and are isolated from British society for years at a time. Although many people imagine the 14,000 members of foreign-service families to be from the upper classes, the social mix has been changing since the 1940s, and the isolation and bureaucratic socialization may be more of an obstacle to consciousness-raising than class background. Still, coming to political awareness has been a slow process for many wives.

In the early 1970s the wife of a British foreign-service officer committed suicide. Her friends believed that she did it out of loneliness. After spending years with her husband on assignments overseas, when she finally came 'home', she was unprepared for the loneliness and lack of support. Her suicide shocked the Treasury's Medical Officer, the official in charge of providing medical care for civil servants and foreign-service personnel. He was one of the first within the government to take seriously the problems facing foreign-service wives. His solution was to set up networks of women volunteers in the different parts of the country, who could help returning foreign-service wives readjust to life in Britain.

But one diplomatic wife who had trained as a psychologist argued that this was only a bandaid; there were deeper problems that the government had to confront. The Foreign Office agreed to employ a civilian psychologist to conduct a more thorough study. Though his report uncovered profound problems and frustrations, little action was taken to rethink the role of the diplomatic wife and thus the way the Foreign Office did business. The DSWA itself remained chiefly concerned with social activities; its members didn't see themselves as political lobbyists.

By the early 1980s more diplomatic wives had absorbed the lessons of the wider women's movement. They were less willing to rely solely on private solutions to problems posed by the way the government chooses to carry on its international relations. They were less willing to sacrifice their own career aspirations for the sake of their husbands'. Still, one of the experiences that helped convince Gay Murphy that a diplomatic wives' association could change the conditions she and her colleagues coped with was being posted with her husband to Washington in the early 1980s. There she had a first-hand look at what American foreign-service wives were doing to push their State Department to officially acknowledge the contributions wives made to state business. They were pressing for salaries or, short of that, for family services.

Soon after their posting to Washington, Gay Murphy and her husband were sent to Mexico City. Trained as a family counselor, she was especially interested in the operations of the US embassy's Family Affairs Officer. American diplomatic wives had won the kinds of services that might help British wives cope with their multiple roles. The US embassy was able to supply information on taxes, schooling, adoption and careers.

American wives have the advantage that the American foreign service is much larger than that of most other governments; there are enough American wives and children to make the provision of such services feasible. In a country like Mexico, the American mission dwarfed those of even major international powers such as Britain. Still, comparing notes with American diplomatic wives helped British women recast the role of their own association. They started to change how foreign relations are conducted when they met resistance from the Foreign Office, Treasury or Parliament.

The 'never complain' ethos hasn't evaporated, however; the 'stiff upper lip' remains a valued attribute, especially among many of the more senior wives. Problems such as alcoholism, drug abuse and depression are still often kept in the closet. Yet in recent years the DSWA has made headway. In the process, diplomacy's dependency on a certain kind of marriage and on the ideology of wifely duty have been exposed.

Acquiring office space inside the Foreign Office and two paid secretaries are only the most visible accomplishments of the DSWA. More significantly, Gay Murphy says, when she visits a civil servant or a cabinet minister on DSWA business, she can go 'as herself'. She is not treated as though she were nothing more than a wife or as though she had her husband's rank. Such autonomy will be hard to sustain, however, when she leaves London to accompany her husband on his next foreign assignment. Once again, she must adjust to being a wife first, a wife of a particular rank. But here in London, working for the association, she has her own political mission and, with it, her own identity.

Thus for many diplomatic wives there are two marriages: the one they and their husbands live while stationed at home; and the one they live while overseas. It is the women who do most of the adjusting from one kind of marriage to the other.

Within the DSWA women have made a conscious effort not to relate to each other according to their husbands' ranks, an all-too-common practice among diplomatic wives when overseas. When an association volunteer said a phone call had come in from 'one of the senior women', she quickly caught herself: 'I'm really trying to break that habit. I meant one of the women married to a senior man.'

DSWA activists have lobbied the Treasury, Foreign Office, the committees of the House of Commons to stop the practice of superiors including a wife's performance in the periodic evaluation of her husband. Her hostessing and volunteer work should not, they argued, be assessed in deciding whether he will be promoted. The Annual Confidential Report may mention a wife's health and any special language skills she has, but thanks to DSWA's successful pressuring, it may no longer include comments on her entertaining or charity work. Of course this political victory has had the effect of pushing out of sight those contributions that a woman makes to her husband's professional performance.[17] However, it has left women somewhat freer to pursue their own jobs at home and abroad if they wish to do so. Until the DSWA objected, a wife who wanted to take a paid job overseas was required to ask permission from the Head of Post, and permission 'was by no means regularly given.'[18]

Activist diplomatic wives have cultivated the media to raise public awareness of what they endure to ensure the foreign-policy machine runs smoothly. While the women are careful not to cross the threshold into 'policy matters' – for instance, discussing under what conditions the government should remove diplomatic families from a dangerous post – they do take every opportunity to raise issues regarding health, education, jobs and pensions. Wives are insisting that the government provide more assistance, instead of assuming that wives can cope on their own with the disruptions to their own and their children's lives that come from the government's need to move their representatives around the world. They have called on the British government to allow women to pursue their own careers, or at least to have gainful employment when overseas. They are also proposing a scheme whereby diplomatic wives who have not pursued their own careers receive pensions in their own right, thus making the government acknowledge that the work they do is an integral part of the diplomatic process.

Letters to the DSWA's magazine suggest that women are imagining alternative ways to run an embassy:

> As more and more wives want to work abroad, could there not be some plan established to incorporate working wives into the Embassy structure . . . as has been done in the American Foreign Service?
>
> Also it's about time that Diplomatic Service Officers were re-educated about wives working in the Office; we can do more than part-time clerical/secretarial jobs, we could be AAOs, Information Officers, Vice Consults, etc. Why should we only have the chance to do the more mundane jobs?[19]

These aren't easy demands for the government to meet. They come at a time when the British government is cutting the cost of conducting foreign affairs. What women are calling for costs money. Furthermore, one of the ways that a government with a major presence overseas tries to win goodwill is by providing paid jobs for local residents in its embassies and consulates. Giving diplomatic wives first call on such jobs clashes with this established strategy. Moreover, if more and more women insist upon having paid jobs of their own, who will do the entertaining? Who will create the environment in which diplomats can build trust on a man-to-man basis, in which British arms and other goods can be sold to international customers? On a deeper level, recognizing diplomatic wives as people with their own skills, financial aspirations and personal identities, makes it harder to treat embassies as 'families', or as 'teams', with all the members pitching in for the sake of achieving their government's global objectives.

Diplomatic wives have to continue to push their governments to alter their view of diplomacy as well as persuade their husbands to alter their notions of marriage. Gay Murphy explains that it is frequently hard for a woman to criticize the foreign service without sounding as if she is criticizing her own husband: 'You are living with part of the bureaucracy.'[20] However, many of the younger men – and now women – joining the service are more willing to acknowledge the stresses that diplomacy imposes on women as wives. Some men have come up to Gay Murphy at gatherings and thanked her for the work the DSWA does.

Still, it is up to women to take the initiative to nudge their husbands, to clarify what they expect of their marriages, to try out alternative visions of what marriage might mean and of what a successful foreign service career might entail. This is political work in the eyes of DSWA activists. Sometimes it doesn't bear fruit. Some marriages cannot withstand the contradictory pressures of the diplomatic life. Divorce is common in the foreign service.

In 1986 diplomatic wives' associations from the twelve countries then belonging to the European Economic Community met for the first time. The idea was introduced by the British government, which at the time held the presidency of the EEC. It seems it was intended to be a relatively harmless public event that would reflect well on the government. But once the women got together, there was a lot of serious discussion, comparing and formulating strategies. The associations that had been in existence longer, such as Britain's and Sweden's, were represented by assertive women who had come to feel autonomous in their own right. Younger associations still at the stage of having to earn their legitimacy were represented by 'senior women' who were more cautious.

The three 'hot' topics at the 1986 meeting were pensions, divorce and the tainted public image of foreign services. Women at the gathering were especially impressed by the success of the Swedish association in lobbying for pensions. A Swedish diplomatic wife now receives her own pension. Divorce raised multiple issues – as it does in the military – because laws governing alimony settlements reflect so clearly just how much – or how little – a government values the unpaid work done by a diplomatic wife. They aroused anger among women whose husbands have divorced them after they have sacrificed their own earning power and invested years of service for the sake of their husband's career, only to be left impoverished in their old age. Divorce rulings also outrage married women who see them as a reflection of the gap between their government's expectations and its actual respect for women's work. When the women from the twelve countries compared their respective conditions they discovered that the Swedish and the Danish wives' associations had been most successful in lobbying their governments to ensure fairness. In Sweden and Denmark a man in the foreign service who divorces his wife must divide his pension between his two (or three) wives according to the number of years each woman has served as a partner in diplomatic postings. Instead of seeing their ex-husbands' new wives as their chief rivals, divorcees have focussed their political efforts on the government, which has benefited from their years of unpaid labor.[21]

Perhaps because they see themselves as doing daily battle with their bureaucracies in order to gain mundane services, financial security and respect, women from all the EEC countries voiced concern and even resentment at the declining public image of foreign services. This has put many of the activist diplomatic wives in an awkward position. On the one hand, they have developed a new appreciation of how inadequate their foreign services' responses are to women's real needs. Even if they speak in discreet tones, they are critics, increasingly savvy critics. On the other hand, their husbands' careers still depend on their wifely skills and the marital partnership. This realization, in turn, draws them into a familial relationship with their government's foreign service. Consequently, women married to foreign-service officers are inclined to defend the foreign service when it is being criticized, even if they feel exploited by it.

WAGES FOR (DIPLOMATIC) HOUSEWORK

The US Association of American Foreign Service Women (AAFSW) has become a political organization. It organizes women – and a few men – married to American foreign-service officers to monitor problems produced by the way the US government conducts its international affairs. It lobbies the State Department and the Congressional Foreign Affairs Committee to improve the conditions under which wives and their children live in Washington and abroad. While its members have learned the lessons of political discretion integral to diplomacy, these women have formidable resources with which to press their case. Not least of these is their own social class status. Many American foreign-service wives are at home in Washington, a predominantly Black city in which the power élite is overwhelmingly white. They have become experienced in sensing the political pulse of the capital as one party replaces another in the White House and Congress. They have the same class backgrounds as the members of Congress they lobby. 'They entertain these guys in their homes,' one feminist observed as she described their political advantage. She was comparing foreign-service wives' resources with those of American military wives, who have also become more vocal in demanding that the government stop taking for granted the unpaid labor of women. While leaders of the military wives groups are usually wives of senior officers, they none the less are less likely to be familiar with the white upper-class milieu in Washington than most foreign-service wives.[22]

Foreign-service wives say that they have learned most about lobbying through watching the CIA wives in action. Until the 1970s the Central Intelligence Agency prohibited its wives from meeting together in groups of more than three. Despite the prohibition, CIA wives started to speak out about the special hardship imposed on women married to secret-service officials serving overseas. Both they and their children suffered: 'Who's the spy?' is a favorite game among diplomatic children. Faced with women no longer willing to remain dutifully silent, CIA administrators decided to be accommodating rather than risk attracting public attention. Today CIA wives have meetings, a formal (carefully guarded) mailing list and an agency office mandated to deal specifically with the problems encountered by CIA families.

CIA wives now press the Congressional Intelligence Committee – behind closed doors, to keep it inside 'the intelligence community' – to adopt benefit packages that address their special needs. Like foreign-service wives, these women generally have had a university education and feel comfortable in Washington policy-making circles. When abroad, they tend to live in the same diplomatic communities as their State Department colleagues which gives them the chance to share information and strategies. In addition, however, CIA wives can go to Congressional Intelligence Committees and hold out the threat, if only implicitly: 'Think of the stories we could tell.' The very notion of an intimate, close-knit 'intelligence community' may create a stifling environment for women married to CIA agents. Yet it also provides them with a lever with which to pry open the coffers.[23]

The first change to send ripples through the US foreign-policy system came in 1971. Women pursuing careers in the State Department took a cue from the American women's movement and called for an end to the government's policy of compelling a woman in the foreign service to resign if she got married. Through their newly created Women's Action Organization, these women successfully pressed the State Department to put an end to the foreign-service marriage rule. This threw into stark relief diplomacy's dependence on marriage. The question being posed by many American women outside the corridors of power finally took on significance for women within government organizations: why should marriage advance a man's capacity to gain money, skills and influence but hinder a woman's chance to acquire the same? Increasing numbers of women marrying foreign-service male careerists in the 1970s had university degrees and career aspirations of their own, but they were expected to put them aside or use them only to advance their husbands' career and the international political interests of the US government. More and more diplomatic wives were refusing to accept this assumption as central to being a loyal wife and a patriotic citizen.

In 1972 the State Department was compelled to drop the other shoe. It declared that henceforth foreign-service spouses were 'private persons'. According to the directive, spouses – most of them wives – were no longer to be treated as if they were unpaid employees. Specifically, wives would cease to be evaluated in the efficiency reports that mean life or death to a foreign-service official's career. The 'twofer' system was dead: theoretically, the United States government would have to conduct its foreign policy without getting a team of two for the price of one. The State Department had been compelled to admit that women had their own lives to live.[24]

But declarations by themselves don't transform political practice. They may simply reveal the distance between formal policy and daily political reality. American women married to foreign-service men still had to travel to the countries where their husbands were posted if they wanted to sustain their marriages. They still felt they had to help their husbands perform the public and social duties that the host country, visiting dignitaries and business people expected. They were still relied on to keep the children happy and healthy despite the frequent moves and unfamiliar surroundings. The State Department declaration, itself a victory for diplomatic wives, didn't change any of that.

In 1984 some foreign-service wives lobbied Congress for an amendment to the pending Foreign Service Act of 1980. The amendment was intended to resolve a persisting contradiction; it proposed that a foreign-service wife be paid. If she was not longer an unpaid handmaiden of diplomacy but a cog in the foreign-policy machine, then she should be paid for her work. The women asked Congress that a spouse who agrees to carry out representational responsibilities be paid a salary equivalent to 40 per cent of the employee's – usually, the husband's – salary. Congress was not convinced.[25]

The wages-for-diplomatic-housework proposal did not resolve the contradictions at the heart of international relations any more than similar proposals have for civilian wives in many countries. American diplomatic wives have not continued to invest their energies in lobbying for pay. They are more concerned today with genuine autonomy and the provision of the services that make their unpaid family work easier. Having taken a closer look at the assumptions behind the wages proposal and the consequences flowing from it, most American diplomatic wives have decided that wages-for-housework only tighten the noose around a woman's neck. The wages don't liberate her. They nail shut the front door.

Today there are approximately 9,000 foreign-service spouses and 13,000 paid professionals in the US government's five overseas civilian agencies: the State Department's Foreign Service, the Agency for International Development (AID), the United States Information Agency (USIA), the Foreign Agricultural Service and the Foreign Commercial Service. The office created by the State Department in 1978 in response to campaigning by foreign-service wives is the Family Liaison Office. At the time it was established, some State Department officials ridiculed the idea of an office to address the needs uncovered by the Association of American Foreign Service Women: 'Why do we need to hold the hands of whining wives?'[26]

Wives' problems weren't deemed to be serious foreign-policy problems and therefore did not deserve bureaucratic recognition. Wives were supposed to be able to cope with these problems privately, while continuing to do all the things that enhanced diplomatic relations. But the AAFSW went directly to the then Secretary of State, Cyrus Vance, with their findings. He was persuaded. And with his backing, resistance to a US Family Liaison Office crumbled. To date, only Australian foreign-service wives have the equivalent of a Family Liaison Office. The director of the Family Liaison Office has been a foreign-service wife for twenty-two years and a past president of the AAFSW. She oversees a staff of thirteen and advises spouses on their own chances for employment, their children's education, taxes, health, moving and coping with crisis evacuations.[27]

Responsibility for supporting wives during evacuations from foreign posts was added to the Family Liaison Office's duties in 1980 in the wake of the public outcry over the taking of US embassy hostages in Iran and outspoken criticism by the wives of some of the hostages. Penelope Laigen, wife of an American chargé d'affaires in Teheran, explained her feelings:

I felt that as the wife of mission there, I had a role to play in this very public international crisis. If I had run to Iran and made a scene, or cried or called the State Department stupid, I would have found out in two minutes from the State Department just how public a person I was.

So Penelope Laigen did her work without criticizing the Department. She played by the pre-1970s rules which categorized her as an unpaid member of the foreign-policy team. 'I stood up in many of those meetings and said, "Look, we cannot go against our Government." ' And yet in the end she never received the thanks or respect due to her for her services as a dutiful governmental wife. 'I have given my whole life to this service and have come up with nothing.'[28]

Foreign-service wives now in their early fifties are married to men who are at a critical turning point in their careers. They may be squeezed out by White House political appointees (who have been taking up more and more of the senior diplomatic posts) or by the 'up or out' system instituted by the Reagan administration, whereby many experienced officers are forced into early retirement unless they achieve promotion. But if they survive, these men will be assigned to embassy posts abroad that still require considerable entertaining and volunteer work on the part of their wives. Furthermore, as a husband rises higher in the embassy hierarchy he oversees a wider range of embassy employees. This makes it still harder for his wife to take a paid job in the embassy without violating the State Department's nepotism rule, which prohibits one spouse from exercising direct supervisory authority over the other. Many of these women and their husbands joined the foreign service during the 1960s. They speak warmly of the 'Kennedy years'. They like to quote John Kennedy's inaugural address: 'Ask not what your country can do for you, but what you can do for your country.' In that call, conventional wifely duty and patriotic duty become compatible. Twenty-five years after Kennedy's inauguration, some of these women look back wistfully at that era when 'sacrifice for your country meant something'. They are reluctant to let go of this ideal. Many feel as if refusing to accompany their husbands to their next overseas assignment for the sake of pursuing their own careers is a betrayal of that 1960s American spirit.[29]

CONFUCIAN EMBASSY POLITICS

How palatable life is for a young foreign-service wife in a given post often depends on the wives above her. Before the 'private person rule' was established in 1972, a young American wife was at the 'beck and call' of the women married to foreign-service officers of higher rank than her husband. The conduct of diplomacy relied on an embassy's senior women being able to mobilize the skills and labor of more junior women. Without this hierarchy among wives, the diplomatic machinery wouldn't work. Junior wives tended to picture some of these senior women as 'dragon ladies'. They looked upon the wife of the Deputy Head of Mission and the wife of the ambassador the way many pre-revolutionary Chinese wives viewed their mothers-in-law.

Mary Ann White, a trained social worker now with the Girl Scouts of America, thinks it was pure luck that she and her husband were sent to Hong Kong at a time when the head of consulate's wife was a woman who understood that a young mother of two infants wouldn't have time for diplomatic tea parties. Their next assignment was in Canada. Because Canada was so close and because its government was so friendly to the United States, the American embassy was 'loaded with senior ranks'. But again Ann was lucky. The ambassador's wife and the other senior wives treated her, now with her four children, as a 'kind of mascot'. Even when she and her husband were invited to play bridge with senior members of the embassy community, it wasn't competitive bridge fraught with potential embarrassments over rank.[30]

It wasn't always like this. When they were posted to Ecuador Mary Ann 'served' under an ambassador's wife who treated junior wives as if they were there to enhance her entertaining.

> She'd call me up and tell me to get all the other wives to bring different dishes for a dinner at the Residence. And then when I got there she would hand me this list with the timing of all the hors-d'oeuvres – what order they were to come out of the kitchen. I was supposed to spend all evening in the kitchen supervising the cook. But by that time I'd gotten to know the cook, so I just went back, gave him the list and then slipped out into the garden and enjoyed myself without the ambassador's wife ever seeing me.

Mary Ann White tells this story to illustrate how she and other foreign-service wives learned to 'slide around' the 'Confucian' rules that confined them in the days before they could cite a formal directive when proclaiming their autonomy. She learned Spanish and became involved in medical projects for children. Even though it, too, was unpaid, it was work she chose to do and which she cared about. As her husband got promotions and she rose up the ladder of embassy wives, she shared her strategies with younger women. At another Latin American posting there was a woman Deputy Chief of Mission, the only woman in the US foreign service at the time to have reached such a senior rank. One day she telephoned Mary Ann, then one of the more senior wives, to say how unhappy she was that three of the younger wives 'stood in a corner and just talked to each other' at a recent embassy reception. Would Mary Ann talk to them and get them back in line? She did, but not in the way the DCM had in mind. Over a cup of coffee, she tutored the three younger women on how to be less visible, how to slip around the expectations: 'Go to the ladies' room; don't go to every reception.'

Not all American foreign-service wives have had the good fortune to be taught the ropes by a senior woman who identifies more with other women than with her husband's career or with the State Department's mission. Alcoholism has been one symptom of the problems. While a male official who dealt with his drinking problem would be looked upon with admiration as he clung to his can of soda during cocktail parties, a wife's alcoholism was more likely to be buried, treated as a community secret. It wouldn't do to have a drunk foreign-service wife. It would reflect badly on American society – wives must represent what is best about their country. Also an alcoholic wife would make the important informal discussions among men awkward, the opposite of the effect that wives are supposed to have on inter-government relations. A common solution was to discreetly transfer the woman and her husband to another post. The wife is left to deal with her drinking problem on her own. The stress of diplomatic marriage and the reliance of diplomacy on a constant round of parties and receptions means that alcoholism remains a problem for wives.

Pamela Moffat, recently president of the AAFSW, is on her way to testify before the Senate Foreign Relations Committee on a bill that would provide a fairer distribution of benefits to divorced foreign-service wives. She gets angry when she hears members of Congress describe foreign-service families as a privileged and indulgent élite. She's grateful that at least some newspapers are carrying more accurate accounts of the stresses that diplomats and their spouses cope with in order to carry out the US government's foreign policies.[31] Pam Moffat is grateful for the 1970s reforms, though she wishes more wives would accept what she sees as the challenges and rewards of going with their husbands overseas. She was thrilled when her husband received a difficult assignment to Chad, a very poor country just emerging from a bitter civil war. When she first arrived she was the only US foreign-service wife there. In the era of the 'private person rule' she doesn't miss the official lunches – 'there are fewer lunches, or no lunches at all' – but she does miss the sense of community that used to bolster a US mission abroad, which depended on wives feeling that they were integral parts of an embassy team.[32]

The 'real crunch' is going to come in the early 1990s, according to diplomatic wives. That is when women who became foreign-service wives after the 1972 directive will become the 'senior' wives, as their husbands are appointed Deputy Chiefs of Mission and ambassadors. There will then be an entire generation of foreign-service wives who have come to expect that a marriage should allow them to earn their own incomes and pursue their own careers. The wife of an ambassador will still be expected to assist in the conduct of diplomacy, but she will have few 'junior wives' to help her with her job.[33]

THIRD WORLD DIPLOMATIC WIVES

There are 160 sovereign governments in the world today. All of them have to build relations with at least several other governments in order to protect their citizens abroad, ensure favorable terms of trade and aid, ward off or integrate themselves into military alliances. But very few of these governments have the resources – or the perception of global importance – it takes to field large diplomatic corps. Some governments may have just a United Nations delegation plus embassies in three or four other capitals they consider strategic priorities. In virtually every country, however, the people who become diplomats are part of the country's political élite, past or present. Yet how they use women and men is likely to vary according to their resources, their role in international relations and their culture's perception of femininity and masculinity.

A Sri Lankan woman was visiting a friend in England. They had come to know each other when both of them were in Colombo, her English friend as wife of the British ambassador to Sri Lanka, she as wife of the Minister of Finance. The Sri Lankan woman was politically astute, fluent in English, an experienced traveller, with children now living in several countries. She too had served as a diplomatic wife, accompanying her husband when he was appointed ambassador to Japan, one of the countries her government hoped would invest more capital in Sri Lanka. Despite the political importance of the Japanese mission for Sri Lanka, the ambassador's wife was relatively unburdened by the expectations that weigh so heavily on British and American diplomatic wives. 'Our government is too poor to entertain constantly.'[34] She did not have to take on the running of a large residence staff. Moreover, as an Asian woman, she found that she could travel around Tokyo without being treated as exceptional. She wasn't always on display as 'the ambassador's wife' and so could enjoy these daily exercises in disguise.

Nien Ling Lieu, a Chinese woman who spent her childhood as the daughter of a pre-revolution diplomat, found her parents' upper-class background quite compatible with the class backgrounds of the other people they met in diplomatic circles. Her mother did her utmost, often to her daughter's dismay, to live up to the contemporary standard of diplomatic hostess. She liked dressing well and being seen at public functions. She took satisfaction in local reporters wanting to interview her about her charity work. To her teenage daughter, though, those reporters' questions sounded frivolous compared to the serious, searching questions she'd overheard local reporters ask her father, the ambassador. As a diplomatic daughter, Nien Ling Lieu was also expected by her parents to represent her government. She once tried to resist when her father, who admired her academic accomplishments, none the less insisted that she attend a puppet show for diplomatic children sponsored by the host government. For her and her sisters not to appear, he contended, would have amounted to an international insult.[35]

Following the Chinese revolution the Communist government laid down new rules for the conduct of diplomacy. Wives no longer were sent abroad to serve as hostesses. Diplomatic relations were to be conducted with less reliance on representation and entertainment, though women who were professional members of the foreign service might be appointed to the same overseas post as their husbands. Other wives were expected to stay at home. The assumption informing this gender transformation of Chinese diplomacy was that women have their own jobs and are not simply husband-followers. A husband being assigned to serve abroad is no justification for his wife to go as well. Yet at the most senior levels, even the Chinese Communist regime has given in to international diplomatic convention and requires wives of ambassadors to accompany husbands. The policy has caused resentment among these women, who have pursued careers at home and achieved considerable public responsibilities of their own.[36]

The Chinese government still imagines an unmarried woman to be a vulnerable creature abroad. Recently women and men attended a course in Beijing training them to become cultural attachés in the government's foreign service. One woman discreetly sought out the instructor to share her dilemma. She didn't want to get married. But she knew that as a single woman, she would not be sent abroad. Her superiors considered unmarried women too open to temptations, especially those offered by Western societies. Single men, however, could be posted abroad. They were considered impervious to foreign temptations.[37]

As more governments feel that they must become full members of the 'diplomatic community', there will be more and more pressure on them to choose a model of diplomacy. Each model is constructed on assumptions about how political trust between government representatives is best nurtured. The current international system pits men against each other so often that their only congenial common ground is a shared notion of masculinity – though, paradoxically, it is an insecurity in their own masculinity that also makes many male government officials eager to prove themselves through combative confrontation. Therefore, élite men have developed a stake in helping to create and preserve that common ground so that the business of international politics will get done. Integral to this conventional model is the belief that negotiations 'man-to-man' are most likely to go smoothly if they can take place outside official settings, in the 'private' sphere of the home or at gatherings that include wives. Poorer governments lacking the resources to support elaborate missions abroad, or governments self-consciously trying to transform the sexual division of labor in their society, may find the reforms introduced by British, Swedish and American diplomatic wives helpful. They could justify their own cost-cutting or efforts to effect social change. But so long as governments presume that masculinity nurtures diplomatic trust, the conventional model may be hard to displace, even as it cracks under the strain of women's demands.

WOMEN AS DIPLOMATS, MEN AS SPOUSES

In 1972, a year after the Americans, the British Foreign Office lifted its ban on married women becoming career diplomats. Until then, because any woman in the foreign service was presumed to be a 'dependent' and so unable to be moved to another posting, the government required women to quit the diplomatic corps upon marriage. As a result, the few women who have risen to Britain's senior diplomatic posts have all been unmarried. In 1983 only 11 per cent of the recruits entering Britain's foreign-service administrative training program were women. By 1985 the proportion had climbed to 25 per cent. With the recent increase in married women diplomats has come an increase in the number of diplomatic husbands.[38]

Once in the British foreign service, a woman confronts special problems. As Britain's ambassador to the US described it, to be successful in the Foreign Office, an aspiring diplomat has to learn to mold his/her character to the corps:

You have to trust each other particularly well. So in the Diplomatic Service you do have the same sort of flavour as you might have in

114

a regiment. You depend upon each other so much more in our sort of job than people do in ordinary life at home.

Women might have a harder time adjusting to 'life in the regiment'.[39]

Some career women have begun to make use of Britain's Sex Discrimination Act to ensure that they receive the promotions they deserve. In 1986 the Foreign Office offered the post of Deputy High Commissioner to Zambia to Mrs Sue Darling Rogerson, an experienced senior diplomat. Then suddenly it withdrew its offer. The Foreign Office explained that there was 'already a female second secretary serving in the political section [in the Zambia embassy], and an all-female political section would have been operationally ineffective in a male-dominated society like Zambia'.[40] Sue Darling Rogerson charged the Foreign Office with a breach of the Sex Discrimination Act. Faced with an embarrassing legal challenge, the government admitted its error and offered her a post of equal seniority, but in Australia, not Zambia. At the time of Sue Darling Rogerson's case, there were only two women in Britain's top 154 foreign-service posts and only twenty-seven women among its 436 first secretaries.[41] This does not make the Foreign Office strikingly different from the rest of the British government's senior bureaucracy. Although nearly half of all British civil servants are women, they are concentrated in the lower-paid jobs with the least responsibility for policy-making. Of the 8,000 top civil-service jobs, 93 per cent are held by men.[42]

In the United States a small group of high-ranking women in the State Department and its 'sister' agencies, USIA and USAID, began having informal lunches in the summer of 1970 to discuss women's issues in the foreign services. They were angered by the way reports supposed to reassess the operations of the State Department completely ignored women. One of the women, Jean Joyce, remembers attending a task-force meeting, chaired by an ambassador, after she had been energized by hearing Gloria Steinem speak. She went to the meeting armed with figures 'showing the frightful state of women's promotions'. She sat in the front row.

I got up and said, 'Mr Ambassador, has your committee looked into the question of the inequity in rate of promotion of men and women in the Foreign Service?' And he said something hastily, 'Of course, we have women on the committee. We don't happen to have one here today but I think she couldn't come' . . . And then he said to me in the kind of unctuous tone that I've heard often at diplomatic parties, when the wife of one ambassador by rank has to sit next to another ambassador and he makes some pleasantry and then turns to the man on the other side or across from him and starts the *real* conversation . . . 'I'm sure that men and women will always get on together very well, as they always have,' with a great big smile, with that kind of unctuous false flattery. . . as if to say, 'Women, you know, need only to be charmed.'

I remained standing . . . I stood there right in front of him and I said, 'Mr Ambassador, you have not answered my question . . .' and I read the list out for all of them to hear and of course all the officials from the Office of Equal Employment and various other officials were there and it was devastating.[43]

The numbers of women attending the lunches grew. 'Our lunches began to be twenty-five, thirty-five people. And the level of indignation, of a sense of grievance, of bitterness, of anger, was immediately apparent. The thing caught fire just like that. As soon as there was a match.'[44] They told each other stories of women who put off getting married until they were fifty so that they could pursue their careers and keep their retirement benefits. They told of secretaries who were 'treated as drones'. They described departmental 'suitability' rating charts used to determine overseas assignments, which ranked a married man as 'most stable' and an unmarried woman as 'least stable'. They decided to organize the Women's Action Organization in order to systematically attack policies that marginalized and exploited women in the foreign policy establishment. Fighting battles as individuals on a case by case basis, as they had in the past, was neither effective nor efficient.[45]

WAO activists knew the ways of Washington. They picked their time wisely. In 1970 State Department officials were demoralized. The Kennedy and Johnson years had brought a decline in State Department influence. Foreign-policy decisions were more likely to be made in the National Security Council than in the State Department. Presidents were increasingly skeptical of the foreign service's ability to give them the advice and information they wanted. Special task forces were being commissioned to reassess all aspects of the State Department's operations. It was this process of examination that the women of WAO believed might permit them to raise their issues at the highest levels of the State Department.

They insisted upon a meeting with the State Department's senior management officials to press for changes in four areas:

● The State Department's policy compelling foreign-service women and secretaries to resign when they got married.

● The policy barring a woman with children from an overseas assignment.

● The policy that prohibited even unmarried women professionals from being posted to any of the 'Iron Curtain' or Muslim countries, though women in secretarial jobs could be sent to those countries.

● The policy of treating foreign-service wives as if they were adjuncts to their husbands.[46]

WAO won on all four points. The US State Department lifted its ban on married women. Today Phyllis Oakley stands for what this has meant for women diplomats. In 1987 she was appointed Deputy Assistant Secretary of State. She appears nightly on the television news speaking for the State Department on questions concerning naval operations in the Persian Gulf, the US position on Palestinian rights, and American policies toward the Nicaraguan Contras. When she was appointed, she recalls, the two questions the press asked repeatedly were: 'How old was I?' and 'Was I married?' Questions she thought would never have been asked of a man.[47] But marriage was more relevant than most reporters might have supposed. For Phyllis Oakley had entered the foreign service in 1957. She was forced to resign from the service after she married another foreign-service officer, becoming a diplomatic wife. She accompanied her husband to Sudan and then from post to post. She refers to these as her 'wilderness years'. Teaching and working with the YMCA 'may have made me a better-rounded person, but they certainly didn't enhance my ability to compete with men who spent those years gaining first-hand experience as diplomats.'[48]

But when WAO successfully lobbied the State Department to abolish its prohibition on women diplomats marrying, Phyllis Oakley quickly re-entered the foreign service. Now she was both a diplomat *and* a diplomatic wife. She and her husband became what the Family Liaison Office calls a 'tandem couple'. In 1975, when her husband was appointed ambassador to Zaïre, an African country which has assumed strategic importance to the United States, Phyllis Oakley became the first American ambassador's wife to work as a foreign-service officer in an embassy where her husband was ambassador.[49]

In 1987, when she was appointed Assistant Secretary of State, her husband was serving on the National Security Council. She speculated that behind her appointment to such a high-profile post was the Reagan administration's desire for a new foreign-policy image. But women remained a distinct minority in the US foreign service: 21.2 per cent, and a mere 5 per cent of senior officers. Of 133 Chiefs of Missions overseas, only nine were women, and a majority of them were political appointees rather than professional careerists like Phyllis Oakley.[50]

Phyllis Oakley, like the overwhelming majority of women – and men – in the US foreign service, is white. In January 1981 there were no women of color in the senior foreign service; and women of color comprised a mere 2.5 per cent of all levels, including support workers.[51] In 1987 the State Department's Equal Opportunities Office could write in its Annual Report to Congress that there had been progress – slight progress. Now there were a total of 2,592 women in the US foreign service; there were 6,847 men. White men and women together comprised 89 per cent of all foreign service employees.[52]

American society at the end of the twentieth century is changing fundamentally. Roughly 25 per cent of the population are people of color, and the proportion is growing. White men comprise only just over a quarter of all Americans, yet they continue to hold most of the senior policy-making posts in the government. At the Pentagon, the State Department's principal rival for foreign-policy influence, there are only fifty-six women out of the 400 who staff the important Under Secretary for Policy. Captain Paula Boggs, one of the very few black women in the office of the Secretary of Defense, blamed the military establishment's tradition of 'mentors' for the persistence of male bias: 'If a high-ranking officer adopts you and grooms you for a position in policy, you are much more likely to obtain that position than someone who does not have that link.'[53]

US Department of State, 1988: breakdown of staff

	White (%)	Black (%)	Hispanic (%)	Asian (%)	Women (%)	Total (number)
Non-foreign-service						
GS 1–4 (lowest grades)	22	68	5	4	82	555
GS 16–18 (senior grades)	95	4	0	1	11	107
Foreign service						
Total foreign service	89	5	4	2	28	9,420
Senior foreign service	96	2	1	0	5	763

Source: Assistant Secretary for Personnel-Civil Service, US Department of State, 'Workforce Statistics – Minority Employment Summary, Permanent Full-Time, as of April 1988', Washington, DC, 1988.

Beyond mere numbers, however, women and men in the State Department have commented on the tendency to assign women and minority men to the sorts of posts that don't lead to the most senior promotions. Women of all racial groups are more likely to be placed in consular posts, jobs that aren't stepping-stones to more policy-oriented posts. Women, furthermore, are far less likely to be chosen by superiors to attend international conferences. The post of delegate to an international conference – on disarmament, trade, the environment – is considered a 'plum' in the State Department and is commonly reserved for officers seen as promising by their superiors. Even those women who do manage to reach senior posts such as Deputy Chief of Mission, Chief of Mission and ambassador, have typically been assigned to countries not considered of great importance by the foreign-policy-makers. London, Paris, Bonn, Moscow, New Delhi and Manila each had no women in key foreign-service posts in the years 1980 and 1983.[54]

In April, 1989 George Bush's new Secretary of State, James Baker, announced that he would comply with federal court rulings that found the State Department guilty of sexist discrimination. The court ordered the Department to revise its foreign-service entrance examinations so that the questions were less biased in favor of male applicants and also to invite any women foreign-service officer to apply for appointment to a better post if she believed her current assignment had been at a level below her formal capabilities. These court rulings were the result of a thirteen-year-long case brought by Alison Palmer, a foreign service officer, in 1976. She charged the State Department with discrimination in both its hiring and promotional practices. The court's ruling could affect as many as 600 women in the US foreign-service.[55]

Similarly, insiders have noticed that Black men and women are likely to be channeled by their superiors into posts in Africa and those countries of Latin America or the Caribbean with large Black populations, which aren't given top priority by most American administrations and thus where it is harder for a career diplomat to catch the eye of his or her superiors.[56]

One arena in which women are making significant progress is trade negotiations. Women make up half of the 100 professional staff members of the Office of the United States Trade Representative. More importantly, women have played leading roles in negotiating major textile and computer-chip agreements, in which the American government has a great political stake. The rise of women in this field, however, should not be taken as a signal that foreign policy is becoming less gendered. Some inside observers see women negotiators as giving the American side a strategic advantage in these tough bargaining sessions: it throws men on the other side of the table off balance. Men representing other countries aren't sure how to react. One even angrily complained that he felt as though he was arguing with his wife, and it was humiliating. Judith Hippler Bello, an American woman who negotiated a computer-chip agreement with Japan, describes the role that gender confusion can play in this foreign-policy contest: 'We're on a steady course when they are thrown off balance, and balance is a critical element in any negotiation.' And, typically, that strategic balance is maintained by informal contacts away from the bargaining table: '[Foreign male negotiators] don't know what to do with us. They can't take us to their usual haunts where they go as men where some business gets done.'[57]

WOMEN IN INTERNATIONAL ORGANIZATIONS

Nearly 90 per cent of the secretaries and clerical personnel at the World Bank are women, but women occupy less than 3 per cent of its 'senior level' positions. At the Inter-American Development Bank there are thirty-three jobs in the 'Executive' category. One is held by a woman.

These were the 1983 findings of the members of the US Congressional Women's Caucus, who began taking a closer look at international organizations in order to determine whether they should cast their legislative votes for continued American funding. They concluded that the situation was 'appalling'.[58]

Catherine Watson, a British development specialist who worked for the World Bank, came away from the job with distinctly mixed feelings. The work was 'gripping'. In an atmosphere of 'confidence, privilege and inviolability' she could pursue her professional interests in agriculture. Then there were the physical comforts – 'the cafés, the shops, the wide streets, and the bookstores'. The neighborhoods of northwest Washington were far removed from local and global impoverished communities. Still, she felt uneasy. The North American and European men who monopolized the highest positions in the bank, together with those men from Third World countries who had attended Western universities and spent years in the cosmopolitan circles of development agencies, were too inclined to speak of Third World countries in disparaging terms.[59]

The men up and down the World Bank's ladder were not carbon copies of each other: there were the 'ex-colonials', the 'career men' and the high-flying 'young professionals'. Each group viewed problems and goals differently; each could become impatient or even patronizing toward the others. Differences notwithstanding, they could relate to each other across their political and cultural differences as men. And this meant the World Bank was a place where women were either secretaries or oddities. The secretaries were

> mostly beautiful young Latin American or Philippine women who wore expensive clothes, or redoubtable British women who had been with the Bank for years, who treated their bosses as though they were ever so slightly daft, and who no doubt would have had a shot at being bosses themselves had they been born 20 years later.[60]

Susana Mendaro, an Argentinian economist and one of the World Bank's few female professionals, discovered that her reports on the mismanagement of a development project in Zambia were turned down; that is, until they were incorporated into reports signed by male staff members. She was denied promotions, despite recommendations from her superior, and had to cope with sexual harassment on a bank trip to Mexico. Finally, she decided to sue the World Bank for flouting anti-sex discrimination constraints imposed on but rarely carried out in international agencies in most countries. 'That's cowboy land out there . . . There are no laws. Men can do anything they please.'[61]

Women inside the United Nations have organized. The Ad Hoc Group on Equal Rights for Women in the United Nations has lobbied the Secretary General and the General Assembly since the early 1980s to demand that women be appointed and promoted to more of the UN jobs that carry policy influence, technical responsibility and material rewards. In 1984 Yolanda Samayoa, president of the Ad Hoc Group, met with Secretary General Javier Perez de Cuellar on International Women's Day to outline the dismal picture of a masculinized United Nations. That year women made up more than half of the Secretary General's staff, but held only 22.3 per cent of the professional international civil-service posts, as compared with 83 per cent of its clerical and secretarial jobs. Of the thirty-five under secretaries running arms of the UN worldwide, only one was a woman; of the organization's forty-nine assistant secretaries-general, only three were women.[62]

For an organization intended to change the world, the United Nations looked remarkably like the patriarchal status quo. The Ad Hoc Group made clear to the Secretary General that they were becoming impatient with token gestures: 'Every year the women of the United Nations meet with you for what has become a ritual philosophical exchange . . . We present the perennial problem and you reiterate your commitment to the principles of equality.'[63]

Three years later the Secretary General appointed a Pakistani woman, Dr Nafis Sadik, to be the new executive director of the UN's Fund for Population Activities (UNFPA). This made Dr Sadik the first woman to direct such an influential and politically sensitive post in the organization. In his announcement, the Secretary General's representative made it clear to the press that he was well aware of Dr Sadik's gender; he also implied that appointing a person from the Third World was part of a calculated effort to get more poor countries' governments to take part in UN-backed population control programs.[64]

Yet Nafis Sadik is hardly part of a wave of women's appointments within the upper reaches of the UN. While the Ad Hoc Group did succeed in making the marginalization of women visible by getting the Secretary General to create the post of Coordinator for the Improvement of the Status of Women in the United Nations Secretariat, the job has proved a difficult one. Mercedes Pulido de Briceno, its first occupant, described the obstacles she faced as Coordinator: 'During the Inquisition in Spain people were forbidden to talk so that there wouldn't be conflicts . . . And I have realized that when it comes to women, it's like the Inquisition here at the UN.'[65] She said this in 1985, the final year of the United Nations' own Decade for Women.

Marriage politics has been holding women back in the United Nations just as it has in governmental foreign services. When pressed by Ad Hoc Group lobbyists and by the Coordinator to nominate more women for senior posts, UN member governments respond that women can't be put on their own in a world where late-night meetings and cocktail parties are *de rigueur*. Furthermore, they plead, single women's presence in such an environment would produce embarrassments, while married women do not enjoy the mobility so essential for UN work: they are likely to get pregnant; they are diverted by family responsibilities. Women working as UN secretaries complain that too often they are used by their male superiors as if they were wives – or domestic servants: they are expected to baby-sit, run errands, help serve at cocktail parties, even balance the family checkbook.[66]

By the end of 1987 there were signs that the Coordinator's refusal to be daunted by these excuses was beginning to bear fruit. Now there were two women in under secretary general posts, comprising 7.7 per cent of the officials at that senior rank. Just below them, in assistant secretary- general posts, there were another two women, representing 9.1 per cent of the holders of that influential rank. But it remained true that the lower one looked on the United Nations civil-service ladder, the more likely one was to find women. Holders of P–5 posts, the upper rungs of the ladder, were only 11.4 per cent female; those in P–1 posts, at the bottom of the ladder, were 74 per cent female.[67]

As is usually the case, within each category are other, telling patterns. The United Nations political system requires that a large number of important posts be subject to geographic quotas. This serves to keep one region from dominating any of the organization's activities. But the Coordinator for the Improvement of the Status of Women reported to the General Assembly in 1987 that women from Eastern Europe, the Middle East and Africa comprised a far smaller proportion of the officials from those regions than was equitable. Whereas 31.0 per cent of all geographically appointed officials from Asian and Pacific countries were women, only 5.4 per cent of all geographically appointed officials from Eastern Europe were women. Second, those Eastern European, Middle Eastern and African women who were appointed were most likely to fill service and administration posts, not posts responsible for technical projects or with policy-making authority.[68]

As in the British and American foreign services, these modest steps toward demasculinizing the machinery of international politics are coming at a time of financial retrenchment. In the United Nations, as in Washington and London, any efforts to make international agencies more truly reflect the societies they represent are met with claims that it is not feasible when every penny has to be counted.

CONCLUSION

Government men depend on women's unpaid labor to carry on relations with their political counterparts. So long as the conventional politics of marriage prevailed, no government needed either to acknowledge or to accommodate diplomatic wives and women careerists. They could use marriage both to grease the wheels of man-to-man negotiations and to ensure that no women reached positions of influence.

But since the 1970s diplomatic wives and women careerists – separately and together – have been organizing in ways that have turned the spotlight on that government dependence. Today the more diplomatic wives refuse to be confined by their traditional marital roles, the more governments try to make token concessions, without fundamentally rethinking the nature of relations between states. Governments have not fully relinquished their control because they still need women. Women remain vital to creating and maintaining trust between men in a hostile world.

6

CARMEN MIRANDA ON MY MIND: INTERNATIONAL POLITICS OF THE BANANA

When she appeared on screen, the tempo quickened. Dressed in her outrageous costumes, topped by hats featuring bananas and other tropical fruits, Carmen Miranda sang and danced her way to Hollywood stardom. While she was best known for her feisty comic performances, she also played a part in a serious political drama: the realignment of American power in the Western hemisphere. Carmen Miranda's movies helped make Latin America safe for American banana companies at a time when US imperialism was coming under wider regional criticism.

Between 1880 and 1930 the United States colonized or invaded Hawaii, the Philippines, Puerto Rico, the Dominican Republic, Cuba and Nicaragua. Each was strategically valuable for its plantation crops. The British, French and Dutch had their plantation colonies producing rubber, tea, coffee, palm oil, coconuts, tobacco, sisal, cotton, jute, rice and, of course, the monarch of plantation crops, sugar. Bananas, sugar, coffee, pineapples – each had become an international commodity that Americans, too, were willing to kill for. But by the time Franklin Roosevelt came into office, sending in the marines was beginning to lose its political value; it was alienating too many potential regional allies. New, less direct means had to be found to guarantee American control of Latin America.

Carmen Miranda was born in Lisbon in 1909, but emigrated as a child to Brazil, where her father established a wholesale fruit business. Despite her parents' hopes that their convent-educated daughter would grow up to be a respectable young woman, she secretly auditioned for and won a regular spot on a Rio de Janeiro radio station. She became a hit and soon was an attraction on the local nightclub circuit. By 1939 Carmen Miranda had recorded over 300 singles, appeared in four Brazilian films and was being referred to by her compatriots as a national institution. It was at this point in her career that Broadway theatrical producer Lee Schubert saw Carmen Miranda perform and offered her a contract to move north. When she stepped off the boat in New York on May 4 1939, Schubert had the press corps already primed to greet his new 'Brazilian bombshell'. With her outrageous headgear and limited but flamboyant English (she spoke French and Spanish as well as Portuguese), she was on her way to being turned into the 1940s American stereotype of the Latin American woman. In response to reporters' questions, Miranda replied, 'Money, money, money . . . hot dog. I say yes, no, and I say money, money money and I say turkey sandwich and I say grape juice.'[1]

The world's fair was attracting throngs to the Sunken Meadow fairgrounds just outside New York City in the summer of 1939, but Carmen Miranda still managed to make Schubert's show, *Streets of Paris*, a commercial success. *Life* magazine's reviewer noted:

> Partly because their unusual melody and heavy accented rhythms are unlike anything ever heard in a Manhattan revue before, partly because there is not a clue to their meaning except the gay rolling of Carmen Miranda's insinuating eyes, these songs, and Miranda herself, are the outstanding hit of the show.[2]

In 1940 Hollywood studio directors were boarding the Latin America bandwagon. Men like Darryl Zanuck, head of Twentieth Century Fox, had long cultivated friendships with politicians in Washington. It was one way of overcoming the barriers of anti-Semitism confronting many of the film industry's moguls. Thus when President Franklin Roosevelt launched his Latin American 'Good Neighbor' policy, the men who ran Hollywood were willing to help the government's campaign to replace a militaristic, imperial approach to US–Latin America diplomacy with a more 'cooperative' strategy. Roosevelt and his advisers were convinced that gunboat diplomacy was arousing too much opposition among precisely those Latin American governments which American businessmen would have to cultivate if the country was to pull itself out of the Depression. Tourism and investment were promoted in glossy brochures. Pan-American Airways flew holiday-makers to Havana and Managua; construction of the Pan-American Highway was started. Nicaragua's

Anastasio Somoza was invited to the world's fair to celebrate regional democracy and progress. Latin American movie stars replaced the marines as the guarantors of regional harmony.[3]

Darryl Zanuck enticed Carmen Miranda away from Broadway to be his studio's contribution to the 'Good Neighbor' policy. She appeared in the

14 Carmen Miranda. A Hollywood publicity shot, n.d.

1940 film *Down Argentine Way*, starring Betty Grable and Don Ameche, singing 'South American Way'. Her film career soared during World War II, when Washington officials believed that it was diplomatically vital to keep Latin American regimes friendly to the United States. Propaganda and censorship agencies urged the entertainment industry to promote Latin actors and popularize Latin music.

Carmen Miranda was confined to light roles, treated by the studios as a comic or character actor, never a romantic lead. Perhaps her most lavish film was Busby Berkeley's *The Gang's All Here* (1943), whose set was adorned with giant bananas and strawberries. She mastered English, but was careful to maintain in her performances a heavily accented pronunciation, which suggested feminine *naïveté*. For many Americans, during the 1940s Carmen Miranda became a guide to Latin culture. While Hollywood's Latin American male was stereotypically a loyal but none-too-bright sidekick, like Donald Duck's parrot pal José Carioca, Miranda personified a culture full of zest and charm, unclouded by intense emotion or political ambivalence. Like the bananas she wore on her head, Miranda was exotic yet mildly amusing.

'Carmen Miranda is the chief export of Brazil. Next comes coffee.' So recalls Uruguayan historian Eduardo Galeano.[4] Brazilians themselves were proud of Miranda's Hollywood success. When she died suddenly of a heart attack in 1955, her body and effects were shipped back to Rio to be memorialized in a Carmen Miranda museum. Brazilian President Kubitschek declared a national day of mourning.

'I'M CHIQUITA BANANA AND I'VE COME TO SAY'

The banana has a history, a gendered history. The fruit has its origins in Southeast Asia and was carried westward by traders. By the fifteenth century it had become a basic food for Africans living on the Guinean coast. When Portuguese and Spanish slave-traders began raiding the coast for Africans to serve as forced labor on colonial estates, they chose bananas as the food to ship with them; it was local and cheap. These were red bananas, a variety still popular in the West Indies and Africa. The yellow banana so familiar today to consumers in Europe, Japan, the Persian Gulf and North America wasn't developed as a distinct variety until the nineteenth century. Then it was imagined to be food fit not for slaves, but for the palates of the wealthy. The first record of bunches of bananas being brought to New York from Havana was in 1804. But it was when the yellow banana was served as an exotic delicacy in the homes of affluent Bostonians in 1875 that it took off as an international commodity. In 1876 the banana was featured at the

United States Centennial Exhibition in Philadelphia. The yellow banana symbolized America's new global reach.[5]

Notions of masculinity and femininity have . been used to shape the international political economy of the banana. Banana plantations were developed in Central America, Latin America, the Caribbean, Africa and the Philippines as a result of alliances between men of different but complementary interests: businessmen and male officials of the importing countries on the one hand, and male landowners and government officials of the exporting countries on the other. To clear the land and harvest the bananas they decided they needed a male workforce, sustained at a distance by women as prostitutes, mothers and wives. However company executives' manly pride was invested not so much in their extensive plantations as in the sophisticated equipment and technology they developed to transport the fragile tropical fruit to far-away markets: railroads, wire services and fleets of refrigerator ships. Even today company officials take special satisfaction in describing their giant cold-storage ships circling the globe, directed by a sophisticated international communications network, all to ensure that bananas that leave Costa Rica or the Philippines by the green tonnage will arrive in New York or Liverpool undamaged and unspoiled, ready for the ripening factory.[6] The companies envisaged their customers to be women: mothers and housewives concerned about their families' nutrition and looking for a reliable product. The most successful way of bonding housewives' loyalty to a particular company was to create a fantasized market woman.

The United Fruit Company, the largest grower and marketer of bananas, made its contribution to America's 'Good Neighbor' culture. In 1943 the company opened a Middle American Information Bureau to encourage 'mutual knowledge and mutual understanding'. The bureau wrote and distributed materials which emphasized the value of Central American products such as hardwoods, coffee, spices and fruits to the US war effort. It targeted school children and housewives: those who ate bananas and those who bought them. *Nicaragua in Story and Pictures* was a company-designed school text celebrating the progress brought to Nicaragua by foreign-financed railroads and imported tractors. 'Fifty Questions on Middle America for North American Women' and 'Middle America and a Woman's World' explained to the North American housewife, United Fruit's chief customer, how the Japanese invasion of Malaysia made imported foods from Nicaragua and Costa Rica all the more important to her wartime security.[7]

United Fruit's biggest contribution to American culture, however, was 'Chiquita Banana'. In 1944, when Carmen Miranda was packing movie houses and American troops were landing on Europe's beaches, United

Fruit advertising executives created a half-banana, half-woman cartoon character destined to rival Donald Duck. Dressed as a Miranda-esque market woman, this feminized banana sang her calypso song from coast to coast. Chiquita Banana helped to establish a twentieth-century art form, the singing commercial. One could hear her singing the praises of the banana on the radio 376 times daily.

Americans who are now in their fifties still can give a rendition of her memorable song:

> *I'm Chiquita Banana*
> *And I've come to say*
> *Bananas have to ripen*
> *In a certain way.*
> *When they are fleck'd with brown*
> *And have a golden hue*
> *Bananas taste the best*
> *And are the best for you.*
>
> *You can put them in a salad*
> *You can put them in a pie-aye*
> *Any way you want to eat them*
> *It's impossible to beat them.*
> *But bananas like the climate*
> *Of the very, very tropical equator.*
> *So you should never put bananas*
> *In the refrigerator. No no no no!*[8]

United Fruit sales strategists set out to do the impossible – to create in housewives a brand-name loyalty for a generic fruit. They wanted women to think 'Chiquita' when they went to the grocery store to buy bananas. Roosevelt's 'Good Neighbor' policy and Carmen Miranda's Hollywood success had set the stage; animated cartoons and the commercial jingle did the rest. Between the woman consumer and the fruit there now was only a corporation with the friendly face of a bouncy Latin American market woman. Forty years later United Fruit Company has become United Brands; its principal subsidiary is Chiquita Brands, bringing us not only bananas, but melons, grapefruits and tropical juices.

Today virtually every affluent, industrialized country imports bananas from mainly poor, still agrarian countries. Each consumer society gets its bananas from two or three large agribusiness corporations which either have large plantations of their own or monopolize the marketing

15   United Brands Company's recording for children of the 'Chiquita Banana' song. (Original music by Len Mackensie, 1945; updated commercial lyrics, 1975, © Maxwell-Wirges, 1945)

system through which small growers sell their fruit. Since United Fruit's advertising coup in 1944, its competitors have followed suit, designing stickers for their own bananas. This allows a shopper to go into any grocery store in Europe, North America or Japan and check at a glance the state of international banana politics: just look for the sticker with its corporate logo and the country of origin. In London one might peel off a Geest sticker that says 'WINBAN' (the Windward Island nations of St Lucia, St Vincent or Dominica) or look for the Fyffes sticker (Fyffes is United Brands' European subsidiary) that gives the country of origin as Surinam. In Detroit or Toronto a shopper would be more likely to find a Chiquita, Del Monte or Dole sticker, with Costa Rica,

Ecuador or Colombia written below the logo in small print, while in Tokyo Sumitomo's Banambo sticker would identify bananas produced in the Philippines.

After a century of banana big business, Americans remain the largest consumers of bananas, eating some 2 million tons of the fruit each year. But with the opening of the Philippines to banana companies, especially under the debt-ridden Marcos regime, hungry for foreign investment, consumers in Japan and the Persian Gulf have become the latest targets for advertising campaigns.

16   Banana logo stickers from some of the largest international banana companies

131

World Consumption of Bananas

Largest consuming countries	Major suppliers	Volume (tons)
United States	Ecuador, Costa Rica, Honduras	2,325,000
Canada	Ecuador, Columbia, Honduras	269,400
West Germany	Panama, Costa Rica, Honduras	503,000
France	Martinique, Guadeloupe	466,800
United Kingdom	Windward Islands, Colombia, Surinam	322,000
Italy	Colombia, Costa Rica, Somalia	330,000
Spain	Canary Islands	415,000
Japan	Philippines, China	757,900
Saudi Arabia	Philippines, Guatemala, Ecuador	120,000
Argentina	Ecuador, Brazil, Colombia	140,000

Source: Green Gold: Bananas and Dependency in the Eastern Caribbean, London, Latin American Bureau, 1987, pp. 14–15. Figures are from the Food and Agriculture Organization for 1982.

Bananas for Bahrain

A giant container ship steams out of the Philippines bound for the Middle East. On its cargo manifest . . . are bananas headed for markets in the region.

The shipment has been arranged by one of Japan's general trading companies, or *sogo shosha* . . .

In the world of the *sogo shosha*, bananas are just the beginning.[9]

Bananas have become big business, declares this advertisement placed by the Japan Foreign Trade Council. The history of Japan's banana industry, however, reaches back to the early 1900s. In 1903 small farmers in Taiwan were Japan's sole banana suppliers and remained its major source until the 1950s. Philippines bananas entered the Japanese market in 1969. In the next six years Philippines bananas grew from just under 3 per cent of the market to 85 per cent of the market. They had several advantages for Japanese fruit traders: they were grown near Japan; they were less vulnerable to typhoons; bananas could be introduced on large-scale plantations whose owners were looking for a new crop; they could be grown by cheap wage-labor readily available to plantation owners. Whereas once bananas were bought as 'hospital gifts' by Japanese consumers, by the 1970s they had become an everyday fruit seen by Japanese housewives as a good source of family nutrition at a reasonable price.[10]

WOMEN IN BANANA REPUBLICS

It is always worth asking, 'Where are the women?' Answering the question reveals the dependence of most political and economic systems not just on women, but on certain kinds of relations between women and men. A great deal has been written about countries derisively labeled 'banana republics'. They are described as countries whose land and soul are in the clutches of a foreign company, supported by the might of its own government. A banana republic's sovereignty has been so thoroughly compromised that it is the butt of jokes, not respect. It has a government, but it is staffed by people who line their own pockets by doing the bidding of the overseas corporation and its political allies. Because it is impossible for such compromised rulers to win the support of their own citizens, many of whom are exploited on the corporation's plantations, the government depends on guns and jails, not ballots and national pride.

The quintessential banana republics were those Central American countries which came to be dominated by the United Fruit Company's monoculture, the US marines and their hand-picked dictators. Their regimes have been backed by American presidents, mocked by Woody Allen, and overthrown by nationalist guerrillas.

Yet these political systems, and the international relationships which underpin them, have been discussed as if women scarcely existed. The principal actors on all sides have been portrayed by conventional commentators as men, and as if their being male was insignificant. Thus the ways in which their shared masculinity allowed agribusiness entrepreneurs to form alliances with men in their own diplomatic corps and with men in Nicaraguan or Honduran society have been left unexamined. Enjoying Cuban cigars together after dinner while wives and mistresses powder their noses has been the stuff of smug cartoons but not of political curiosity. Similarly, a banana republic's militarized ethos has been taken for granted, without an investigation of how militarism feeds on masculinist values to sustain it. Marines, diplomats, corporate managers and military dictators may mostly be male, but they tend to need the feminine 'other' to maintain their self-assurance.

One of the conditions that has pushed women off the banana republic stage has been the masculinization of the banana plantation. Banana-company executives imagined that most of the jobs on their large plantations could be done only by men. Banana plantations were carved out of wooded acres. Clearing the brush required workers who could use a machete, live in rude barracks, and who, once the plantation's trees were bearing fruit, could chop down the heavy bunches and carry them to central loading areas and from there to the docks, to be loaded by the ton on to refrigerator ships. This was men's work.

Not all plantation work has been masculinized. Generally, crops that call for the use of machetes – tools that can also be used as weapons – are produced with large inputs of male labor: bananas, sugar, palm oil. Producers of crops that require a lot of weeding, tapping and picking hire large numbers of women, sometimes comprising a majority of workers: tea, coffee, rubber.

Nor is the gendered labor formula on any plantation fixed. Plantation managers who once relied heavily on male workers may decide to bring in more women if the men become too costly; if their union becomes too threatening; if the international market for the crop declines necessitating cost-cutting measures such as hiring more part-time workers; if new technology allows some physically demanding tasks to be done by workers with less strength. Today both sugar and rubber are being produced by plantation companies using more women workers than they did a generation ago.[11] What has remained constant, however, is the presumption of international corporations that their position in the world market depends on manipulations of masculinity and femininity. Gender is injected into every Brooke Bond or Lipton tea leaf, every Unilever or Lonrho palm-oil nut, every bucket of Dunlop or Michelin latex, every stalk of Tate & Lyle sugar cane.

Like all plantation managers, banana company executives considered race as well as gender when employing what they thought would be the most skilled and compliant workforce. Thus although the majority of banana workers were men, race was used to divide them. On United Brands' plantations in Costa Rica and Panama, for instance, managers recruited Amerindian men from the Guaymi and Kuna communities, as well as West Indian Black men and hispanicized Ladino men. They placed them in different, unequally paid jobs, Ladino men at the top (below white male managers), Amerindian men at the bottom. Amerindian men were assigned to menial jobs such as chopping grass and overgrown bush, thus ensuring that Ladino men's negative stereotypes of Amerindians – *cholos*, unskilled, uncultured natives – would be perpetuated. The stereotypes were valuable to the company because they forestalled potential alliances between Ladino, Black and Amerindian men over common grievances.[12]

> *Manager*: It's easier to work with *cholos*. They're not as smart and don't speak good Spanish. They can't argue back at you even when they're right ... Hell, you can make a *cholo* do anything.

Ladino foreman: My workers are [not] *cholos* . . . It's different here. Sure I can grab them [Ladino and Black male workers] and make them work faster; but the consequences will catch up with me tomorrow. We're not *cholos* here . . . you understand?

Guaymi worker: They used to have up to 200 of us crammed into shacks eating boiled bananas out of empty kerosene cans.[13]

To say, therefore, that a banana plantation is masculinized is not to say that masculinity, even when combined with social class, is sufficient to forge political unity. On the other hand, the presumption that a banana plantation is a man's world does affect the politics of any movement attempting to improve workers' conditions, or to transform the power relationships that comprise a 'banana republic'.

A banana plantation's politics are deeply affected not just by the fact that the majority of its workers – and virtually all of its managers and owners – are men, but by the *meaning* that has been attached to that masculinization. Even male banana workers employed by a foreign company that, in alliance with local élites, had turned their country into a proverbial banana republic, could feel some pride. For they were unquestionably performing men's work. They knew how to wield a machete; they knew how to lift great weights; they worked outside in close coordination with trains and ships. Whether a smallholder or a plantation employee, a banana man was a *man*.

> *Touris, white man, wipin his*
>   *face,*
> *Met me in Golden Grove*
>   *market place.*
>
> *He looked at m'ol'clothes brown*
>   *wid stain,*
> *An soaked tight through wid de*
>   *Portlan rain,*
> *He cas his eye, turned up his*
>   *nose,*
> *He says, 'You're a beggar man, I*
>   *suppose?'*
> *He says, 'Boy, get some*
>   *occupation,*
> *Be of some value to your*
>   *nation.'*

I said, 'By God and dis big right
  han
You mus recognise a banana
  man . . .

Don't judge a man by his patchy
  clothes,
I'm a strong man, a proud man,
  an I'm free
Free as dese mountains, free as
  dis sea,
I know myself, an I know my
  ways,
An will say wid pride to de end
  o my days.

Praise God an m'big right
  han
I will live an die a banana man.[14]

In the 1920s when banana workers began to organize and to conduct strikes that even the US government and local élites had to pay attention to, their demands reached beyond working conditions to political structures. These workers' protests took on strong nationalist overtones: the local regime and foreign troops were as much the target of their protests as the plantation companies. But so long as banana plantation work was imagined to be men's work, and so long as the banana workers' unions were organized as if they were men's organizations, the nationalist cause would be masculinized. A banana republic might fall, but patriarchy remained in place.

WOMEN WEED, WOMEN CLEAN

The banana plantation has never been as exclusively male as popular imagery suggests. It takes women's paid and unpaid labor to bring the golden fruit to the world's breakfast tables.

A banana plantation is closest to a male enclave at the beginning, when the principal task is bulldozing and clearing the land for planting. But even at this stage women are depended upon by the companies – and their male employees – to play their roles. As in the male-dominated mining industry from Chile to South Africa and Indonesia, companies can recruit men to live away from home only if someone back home takes care of their families and maintains their land. The 'feminization of agriculture' – that is, leaving small-scale farming to women, typically without giving them training, equipment or extra finance – has always been part and parcel of the masculinization of mining and banana plantations.[15] The male labor force has to make private arrangements with wives, mothers or sisters to assure them of a place to return to when their contracts expire, when they get fed up with supervisors' contemptuous treatment or when they are laid off because world prices have plummeted. Behind every all-male banana plantation stand scores of women performing unpaid domestic and productive labor. Company executives, union spokesmen and export-driven government officials have all preferred not to take this into account when working out their bargaining positions. International agencies such as the International Monetary Fund scarcely give a thought to women as wives and subsistence farmers when they press indebted governments to open up more land to plantation companies in order to correct their trade imbalances and pay off foreign bankers.

Once the banana trees have been planted, women are likely to become residents and workers on the plantations. Plantation managers, like their diplomatic and military counterparts, have found marriage both a political asset and a liability. On the one hand, having young male workers without wives and children has advantages: the men are in their physical prime, they are likely to view life as an adventure and be willing to tolerate harsh working and living conditions. On the other hand, young unattached men are more volatile and are willing to take risks if angered precisely because they will not jeopardize anyone's security aside from their own. This makes the married male worker seem more stable to a calculating plantation manager. He may demand more from the company in the form of rudimentary amenities for his wife and children, but he is more likely to toe the company line for their sake.[16]

Women are most likely to be employed by the banana companies if the plantation cannot recruit men from a low-status ethnic group, like Amerindians in Central America, to do the least prestigious and lowest-paid jobs. In all sorts of agribusiness, women tend to be given the most tedious, least 'skilled' jobs, those that are most seasonal, the least likely to offer year-round employment and those company benefits awarded to full-time employees. Weeding and cleaning are the quintessential 'women's' jobs in agriculture, both in socialist and capitalist countries.[17]

Bananas today are washed, weighed and packed in factories on the plantations before being transported to the docks for shipment overseas. Inside these packing houses one finds the women on the modern banana plantation. They remove the bunches of fruit from the thick stems, an operation that has to be done carefully (one might say skillfully) so that the bananas are not damaged. They wash the bananas in a chemical solution, a hazardous job. They select the rejects, which can amount to up to half the bananas picked in the fields. Companies often dump rejected bananas in nearby streams, causing pollution which kills local fish. Women weigh the fruit and finally attach the company's tell-tale sticker on each bunch. They are paid piece-rates and foremen expect them to work at high speed. In between harvests they may have little work to do and not receive any pay. At harvest time they are expected to be available for long stretches, sometimes around the clock, to meet the company's tight shipping schedule.[18]

Tess is a Filipino woman who works for TADECO, a subsidiary of United Brands, Philippines. She works on a plantation on the country's southern island, Mindanao. A decade-long war has been fought in the area between government troops and indigenous Muslim groups protesting against the leasing of large tracts of land either to multinational pineapple and banana companies or to wealthy Filipino landowners, who then work out lucrative contracts with those corporations. Tess herself is a Christian Filipina. She, like thousands of other women and men, migrated, with government encouragement, to Mindanao from other islands in search of work once the bottom fell out of the once-dominant sugar industry. She works with other young women in the plantation's packing plant, preparing bananas to be shipped to Japan by Japanese and American import companies. She is paid approximately $1 a day. With an additional living allowance, Tess can make about $45 a month; she sends a third of this home to her family in the Visayas.

Tess uses a chemical solution to wash the company's bananas. There is a large, reddish splotch on her leg where some of the chemical spilled accidentally. At the end of a day spent standing for hours at a time, Tess goes 'home' to a bunkhouse she shares with 100 other women, twenty-four to a room, sleeping in eight sets of three-tiered bunks.[19]

Many women working on banana plantations are young and single, and, in the Philippines, often have secondary-school or even college educations. They may be the daughters of male employees, or they may be recruited from outside. They are subjected to sexual harassment in the packing plants and can be fired if found to be pregnant. The life of a banana washer is dull and isolated: 'We have no choice than to stay here. First, the company is quite far from the highway and if we . . . spend our fare what else would be left for our food?'[20]

Large banana companies – Geest in Britain, United Brands, Del Monte and Dole in the United States and Japan's Sumitomo – also require workers at the other end of the food chain, in the countries where they market their bananas. The docks, the trucks and the ripening plants reveal

17 Women using chemicals to clean bananas in a Honduran packing
plant. (photo: Jenny Matthews, 1983)

how company managers shape the sexual division of labor. Stevedors in
every country are thought of as doing a classic 'man's' job, though again
ethnic politics may determine which men will unload the bananas from
the company's ships. Today in Japan, where immigrant labor is being
increasingly relied upon to do the low-status, low-paid jobs, Filipino
men do the heavy work of transferring bananas from ships to trucks.
The job has become so closely associated with the fruit that to be a
longshoreman in Japan is to be a 'banana'. Women are hired in all the
consumer countries to weigh and sort at the ripening plant before the
fruit heads for the supermarket. Food processing is as feminized – as
dependent on ideas about femininity – as nursing, secretarial work and
sewing.

Women are hired by the banana companies to do low-paid, often
seasonal jobs that offer little chance of training and promotion; some involve the hazards of chemical pollution and sexual harassment. But many
women still seek these jobs because they seem better than the alternatives: dependence on fathers or husbands (if they are employed), life on the
dole (if work is not available), work in the entertainment industry around
a military base, subsistence farming with few resources, emigration.

Many women are heads of households and take exploitative jobs in
order to support their children; other women see their employment as

part of being dutiful daughters, sending part of their meager earnings back to parents, who may be losing farm land to agribusinesses. Neither women nor men working on any plantation – banana, tea, rubber, sugar, pineapple, palm oil, coffee – are simply 'workers'. They are wives, husbands, daughters, sons, mothers, fathers, lovers; and each role has its own politics. The politics of being a daughter, a mother or a wife allows First World and Third World governments to rely on international plantation companies, which in turn are able to recruit and control women workers and win the consumer loyalty of women buyers. 'Daughter', 'mother', and 'wife' are ideas on which the international political system today depends.

BROTHELS AND BANANAS

Bananas have long been the objects of sexual jokes and pranks. One food company recently complained when an AIDS education campaign used a banana to demonstrate how a man should put on a condom. But the banana industry – not the banana itself – is far more seriously sexualized. Sexual harassment helps to control women working in the plantation factories; prostitution has been permitted in order to control the still largely male plantation workforce.

> They were no more than lost villages on the Colombian coast, a strip of dust between river and cemetery, a yawn between two siestas, when the yellow train of the United Fruit Company pulled in . . . The age of the banana had come.
>
> The region awoke to find itself an immense plantation. Cienaga, Aracataca, and Fundacion got telegraph and post offices and new streets with poolrooms and brothels. Campesinos, who arrived by the thousands, left their mules at the hitching posts and went to work.[21]

Plantations are self-contained worlds. Workers, managers and the crops they cultivate live together side by side, but regulated by strict hierarchies, the more blatant because they are carved into the landscape. Male managers and their wives live in comfortable houses with gardens and kitchens maintained by local employees and have access to their own clubs with well-stocked bars and refreshing swimming pools. Foremen and their families have their own more modest housing compound and privileges. Workers live in spartan accommodation that often lacks minimal sanitary facilities. Some plantations are better equipped than others. Head offices like to talk about the clinics and schools they provide. They rarely talk about the isolation, or the paralyzing debts accumulated by employees at the company store. Some companies have had to provide basic necessities for workers in order to obtain land rights and tax concessions from local governments. Caribbean critics of their countries' past dependency on monoculture have coined the term 'plantation economy': foreign agribusiness giants have so dominated an entire society that it is reduced to a community permeated by dependency and paternalistic control.[22]

Plantations that depend on a predominately male workforce operate much like military bases. Women's sexual availability just outside the gates (thus supposedly beyond the plantation manager's control) has been offered as one of the rewards for enduring the isolated, harsh conditions of plantation life.

Few commentators on 'plantation economies' have thought to ask about the ways that sexuality has been used to control male workers. One who has is historian Ann Laura Stoler. When investigating life on Dutch-owned sisal, tea, rubber and palm-oil plantations in colonial Indonesia she asked about sexual politics.[23] Stoler found that prostitution was integral to the way managers recruited and controlled male workers from several different ethnic groups. There were many more men than women on these estates. Women were hired at half the rates paid to men, not enough to meet daily necessities. Most were single Javanese women, hired on contract and living far away from home. To make ends meet many of these women provided sexual services to Chinese male workers living in the plantation barracks. Some young women were pushed into prostitution by being sexually harassed by foremen in the packing plants. White plantation supervisors enjoyed the privilege of selecting their sexual partners from the most recent female arrivals.

Prostitution became the norm on many plantations by design, not simply by chance. There are records revealing that managers debated the advantages and disadvantages of prostitution for their company. The debates have a familiar ring; they echo debates about military prostitution. Some Dutch commentators were alarmed at the high incidence of venereal disease among plantation workers and blamed the prostitutes. Others noted that white supervisors were assaulted by male Javanese workers who believed their daughters were being lured into prostitution. But the prevailing view was that it would be too difficult to recruit male workers for plantation work if they were not provided with female sexual services. Furthermore, in the eyes of many plantation managers, prostitution was a lesser evil than homosexual relations between male workers deprived of female companionship. Finally, devoting a sizeable portion of their wages to prostitution left many male workers further in debt and thus made it harder for them to abandon estate work when their current contracts expired.

Around some United Brands plantations in Central America brothels are commonplace. They are situated just outside the company gates. While the men on banana plantations are Amerindian, Black and Ladino, the women working in the brothels are overwhelmingly Ladino. Information is limited, but most women servicing banana workers seem to have done other sorts of work before becoming prostitutes, and many are the sole supporters of their children. Racism and sexism are woven together in Central America's banana plantation brothels, as is so often the case in prostitution politics. Ladino prostitutes told one researcher that they preferred Amerindian customers because, they said, these men were too shy to fully undress and got their intercourse over with quickly. This was not necessarily meant as a compliment to Amerindian masculinity and may have reinforced negative stereotypes among Ladino and Black male workers.[24]

PATRIARCHAL LAND REFORM

Not all bananas are grown on plantations owned or leased by large corporations. Many people in Africa, Asia, the Caribbean and Latin America eat bananas that are grown in their own yards or by small-scale independent farmers, a large proportion of them women, and sold by market women – Carmen Miranda's and Chiquita's inspiration – in provincial towns. Even some of the bananas reaching the supermarkets of industrialized countries – for instance, many Philippines bananas shipped to Japan – are cultivated by smallholders. Geest, one of Britain's largest food companies, buys its bananas from smallholders in the Windward Islands: St Lucia, Dominica, Grenada and St Vincent.[25]

In 1985 Britons consumed nearly 2 billion bananas; over half of them were Windward Island bananas imported and marketed by Geest. Charles Geest, one of two Dutch brothers who founded the company, was listed in 1989 as one of 200 Britons personally worth over £30 million.[26] But Geest operates quite differently to Dole, United Brands or other large-scale plantation companies. Its suppliers may have as much as twelve acres of land or as little as half an acre of land. These smallholders sell their bananas to the local Banana Growers Association, which in turn sells them to Geest. As the sole purchaser of Windward bananas and as the operator of the shipping company, the ripening plants and the wholesale network, Geest is able to impose quality standards, rules and a pricing formula that determine how its Caribbean suppliers must operate. Critics in the Caribbean and Britain charge that Geest makes unfair profits and controls local farmers without having to assume direct responsibility.

It is all too easy to carry out an analysis of Geest without asking where the women are. The question seems unnecessary if one assumes that once the plantation system is removed and a crop is grown by smallholders on their own land, women and men within a household will work together as equals. The only political question then worth pursuing is whether the smallholders are dealt with fairly by the international marketing firm and the governments which link the farmers and the ultimate consumers.

But scratch the surface of small-scale farming and a more complex reality appears. In Dominica a survey of 120 banana farms ranging from one to five acres in size revealed that 82 per cent were owned by men; only 18 per cent were owned by women. This, despite the fact that on virtually every farm it took both women's and men's labor to nurture and harvest bananas that met Geest's high standards. In neighboring St Lucia 95 per cent of the small farms surveyed were owned by the men of the household, only 5 per cent by the women. In St Vincent the same pattern was repeated: men owned 70 per cent, women owned 30 per cent.[27]

The Banana Growers Association and Geest's managers are overwhelmingly male. They deal with small-scale owners who are mostly male. 'The smallholder and his wife' is the phrase commonly heard in international development circles. The phrase is not just sloppy semantics. It permits development agencies and local agricultural ministries to imagine that the person in the rural household to whom technical training, new seeds or agricultural credit should be given is the adult man. The unspoken corollary is that what is progress for a husband will turn into progress for his wife.

Women *grow* more food than men.

Women *buy* more food than men.

Women *cook* more food than men.

But women *own* less land on which food is grown.

And women *eat* less food than men.

'The farmer and his wife' disguises the reality of the world's food production. Most technical agencies agree that women produce at least half of the world's food. In Africa they produce between 60 per cent and 80 per cent. It is the politics of land *ownership* that obscures this reality. If one is talking about food production, not land ownership, it might be more accurate to refer to 'the farmer and her husband'.

More seriously, 'the farmer and his wife' not only obscures the gendered politics of land ownership; it also makes invisible the ways in which women organize their daily lives to sustain families and still produce bananas on their smallholdings. The use of 'the household' as the unit for measuring the success or failure of any project or policy is radically flawed. It presumes – without testing that presumption against reality – that the relationships within any house are equal, that emotional, sexual and economic relationships between men and women and sons and daughters are naturally harmonious, without tension, without intimidation or coercion. This was the presumption used in Britain, France, Canada and the United States to deny women the right to vote: why would a woman need a vote of her own when her father, husband or brother would 'naturally' cast his ballot with her best interest in mind? What was a naïve assumption in the suffrage debate is an unfounded argument in the politics of the banana.[28]

Feminists in Third World countries who have made land reform a political cause have insisted that dismantling large plantations – whether locally or foreign-owned – must not be seen as sufficient to ensure that women gain the power and resources they need to shape rural development so that women as well as men benefit. If land reform is implemented without a critical examination of *which* small farmers will receive the precious land title, land reform can serve to perpetuate patriarchal inequities in the countryside.

In several countries where plantation agriculture has been dominant, women's groups are challenging relations between men and women that shape the way food is produced. In Kenya, where both high-ranking government officials and foreign agribusinesses have profited from the opening of more land to large-scale plantations, Kikuyu women working in a Del Monte pineapple packing plant went on strike in 1987 to protest at working conditions.[29] Honduran peasant organizations with strong women leaders have created autonomous women peasants' groups to permit women to develop political skills. Honduras depends on bananas for over 30 per cent of its export earnings, and the government is closely allied militarily to the United States; the organized peasant women take part in land seizures and call on the government to revise its modest land distribution law so that women other than widows can gain direct title to land.[30] A small group of Honduran women, who have to support their children on $2 a day earned by picking melons and cantaloupes for a multinational, joined the Honduran Federation of Peasant Women (FEHMUC) and began thinking about ways to generate income for themselves. They learned carpentry skills and made the broomsticks and bookshelves. With the money she earned one woman bought the village's first sewing machine, while another woman saved enough to send her daughter to secondary school.[31]

On rubber plantations in Malaysia, the world's largest exporter of rubber, most workers are Indian Malaysians, descendants of workers brought from India at the turn of the century to supply cheap labor for Britain's colonial estates. Women started to work on rubber plantations decades ago, but with the decline in world rubber prices, plantation owners have been turning more and more to women to tap their trees. They are hired as casual labor and thus are less costly than full-time male employees. Britain's legacy of ethnic divide-and-rule and Malaysia's anti-union laws have made bridge-building between Malay, Chinese and Indian women difficult. In addition, the rubber workers' union has been run by Indian Malaysian men. Despite the formidable obstacles, one Malaysian working-women's organization has begun performing dramas on rubber plantations to highlight the dangers for women tappers of the widely used pesticide paraquat. Some plantation women have gone blind from accidental spraying of paraquat, but with rubber prices falling and tappers earning as little as $35 per month, women workers have little time or energy to read, and newspapers cost money that must be spent on food and clothing. So the combination of dramatic performances and sending press clippings to be shared is the Malaysian women activists' strategy for making a small dent in the gender structure on which the rubber industry depends.[32] In using drama to give rural women a new sense of their worth and their political capabilities, the Malaysian women are paralleling Sistren, a Jamaican feminist theater group, whose members are tackling the complex problems flowing from the decline of Jamaica's one-time sugar-dependent economy.[33]

In Nicaragua coffee and banana plantations that have been collectivized have not radically altered the sexual division of labor – there is still 'men's work' and 'women's work' outside and especially inside the rural home. But more Nicaraguan women are beginning to do field jobs, not just packaging, on the banana estates. In coffee cultivation, where women in the past were expected to plant and transplant seedlings, women are starting to use flame throwers in the clearing of hillsides. Later in the coffee-growing cycle women are beginning to join men in what used to be a 'men's job', the pruning of coffee trees. These small steps toward redefining the division of labor have led to an unexpected change in sexual politics. When only men worked together, they forged friendships that spilled over into their after-work socializing. Nicaraguan women on one coffee estate describe how men used to go off together to town to drink and visit brothels. Working buddies became brothel buddies. But, according to these women, now that men are more likely to work alongside women when they clear the land or prune the trees, they form friendships with those women and are less inclined to see drinking and going to prostitutes as the only after-work recreation.[34]

Developing a politics of land reform and agricultural labor that does not reproduce patriarchal relationships between rural women and men is not something that happens automatically. It does not derive necessarily from either a class-conscious or a nationalist politics of food. Where unequal and unfair relations between rural women and men have been seriously challenged, it has usually required women's own analysis and autonomous organizing. Both have been seen by some male land-reform activists either as a waste of time or as a threat to peasant unity. In 1985, as rural Filipinos were mobilizing to overthrow the Marcos regime, some activist peasant women decided that if land reform, a principal demand of the anti-Marcos movement, was to benefit women as well as men, women would have to organize autonomously. They created RICE (not an acronym). Eighteen months later, with Marcos replaced by Corazon Aquino, RICE had grown to 100 members and had affiliated with Gabriela, the umbrella women's group. RICE members also affiliated with the National Peasant Movement, popularly known as the KMP. Although the KMP is perhaps the most visible advocate of genuine land reform, the women in RICE saw it as a male-dominated organization. In villages where KMP was formed before RICE became active, KM P has remained dominated by male peasants. But where a branch of RICE brought together local women for discussions before KMP organized villagers, KMP's local councils have had more women participants and have accorded serious attention to matters of concern to women. One such issue is husbands' refusal to acknowledge the economic contributions made by their wives.

> In my experience before, my husband didn't care about my financial contribution to the family. I worked in the fields like my husband. I did planting and weeding, etc., but he did not recognize this. If I was sick, my husband did not care, he just got mad at me. And I had no say over money matters.
>
> Before, I used to take these things silently; I didn't answer back to my husband. But after being involved in RICE, I got up the courage to reason out why I was being treated like that and answer back to him.[35]

RICE was not the name these women peasants gave themselves. But they soon adopted this English name in the hope that it would sound less threatening to local military commanders. It has been difficult for RICE to criticize the KMP's male domination in part because the army and military-supported vigilante groups have continued to torture and murder KMP activists.

Bananas, like anything else, can be militarized. In the Philippines, as in Honduras and Colombia, banana-plantation union activists have been assassinated by troops loyal to a government that sees multinational agribusiness as good for the economy. The current land system has been maintained in part by intimidation and force.[36] But militarization not only bolsters the plantation system and undermines land-reform movements in general; it also makes any woman's criticism of a progressive movement's male leaders and masculinized agenda appear illegitimate, even dangerous. How can a woman dare to criticize a fellow peasant activist when he is the target of military harassment? An army which uses coercion to maintain the rural status quo makes it hard to shake a nationalist land-reform movement free from its patriarchal base.

Women peasant activists in Honduras and the Philippines have themselves become the objects of an American counter-insurgency doctrine called 'Low-Intensity Conflict'. LIC employs a sprawling definition of 'insurgency' to justify harassment, intimidation and local disruption, and relies on vigilante groups as well as uniformed troops. Its implementation in the Philippines and Central America has made it politically hazardous for rural women to challenge rural men. It has also undermined rural women's independent efforts. To a national-security official who views 'development' through the prism of low-intensity conflict, day-care centers and food cooperatives – projects rural women believe are integral to real land reform – are subversive; they are thus legitimate targets for counter-insurgency operations. In 1987 RICE had twelve groups on Mindanao; a year later only five had survived.[37]

CONCLUSION

Today's affluent consumers are increasingly conscious of the nutritional content of their daily food. Walk into any supermarket and you see the aisles crowded with customers reading the fine print on labels. As affluent consumers' tastes change, the international agribusinesses prick up their ears. So do the bankers, foreign advisors and politicians who work with them to shape international food policies. If the banana was the 'new food' of 1880s America and 1920s Japan, broccoli, raddicchio and winter strawberries are the 'new foods' of the 1990s. This affects not only what women buy and cook in Saucilito and in Hampstead; it affects what women and men produce for plantation companies in Kenya, Malaysia, Guatemala and Jamaica.

147

It may be tempting to imagine plantations as part of an 'old-fashioned' way of life. They seem to symbolize the bad old days of slavery and colonialism. They conjure up the American ante-bellum South or the British empire according to Somerset Maugham. In reality plantations are as modern (or 'post-modern') as the home computer or toxic waste. Large plantation companies such as Castle and Cook (owner of Dole and Standard Fruit), Unilever (owner of both Liptons and Brooke Bond), Del Monte (recently purchased by R. J. Reynolds as part of its buyout of RJR Nabisco) and United Brands, are some of the largest multinational companies in the world today, wielding influence over their own as well as foreign governments.

Furthermore, plantation company executives don't stand still. When the political climate where they are operating becomes chilly – with the passage of land-reform laws or the successful unionization of agricultural workers – they try to persuade new governments to open up lands for plantation crops. When Honduran banana workers used strikes to compel their government to deny recognition to a company-controlled union, their employer, United Brands, began to look more favorably on the Philippines. Similarly, as 1992 looms in Europe, Del Monte has taken steps to persuade the government of Cameroon to open its lands to banana cultivation. Del Monte's Cameroon bananas will be marketed in Europe with the benefit of EEC trade concessions given to former European colonies. Other companies switch to new crops when the market begins to decline in once-profitable products. Thus nowadays the Chiquita label is turning up on melons. Britain's Brooke Bond, once synonymous with tea and still known by the woman tea-picker on its label, has moved into the flower business. Brooke Bond has convinced senior Kenyan government officials that it is in their interest to open extensive flower plantations. Carnations-for-export have become part of the international political economy.[38]

Similarly, Coca Cola, world-famous for its soft drinks, has become one of the world's largest growers of citrus fruits. Its executives have persuaded the government of Belize, still hosting British troops but increasingly pressed to further American interests, to allow it to develop thousands of acres for exported oranges. Palm oil was seen in the 1970s and early 1980s by many export-sensitive governments and their foreign bankers as an attractive substitute for less stable plantation crops such as rubber; now oil-palm plantations are being threatened by Americans' aversion to cholesterol. Companies such as Unilever may rethink their investments in Zaïre, Malaysia and Ecuador if Europeans follow the Americans in insisting that food-processing companies eliminate saturated fats from their cereals, cookie batter and other foods. In Guatemala and Chile, nervous governments and their military commanders are looking to grape and broccoli farming to pacify their rural populations and stabilize their currencies. General Pinochet has given governmental assistance to large-scale fruit estates owned by supporters of his regime so that they and fruit exports have become a principal prop for his government at a time when popular opposition has become alarmingly bold. Military counter-insurgency strategists in Guatemala are pinning their hopes on the opening of large broccoli, cauliflower and cabbage estates to pacify alienated highland Indians.[39]

These plantation companies and the importing and exporting governments that rely on them for tax revenues and political support each make gendered calculations. They appeal to women as food purchasers and as food preparers. If Carmen Miranda helped smooth the way for a more subtle form of American regional influence, 'Chiquita Banana' helped create consumer loyalty for a product that yielded huge profits for an American corporation; the real market women of Latin America were marginalized by a potent combination of 'Good Neighbor' diplomacy and agribusiness advertising.[40] On the other hand, while women consumers often have a difficult time acquiring accurate nutritional information, acting together they have helped open up the files of food corporations. Women who today buy more fresh broccoli than canned peas are not merely passive creatures in an advertising agency's scenario.

As women consumers – in Third World as well as First World countries – try to reorganize the politics of food, women food-industry workers – in the First World as well as the Third World – try to reorganize the politics of land and labor. Plantation companies and the governments who need them have depended on the control of women in order to profitably produce every one of their agricultural products. This has been especially obvious in those sectors where plantation managers have defined most of the tasks as 'women's work': tea, coffee and to a lesser extent rubber. The dependence on women has been harder to recognize in sectors where work has been masculinized: bananas, palm oil, and to a lesser extent sugar. But in *both* masculinized and feminized plantation agriculture women have been crucial to the success of the company and its governmental allies. For even where women do not supply the bulk of the paid labor, they perform certain crucial jobs – as seasonal weeders, as processing-plant workers – and they supply cheap, part-time labor, to be called on when the world price drops for the company's product. Women also provide a plantation's male workers with unpaid food cultivation, child care and sexual satisfaction. Women plantation workers and women farmers share a politics of invisibility. A woman agriculturalist is transformed by writers, policy-makers and economists into 'the farmer's wife'. This transformation is a political process that is being challenged by women farmers not only in Third World countries, but also in West Germany, France, Spain and the United States.[41]

All too often the international politics of bananas (and sugar, rubber and broccoli) are discussed as if they were formulated only in bankers' board rooms or union leaders' meetings. Because both of these settings have been so male-dominated, the dependence of food politics on women and on ideas about masculinity and femininity has been ignored. This in turn has meant that even genuine non-feminist attempts to reform agrarian politics – in the name of nationalism or development – have failed to change patriarchal relationships. The politics of bananas and broccoli cannot be fully transformed until both women and men are made visible, as consumers, producers, managers and policy-makers.

7

BLUE JEANS
AND BANKERS

Polyester. The very word conjures up an entire era. Shopping malls. Drip-dry. Consciousness-raising groups. Ho, ho, ho, we won't go. Hard hats for Nixon.

Polyester caused a major shift in American fashion in the late 1960s that lasted until the mid-1970s. Although it was invented during World War II, polyester, a plastics-based cloth, didn't become a household word until twenty-five years later, when chemical companies, textile manufacturers, machinery producers, fashion designers and garment manufacturers got together to create polyester double-knit clothing for women. At about the same time British consumers were switching from fish and chips to Indian take-aways and from Indian cotton to chemical-based brushed nylon.

Paris Knitting Mills is a clothing company in Ozone Park, across the river from Manhattan in Queens, an industrial neighborhood and home of generations of new American immigrants. Paris joined other garment companies in targeting a particular class of women for the new textile. Polyester double-knit suits were to be a godsend for 'the working mother'. Joseph Lombardo, formerly a presser for Paris and now a union organizer working for Queens' steadily shrinking membership, was clear about this targeted consumer.

> Paris did not sell to the designer group . . . Paris made double-knit suits for your mother or my mother – three-piece suits, with a blouse, a Chanel-type jacket, and a skirt or a pair of pants. They sold for thirty-five or forty dollars . . .
> For a forty-year-old woman who was going back to work after raising her kids it was ideal, because she could have three suits for a hundred dollar investment. She could mix and match.[1]

Polyester and the working mother. This was America in the early 1970s. Whereas in 1950 only 11.9 per cent of American married women with children under six had paid jobs, by 1970 the proportion had risen to 30.3 per cent. Two decades later it would reach 56 per cent.[2]

The polyester formula was inspired by anxiety over global competition. While the peace movement and Henry Kissinger had their eyes on Vietnam, Al Paris of Paris Knitting Mills fixed his attention on Hong Kong and Taiwan. In the US and Europe managers of textile and garment companies were beginning to worry about the rising tide of Asian-made goods that were attracting their customers. 'Buy American.' 'Buy British.' These were the calls made to post-empire women. When they shopped for clothes at Sears or Marks and Spencer women were to be patriotic. This was off-the-rack nationalism. Manufacturers hoped women in polyester and brushed-nylon suits would stave off foreign competition. They counted on the working-class working woman to be attracted to its wash-and-wear convenience, its low cost, its indestructibility. She could balance her family's check book and meet the demands of femininity by purchasing a locally produced, chemical-based wardrobe.

Polyester permitted Western manufacturers to play their strong cards: capital and technology. Their new Asian rivals had cheap female labor, but that wasn't the only asset in the international garments competition. The new fabric and new knitting machines required large investments and engineering know-how that Taiwan and Hong Kong companies couldn't yet afford. Looking back at the polyester era, Art Ortenberg, one of the founders of Liz Claiborne clothing, saw a 'natural marriage between the international knitting-machinery manufacturers and the large chemical companies in the United States – mainly DuPont'.[3]

At the same time, European and North American working mothers' fashion sense was presumed to be unsophisticated. Thus the clothes marketed to them could be kept simple. Paris Knitting Mills could grow only if its women sewing-machinists didn't have to be paid a lot to acquire complicated new skills: 'The beauty of Paris was that the jackets were all so much alike that the girls could sew them with their eyes closed.'[4]

But polyester turned shiny after several washings. And the colors that worked best were bland – pastel blue, pink, yellow, aqua. Chemical engineers may have liked polyester, but the designers didn't. Moreover, Asian manufacturers began to learn how to produce their own double-knit suits. By the mid-1970s Asian-produced polyester clothes were turning up in the ladies-wear department of J. C. Penney's in Ozone Park. The final straw was blue jeans. Women began to wear jeans – 'designer jeans' – where before they would have felt they had to wear the more formal double-knit suits to be publicly presentable: the dress code was shifting, if not crumbling. As feminine respectability was redefined, the international political economy lurched in a new direction.

Al Paris, who in his heyday had opened up plants in Montreal and Dublin, began to lay off workers. Pressers like Joseph Lombardo lost their jobs. But most of the laid-off workers were women, since they comprised the majority of the garment factories' workers. Unemployment soared in the working-class neighborhoods of Queens and in scattered rural towns where many American garment companies now had their plants. Between 1970 and 1986 the International Ladies Garment Workers Union, one of the two major unions in the US garment industry, lost more than 200,000 members. The cause was easy to spot: production of women's and children's clothes in the United States had dropped by more than 50 per cent. Still, the New York metropolitan area remained home for thousands of women and men working in garment factories. In 1986 the ILGWU, with its mainly male leadership and overwhelmingly female rank and file, had 75,400 New York members.[5] 'Deindustrialization' has become a political catchword since industrial decline meant the lay-off of male factory workers in steel and automobile towns. Garment workers' earlier economic hardships and the international transformations they reflected had been easier to overlook because the workers were women, many of them immigrant or poor rural women.

THE BENETTON MODEL

Some Western manufacturers and design houses tried to beat the overseas competition by seeking out lower-paid workers in their own countries. British companies looked to Black and Asian British women, many of them recent arrivals and thus vulnerable to isolation in seasonal employment at low pay with minimum benefits and maximum health hazards. Large retailers such as Marks and Spencer, which sells one fifth of all garments bought in Britain, decided to become 'manufacturers without factories'. Their managers began farming out contracts to smaller producers, who hired workers or employed another layer of subcontractors. Today some 600 different suppliers feed Marks and Spencer alone. Each tries to cope with the constant adjustments as giant retailers refine their strategies to compete with Benetton, Next and other up-market entrepreneurs. Subcontractors prop up their profits yet satisfy their large clients by keeping costs low while offering garments with ever more fashionable stitching.[6]

This has meant finding a way to pass on the costs and the work pressures. British contractors and subcontractors have passed them on to women, especially Asian and Black British women. Some were hired to work in factories. Others were hired by subcontractors to work in their own homes. These arrangements often appealed to women with small children. Despite lower wages and the lack of benefits and health protection, many women believed that at least they could look after their children while earning an income for their families, thus not having to choose between motherhood and paid work. Home work also appealed to many of the women's fathers or husbands. They believed that the women of their communities should be protected from the harsh realities – and perhaps immoral temptations – of white-dominated British society. The sexual and racial politics of post-imperial British immigration were woven into blouses destined for Marks and Spencer.

> When you live in Newham [in the East End of London], you have little choice, sister. Burning down of an Asian home does not even make news any longer . . . How can I look for jobs outside my home in such a situation? I want to remain invisible, literally.
>
> Also, sister, I am a widow and I really do not know what my legal status is . . . At the moment, my uncle brings machining work to my home. It works out to be 50 pence per hour, not great! But I earn and I feed my children somehow. Most of all, I do not have to deal with the fear of racist abuse in this white world.[7]

In the United States, manufacturers, encouraged by regional governors, moved their factories south in search of cheaper, non-unionized workers, who would enable them to compete with the Asian and Latin American imports. Black, Latina and rural white women became America's secret weapon against Mexican, Haitian and Korean goods. American companies also moved off the mainland to Puerto Rico, which fell under US customs protection and thus provided the best of all worlds: a Third World labor force inside the American trade sphere.[8] At the same time, smaller firms in the US and Canada adopted the home-work strategy. As in Britain, the majority of home workers were women of color, again recent immigrants, often fearful of deportation. In Montreal, Toronto, Winnipeg, New York, Miami and Los Angeles, it was Filipino, Vietnamese, Chinese, Greek, Dominican, Cuban, Salvadorean, Haitian and Jamaican women who became essential to garment companies' global strategies.[9]

Feminized patterns of racial and regional inequality – interwoven with ideas about motherhood and feminine respectability – helped those European and North American garment companies who felt threatened by the restructured world economy but who did not possess the resources necessary to move their factories overseas. Garment-company executives in alliance with local officials came up with a formula that has suited electronics companies, toy manufacturers and food processors as well: if you can't move to the Third World, create a feminized Third World in your own back yard.[10]

The re-emergence of sweatshops and home working might seem to be a turning back of the modernist clock. But just as plantations are being fashioned to fit the 1990s, so sweatshops and home working are being given a contemporary look.

Benetton is the successful garment company based in northern Italy, a region of farms and small towns whose newly prosperous industrial companies have earned it the nickname of 'the Third Italy'. With its revolutionary knitting technology and its scores of computer-coordinated small shops, Benetton is being heralded by business-school professors and financial reporters as a model of the way to do business in the era of global competition.

[Luciano] Benetton, whose leonine curling gray-brown hair and horn-rimmed glasses are familiar to millions of Italians from endless photographs in the press, was dressed in his usual assortment of casual clothes: voluminous khaki pants, brown L. L. Bean-style oxfords, a tweed jacket, and a shirt with a button-down collar . . . [He was on his way to do something that] excited him more than anything else in life: the opening of a Benetton store in a 'remote, almost unbelievable' part of the world. We were going that morning to attend a Benetton opening in Prague . . .[11]

Benetton is admired for its stylish designs and its ability to change fashions as rapidly as consumers change their fickle tastes. This combination depends on *flexibility*. In practice, this means that Benetton has to be able to employ advanced computer technology to redesign patterns at a moment's notice. That is the high-tech side. Simultaneously, maximizing flexibility means Benetton's executives being able to call on small-scale local sewing workshops to change their products faster than most big companies can. However, prices must be low enough to enable Benetton to keep ahead of Marks and Spencer. The solution: Italian family-based subcontractors hiring women to work in their homes or in small non-unionized workshops. Although Benetton has eight plants of its own in northern Italy, these operations employ only 2,000 of its 8,000 garment workers. Most of the Italian women who depend on Benetton for their livelihood don't work directly for the company. This is one of the secrets of a corporate model that maximizes flexibility. When the company gives tours to visiting reporters it doesn't include the small, non-unionized shops clustered around Benetton's impressive new plants, even though those subcontractors perform about 40 per cent of Benetton's knitting and 60 per cent of the garment assembly.[12]

Girls, now a prime consumer market, began to adopt the 'Benetton look' in the mid-1980s. With their 'colors of the world' advertising campaign, Benetton executives set out to create a style that could dissolve national borders. Benetton was preparing Europe's adolescents for 1992. Economic planners were taking notice. Benetton's flexibility formula, relying on subcontracting and using women workers in small workshops, has attracted foreign imitators as this advertisement by the government of the Republic of Cyprus makes clear.

The Benetton Approach: A Turning Point for Cyprus

We are thinking in terms of the Italian model rather than the Korean and the Taiwanese. That means flexible socialization where you create for a high quality market like Europe: the Benetton approach.[13]

The cult of flexibility has also taken hold in Cyprus's competitor, Ireland, as well as in countries past their industrial prime. Government policy-makers and company officials both see new methods of controlling women's work as ammunition in current international politics. But those methods require that women – in Italy, Cyprus, Ireland, Britain, Canada – find flexibility attractive for their own reasons, appeals which off-set the lack of promotion, training, benefits or bargaining power. 'Mother's hours' are being joined to communications satellites as international politics enter the twenty-first century.[14]

THE BANKER AND THE SEAMSTRESS

Despite the 'Benetton model' and the attractions of employing low-paid women of color at home, during the 1980s American and European fashion designers and their clothing marketers increasingly contracted directly with garment firms abroad, especially in Asia, North Africa, Latin America and the Caribbean. American industry analysts predict that by the mid-1990s over half of all clothes sold in the United States will be manufactured in foreign factories.[15] The US executives who are moving their orders overseas – either under contract with a foreign firm or investing in plants of their own – claim that the more American consumers demand styles with complicated stitching, the more they must search out the lowest-priced seamstresses: 'A polyester-wool blazer costs $65 to make

156

domestically . . . We can produce the same garment with hand tailoring in the Orient for $47.50.'[16]

Overseas imports may have been hurting garment factory owners like Al Paris, but they were proving very profitable for other American and European clothing companies. Liz Claiborne, Jean Pierre and The Gap, for instance, all contract with the same Hong Kong company, Fang Brothers. Thanks to their business, the Fang Brothers themselves have built up a multinational operation. By the late 1980s these Hong Kong entrepreneurs had factories employing women in Panama, Ireland, Thailand and San Francisco. Such is the current international political system that Hong Kong Chinese businessmen fill orders for American clothing companies by hiring Panamanian women; Panama is the Caribbean's largest Export Processing Zone and thrives despite the US government's efforts to bring down the Panamanian government.[17]

A consumer in Boston, Rome or Osaka can trace the complexities of international garment-trade politics by reading the labels on her jeans, bras or sweaters. Just as Chiquita and Geest stickers are clues to the origins of bananas, so clothing labels tell where a garment was made. Two decades ago the labels were likely to read: USA, Britain, Canada, Ireland, Taiwan, Portugal, Hong Kong. Today, those labels are still on the racks, but they have been joined by labels that say: Panama, Indonesia, China, Bangladesh, Mexico, Jamaica, Morocco, the United Arab Emirates, Sri Lanka or Lesotho.

Garment factories have become part of the local landscape in countries which otherwise are radically different. White South African government officials have encouraged foreign companies to set up shop in bantustans, a scheme intended to bolster apartheid and the fiction of self-sustaining Black 'homelands'. Companies from Hong Kong, Taiwan and Israel have been among those to accept Pretoria's invitation.[18] For their part, Vietnamese government officials have introduced policies to encourage garment factories to produce clothing for sale on the international market. In 1986 6,000 Vietnamese shirts were exported to Canada via Hungary. Under a joint-venture agreement with the Vietnamese government, a Hungarian firm sends cloth to Vietnam; Vietnamese workers sew the shirts; the shirts then are sent back to Hungary for sale or export to buyers in countries such as Canada.[19] In Fiji the government has been nervously courting foreign garment manufacturers. The government has been trying to compensate for a long-term slump in world sugar prices and a more recent sharp fall in tourism revenues following Fiji's military coup in 1988. Its Trade and Investments Board has tried to entice Australian and New Zealand companies to set up factories with a special offer intended to undercut Fiji's Asian neighbors. In so doing, it is hoped, Fijian women's sewing will bandaid over the problems caused by a plantation economy, ethnic strife and militarization.[20]

The international politics of garments stretches from the women at their sewing machines stitching polyester sleeves to the men in board rooms and ministerial offices drafting memos on investments. It is impossible to make sense of the actions and beliefs of one without being curious about the actions and assumptions of the others. And, increasingly, the board rooms and ministerial offices have resonated with bankers' voices. Bankers need to make loans. Bankers need to assess risks. Bankers need to collect on their loans. In the last two decades American, European and Japanese bankers have made high-risk, high-interest loans to Third World governments. For risk-taking has been at the core of the masculinized conception of banking. Just as travel to exotic regions was once imagined to be a risky and therefore peculiarly masculine form of adventure, so today risk-taking is thought by many financiers to be integral to doing

ARE MY HANDS CLEAN? (3:03)

I wear garments touched by hands from all over the world
35% cotton, 65% polyester, the journey begins in Central America
In the cotton fields of El Salvador
In a province soaked in blood, pesticide-sprayed workers toil in a broiling sun
Pulling cotton for two dollars a day

Then we move on up to another rung—Cargill
A top forty trading conglomerate, takes the cotton thru
the Panama Canal
Up the Eastern seaboard, coming to the U.S. of A. for
the first time

In South Carolina
At the Burlington mills
Joins a shipment of polyester filament courtesy of the New Jersey petro-chemical mills of Dupont

Dupont strands of filament begin in the South American country of Venezuela
Where oil riggers bring up oil from the earth for six dollars a day
Then Exxon, largest oil company in the world
Upgrades the product in the country of Trinidad and Tobago
Then back into the Caribbean and Atlantic Seas
To the factories of Dupont
On the way to the Burlington mills

In South Carolina

To meet the cotton from the blood-soaked fields of El Salvadore

In South Carolina
Burlington factories hum with the business of weaving oil and cotton into miles of fabric for Sears
Who takes this bounty back into the Caribbean Sea
Headed for Haiti this time
May she be one day soon free

Far from the Port-au-Prince palace
Third world women toil doing piece work to Sears specifications
For three dollars a day my sisters make my blouse
It leaves the third world for the last time
Coming back into the sea to be sealed in plastic for me
This third world sister
And I go to the Sears department store where I buy my
blouse
On sale for 20% discount

Are my hands clean?

Composed for Winterfest, Institute of Policy Studies.
The lyrics are based on an article by Institute fellow John Cavanagh, "The Journey of the Blouse: A Global Assembly."

Lyrics and music by Bernice Johnson Reagon.
Songtalk Publishing Co. ©1985

18 'Are My Hands Clean?' sung by Sweet Honey in the Rock. Lyrics by Bernice Johnson Reagon ©Songtalk Publishing Company, 1985

competitive international business. The value assigned to risk-taking, furthermore, has become even greater since the 'Big Bang' in 1987 – governments' deregulation of banking. 'Big Bang' reforms made a distinctly American, masculinized style of banking more popular in Britain, France, West Germany and Japan. This masculinized style has helped sustain cooperative relations between otherwise fiercely competitive male bankers. It has also helped keep women on the margins of the financial world, providing crucial support services but only occasionally gaining promotions that give them the chance to make policy decisions. By 1982, after a decade of rapid expansion and computer revolution in the finance industry, women comprised 57 per cent of all banking employees in Britain. Yet at the managerial level, 90 per cent of all posts were filled by men. Only 5 per cent of the thousands of British women working for local and multinational banks hold policy-making posts.[21] Likewise, women are barely visible when the major banking countries, the Group of Ten, gather to resolve problems of trade imbalances and international debt.

This sort of masculinized international banking has been politically costly. It has destabilized more governmental regimes than all the world's terrorists combined. Most Third World countries scarcely have the currency to keep up with the astronomical interest payments due to their foreign creditors, much less to repay the principal. But Japanese, British, American and other large lenders and their governments fear that global default would topple the international political economy so carefully constructed in the years following World War II. So lenders and their allies, who include their own governments and the International Monetary Fund (in which the US and Japanese governments now wield the most votes), are trying to make the debtor countries make good their mammoth debts. The most popular formula pressed on debtor governments combines cuts in government expenditure on 'non-productive' public services with an expansion of exports.

The centerpiece of the bankers' export strategy has been the 'Export Processing Zone'. Indebted governments set aside territory specifically for factories producing goods for the international market. Governments lure overseas companies to move their plants to these EPZs by offering them sewers, electricity, ports, runways, tax holidays and police protection. Most attractive of all is the governments' offer of cheap labor. Women's labor has been the easiest to cheapen, so it shouldn't be surprising that in most Export Processing Zones at least 70 per cent of the workers are women, especially young women. The eighteen-year-old woman at the sewing machine – or electronics assembly line or food-processing plant – in Panama's Colon Export Processing Zone has become the essential though unequal partner of the banker in his glass and chrome office in London or Chicago. The risk-taking banker needs the conscientious seamstress to hold his world together. The politician and his technocratic advisor need the seamstress to keep the banker and his home government pacified. If the seamstress rebels, if she rethinks what it means to be a woman who sews for a living, her country may turn up on the list of 'unstable regimes' now kept by politically sensitive bankers.

MAKING WOMEN'S LABOR CHEAP

It has become commonplace to speak of 'cheap women's labor'. The phrase is used in public policy discussions as if cheapness were somehow inherent in women's work. In reality women's work is only as unrewarded or as low-paid as it is made to be.

The international political economy works the way it does, and has done for the last two centuries, in part because of the decisions which have cheapened the value of women's work. These decisions have first feminized certain home and workplace tasks – turning them into 'women's work' – and then rationalized the devaluation of that work. Without laws and cultural presumptions about sexuality, marriage and feminine respectability these transformations wouldn't have been possible.

Organizing factory jobs, designing machinery and factory rules to keep women productive and feminine – these were crucial strategies in Europe's industrial growth. Industrialized textile production and garment-making were central to Britain's global power. Both industries feminized labor in order to make it profitable and internationally competitive. Other countries learned the British lesson in order to compete in the emerging global political economy and to stave off foreign control. The making of the 'mill girl' proved crucial. American textile investors travelled from Boston to England to learn the formula in the early decades of the nineteenth century. Japanese entrepreneurs, backed by their government's Meiji reforms to resist Western colonization, also chose young rural women as their first industrial workers. In industrializing Tsarist Russia, owners of new textile factories steadily increased the proportion of women workers, with government approval. In the pre-World War I period gendered formulas for factory-fueled capitalism seemed to be traded as energetically as railroad stocks.[22] Neither war nor revolution has done much to transform the feminizing strategies used by both capitalist and socialist garment-factory managers. In the Soviet Union, which has undergone a radical reordering of its political system as well as Draconian industrialization, women in 1970 still comprised 93 per cent of all sewing-machine operators.[23]

Feminization, however, has never been as easy as later historians, through their own lack of curiosity, make it seem. Textile and garment workers frequently shrugged off, even laughed derisively at their employers' efforts to lecture to them on Victorian propriety.[24] Sometimes women went on strike. It took threats, coercion and revised legal structures to bring them back into line. Occasionally the very technology factory owners installed to feminize labor threw feminine respectability into question.

In June 1853 an advertisement appeared in the American *Illustrated News* celebrating Singer's newly patented sewing machine:

The sewing machine has within the last two years acquired a wide celebrity and established its character as one of the most efficient labour-saving instruments ever introduced to public notice . . .

We must not forget to call attention to the fact that this instrument is peculiarly calculated for female operatives. They should never allow its use to be monopolized by men.[25]

The sewing machine was praised by feminists. It drew crowds when it was demonstrated at the 1851 Exposition in London and at the 1855 Exposition in Paris.[26] Thomas Cook's guided tourists were among the throngs who heard the sewing machine being heralded as woman's liberator. It symbolized progress: technology was a liberator of women and men. Countries whose women had access to sewing machines could congratulate themselves on their women's freedom from the sort of physical toil that characterized the benighted societies crowded at the bottom of the global ladder.

While women were encouraged to see the sewing machine as a home appliance, entrepreneurs were being urged to purchase the machines by the dozen for women who would work outside the home in factories. The sewing machine allowed company owners to break down the process of making a dress or a pair of pants into discrete operations and thus impose a rationalized factory system on the seamstresses: each woman would sew only a small part of the garment – a sleeve, a tuck, a back pocket. It also allowed owners to pay their employees by the piece, rather than by the hour or by an entire finished product. The piece-rates increased competitiveness between women workers as well as extending a factory manager's control over the entire production process.

None the less, the sewing machine had its detractors. In French towns large numbers of women were employed to work sewing machines by the 1860s, and many complained of fatigue and ill health. Eugène Guibout, a Parisian physician, reported to the Société Médicale des Hospitaux in 1866 that he believed that the extended use of the machine produced extensive vaginal discharges, sometimes haemorrhages, and extreme genital excitement, due to rubbing of the thighs during operation of the double pedal mechanism that then powered the machines used in industrial production.

The debate spilled over to Germany and Italy. Some male scientists were less alarmed than Dr Guibout, but they, too, raised their eyebrows at the potentially masturbatory effects of the bi-pedal sewing machine. There was palpable relief in international medical circles when a single-pedal machine was introduced. Still, it wasn't until the advent of the electrically powered sewing machine in the next century that the controversy over the sewing machine's sexual consequences was laid to rest.[27]

Garment-company managers have drawn on various patriarchal assumptions to help them keep wages and benefits low in their factories. First, they have defined sewing as something that girls and women do 'naturally' or 'traditionally'. An operation that a person does 'naturally' is not a 'skill', for a skill is something one has to be trained to do, for which one should then be rewarded. Such thinking may be convenient and save money, but is it accurate? Many a schoolgirl has struggled through a home economics class trying to make the required skirt or apron without much success. One garment-factory manager explained that he preferred to hire young Filipino women who *didn't* know how to sew, so that 'we don't have to undo the bad habits they've learned'.[28] But the myth of women as natural sewers persists and is used to deflate women garment workers' actual skills.

Second, a women's labor can be kept cheap if those jobs which even the factory managers acknowledge are 'skilled' can be reserved for men. Levis Jeans in Manila is remarkably like garment factories in New York, Manchester, Toronto, Moscow or Colombo: women are the sewing-machinists; men are the cutters and the pressers. Men also are selected to run specialized machines, like the zipper inserters. Cutting, pressing and zippering all are paid more than sewing. The managerial rationale for this sexual division of labor is that cutting, pressing and running specialized machinery require physical strength that only men have. This argument ignores the options available when technology is designed, the physical demands made on women by housework and farming, and the fact that some men are weaker than some women.

Third, managers justify paying women workers less by imagining that women are merely secondary wage earners in their families. They assume that men – as fathers and husbands – are the 'breadwinners'. This

19 A Levis factory in the Philippines: women sew the distinctive back pocket design. (photo: Cynthia Enloe, 1980)

presumption prevails not just in popular thinking but in the statistical reports of bodies such as the national census bureau, the World Bank, and development agencies.[29] Such reports are a boon to garment-factory managers. They make the practice of paying their women workers *as if* they were being supported at home by a man seem up-to-date and sophisticated. Thus the international garment industry, on which so many governments rely for foreign currency, is deeply dependent on ideas about the family and marriage.

Even those managers who prefer to hire single women – as many do – use the marriage factor to suppress wages. They can presume that the single woman is just earning 'pin money' for herself because she has a wage-earning father who supports her and her mother. Or they can claim

20 At the same factory, men are assigned the higher-paid cutting jobs.
(photo: Cynthia Enloe, 1980)

that the single woman is not a 'serious' member of the laborforce because she intends to work only until she finds a husband and 'settles down', supported by him. Therefore, she does not need to be paid as if she were a career worker; when she is sewing sleeves for the Fang Brothers or a back pocket for Levis she is just going through 'a phase'.

If their own parents, teachers and religious leaders encourage them to think of their 'real' vocation – what will bring them community respect, personal gratification and moral reward – as being a wife and a mother, then it is not surprising that the young women themselves find it difficult to question their employers' contention that they don't deserve better pay because they are 'only working until they marry'. Local community expectations thus combine with World Bank statistical practices to strengthen the garment-factory manager's cost-cutting hand. Take away or transform either and it might prove far more difficult for managers in garment manufacturing and other light industries to use 'cheap women's labor' to ensure international competitiveness.

At the turn of the century many Jewish and Italian women working in New York City's then thriving garment factories endured the low pay, lint dust, eye strain and six-day working week dreaming of marriage and of becoming housewives. It was a dream that made their parents and their employers comfortable. It was a dream that frustrated their coworkers who wanted them to organize, to protest, to strike. Even today, marriage is not just about heterosexual conformity. It is an escape. A husband, many women workers hope, will be a way out of patriarchal factory toil.

It's not easy to teach us union.
Garment girls shift like sand, start
too young in the trade, wait for

Prince Charming to take em away . . .[30]

Feminist researchers in Sri Lanka interviewed women working for garment and electronics companies in the government-supported Export Processing Zone outside Cclombo. Workers told them that they saw their jobs as lasting only a few years; they hoped they would be 'phase jobs', not careers. They also realized that their employers preferred single women. Because so many women in the Export Processing Zone didn't see themselves as 'workers', but as daughters, prospective wives and members of their community, feminists trying to build support around work issues had to radically rethink what a 'work issue' was. They discovered that women working in the factories felt intimidated by men who harassed them as they traveled to and from the Export Processing Zone. This wasn't the sort of issue that an orthodox union would take seriously, but it was significant for these young women workers. Working together, the activists outside the factories and the women employees built a coalition of village elders, religious groups and the women themselves to reduce the harassment. Had they confined their organizing to the factory floor, they would have been subject to dismissal, failed to engage many of the women workers and lost the chance to mobilize the groups with whom the women workers still chiefly identified.[31]

To make women's labor cheap garment-factory managers also find it useful to imagine marriage an inevitable and lasting state for adult women. If factory managers do have to hire married women, and if governments have to acknowledge that balance of trade depends on women over twenty being part of the laborforce, then both are most comfortable assuming that, as a wife, a woman will be economically dependent on a man and put her wifely and motherly roles before any other.

This hardly matches contemporary reality. Today one third of the world's households are headed by women. The single mother – the woman responsible for supporting herself and at least one child – is not simply a phenomenon of affluent societies. In Kenya as well as in Denmark over 30 per cent of households are headed by women. The same is true in Barbados, Vietnam, Zimbabwe, Nicaragua, Jamaica and Lesotho.[32]

Finally, women's labor is made cheap by preventing women from organizing. This tactic rarely succeeds unless managers have assistance from government officials and women workers' male relatives. Fathers, brothers and husbands of women workers sometimes try to keep them from becoming politically involved because it might jeopardize the income they bring into the family. They also often object because political activity seems to violate codes of feminine respectability by involving women in public conflict, conflict with men of authority. Male workmates are not always supportive, seeing some of the women's demands (for protection against sexual harassment, for maternity leave) as irrelevant to 'serious' trade-union activity. Government officials have done their part to keep women's labor cheap by passing laws banning unions or authorizing only unions friendly to management. On occasion also they have called out their police to support managers. This can create a hostile confrontation that seriously jeopardizes a woman's reputation.

Thus keeping women's labor cheap requires vigilance and daily effort. That effort is an integral part of what is called 'international political economy'. Factory managers alone cannot keep women's labor cheap: it takes a combination of allies and ideas – about skills, marriage, feminine respectability, fashion. The politics of the international garment industry are sustained by relationships inside the home, in the community, in and between governments, as well as on the factory floor.

'THE LIGHT INDUSTRY GIRLS'

Those most eager to pay as little as possible for human labor are those who run firms that are most dependent on human labor to produce their product. The more a firm can design its production system to minimize that dependence, the less preoccupied its managers will be about cutting labor costs. Nowadays the kinds of industries that are most labor-intensive are 'light industries'. Light industries and heavy industries differ in the

166

mix of capital equipment – furnaces, turbines, computers, robots, looms, sewing machines – and human labor each needs to turn out a saleable product.

Because light industries are more labor-intensive and less reliant on large infusions of capital, they are also less likely to be concentrated in the hands of a few owners. There are many more players in any light-industry market. This makes light industries more decentralized and more competitive.

This sounds reassuringly democratic and efficient. But for the workers – sewing polyester suits for Al Paris or Liz Claiborne jeans for the Fang Brothers – light industry's decentralized competitiveness may not be benign. For the very intensity of the competition only heightens the determination of owners and managers to keep labor costs as low as possible. Cutting labor costs is seen as one of the chief strategies for beating one's rivals. And the industry's decentralization makes it hard for even a committed government to implement worker safety laws effectively. It is much easier to hide an illegal dress factory than to conceal an illegal automobile plant.

'Light industries' have been most feminized, while 'heavy industries' have been most masculinized. Thus how light and heavy industries relate to each other politically may depend in part on the relative influence possessed by women and men in a country. If women are seen mainly as mothers, part-time employees and unskilled workers, if they do not have control over the unions they are members of or have no unions at all, if they are not considered serious allies or opponents by men in government ministries or political parties, then it will be especially difficult for light industry to hold its own in politics in a way that benefits not only the managers but also the workers. Put another way, the power that men working in mining, aerospace, automobile, steel or petrochemical

LIGHT INDUSTRIES	HEAVY INDUSTRIES
Textiles	Steel
Garments	Automobiles (including tanks and armored vehicles)
Food processing	Chemicals and petrochemicals
Cigarettes	Aircraft and aerospace
Toys	Shipbuilding
Shoes	Machinery
Electronics	
Data entry (insurance data, airline reservations, etc.)	

industries can bring to bear on their country's political system not only privileges heavy industry, it serves to undercut women bunched together in light industry.

This sexual division of labor has had the effect of further masculinizing national and international politics. For government officials in most countries have come to think of 'heavy industries' as the very stuff of national power. Having its own steel industry is held as proof that a country has 'graduated', *arrived*.

While officials in South Korea, Brazil, and other countries that have developed masculinized heavy industries express pride in their elevated international status, their counterparts in 'mature' countries such as the United States, Britain and France feel as though they are losing their grip on world politics because of the decline of their steel and automobile companies. When political commentators accord the fortunes of their countries' steel, aircraft or automobile companies the seriousness reserved for issues of 'national security', they are further entrenching the masculinization of international politics.

First the Japanese and more recently the South Korean economies have 'graduated' from garments to steel.[33] That is, they have moved up from feminized industries to masculinized industries. Hosting the Olympics has become the world's graduation present.

As South Korean government officials were bidding to have their country chosen as the site of the 1988 Olympics, some commentators were talking about the 'two Koreas'. They didn't mean North and South. They were referring to the South Korea of large, capitalized heavy industries and the South Korea of the back-alley garment workshop. In 1988 women made up an estimated two thirds of workers in South Korea's world-famous export-oriented factories. They were working more hours per week than their male counterparts and being paid on average one third less, producing clothes, electronics, shoes and data services – industries that enabled South Korean businessmen to accumulate enough capital to launch their own companies. Those Korean women factory workers who went on strike in the 1980s to bring down the authoritarian military government were protesting against both the myth of the successful South Korea and the price that South Korean factory women were expected to pay to sustain that myth.

Past the rows of charred sewing machines, amid the smoke-blackened piles of timber and cinder, lie the keepsakes of the women who worked and died here. These were among the remains of the Green Hill Textile Company: a snapshot of a young girl smiling in a field of red flowers, a magazine clipping of a singer, a letter from a young man in the army.[34]

In March 1988 a fire tore through the Green Hill Textile Company's small factory, squeezed between a billiard parlor, a restaurant and a church in a dormitory community outside Seoul. Lee Pung Won, the 44-year-old owner, was considered a good employer, who treated his workers 'more like a family'. Most of his employees were young single women who had come from the countryside to the city in hope of finding a waged job. They were paid approximately $1.75 per hour by Lee Pung Won, who expected them to work fifty-seven hours a week. In this, their lives were similar to those of other Korean women working in nearby factories producing shoes and televisions for export. When the factory received a big order, as often happened in the seasonal garment trade, their employer expected the women to work even longer hours:

> The fire broke out in late March as twenty-eight young textile workers lay sleeping in the factory that doubled as their dormitory in this suburb of Seoul. With the stairways locked and heaped with sweaters the women had knit that day, only a few escaped. Twenty-two workers died.[35]

Making it as a 'world class' player has come with a gendered price tag.

AN EARTHQUAKE IS ONLY THE BEGINNING

At 7:19 on the morning of September 19 1985, Mexico City experienced one of North America's worst earthquakes. It left thousands of people homeless, modern office buildings cracked and useless and Mexico's ruling Institutionalized Revolutionary Party (the PRI) badly shaken. For the seamstresses who worked in the factories clustered in the neighborhood of San Antonio Abad, the earthquake marked a political and personal turning point. An estimated 800 small garment factories in Mexico City were destroyed that morning, killing over 1,000 garment workers and leaving another 40,000 without jobs.[36]

Women who were just arriving at work as the quake shook Mexico City stood looking at the rubble that an hour before had been their source of livelihood. It was a Thursday, payday. Many of them were single mothers and their families depended on their wages. But their first thought was of those women, already at work at 7: a.m., who were trapped inside the flattened buildings. Managers usually kept windows closed and doors locked to stop women from taking work breaks or stealing materials, so few of their coworkers inside had had any chance of escaping. Some buildings held up to fifty different garment companies, several per floor. The floors and cement pillars on which they rested could hardly have been expected to hold the weight of heavy industrial sewing machines and tons of fabric, though no government inspector had complained. Most companies were small subcontractors, usually backed by foreign money. Though not as well-known as the more visible 'maquiladoras' strung along the US – Mexican border, these firms were part of the Mexican government's policy of using tourism and light-industry exports to pay off its spiraling debt. By 1986 foreign-owned and joint-venture factories such as those in San Antonio Abad had displaced tourism as the country's second largest source of foreign exchange.[37]

Women outside the collapsed building tried to climb over the debris to rescue their coworkers trapped inside. Hastily mobilized government soldiers told them to get back and cordoned off the building. Within a day the company owners arrived, accompanied by the army. Equipped with cranes, soldiers began to pull away piles of fallen cement so that owners' could retrieve their machinery. Employees still standing in the sun on the other side of the ropes watched with mounting horror and indignation as their bosses and the soldiers chose to rescue sewing machines before women.

At this point something new began to happen. Mexican women who worked in garment factories had tried to organize and strike before. But each time they had been defeated. Employers fired the 'troublemakers', while adopting a fatherly attitude toward those women who accepted the terms of work. Many women needed their meager paychecks to support their children especially as the indebted Mexican government, which had counted on oil to solve the country's problems, was now cutting food subsidies and devaluing the peso to meet foreign bankers' demands. Even those women who were willing to risk being fired had to face male partners who resented their staying out after work to attend meetings. On top of these obstacles, left-wing opposition parties paid scant attention to women working in small sweatshops, preferring to court the more politically influential male oil workers. Small groups of Mexican feminists were active, but they were mostly middle-class and scarcely understood the needs of poor women with only primary-school education. Previously these obstacles had prevented independent women workers organizing. But the earthquake made blatantly clear what hesitant women workers had once been able to overlook: behind a façade of paternalism, employers and their government allied in valuing machines over the women who worked and voted for them.

Becoming more and more angry at what they saw, women at the scene of the disaster began to talk to each other about what this meant. Some women spontaneously moved to block the trucks that were about to carry off the owners' precious machines. Other women confronted the owners. They wanted their paychecks. They wanted to be compensated for the days of lost work. When the owners shrugged their shoulders and claimed they had no money, women began to shout: 'Compensation! Compensation.' Several dozen women decided that they would have to stay at the site over night in order to prevent the army trucks from moving and thus the owners from leaving the scene of death and destruction without fulfilling their legal responsibilities. Staying over night meant having to stay away from male partners and children who expected them at home.

At about this time, middle-class women from feminist groups in Mexico City – some affiliated with political parties and some independent – began to hear of the garment workers' distress and came to several building sites to offer assistance. It wasn't immediately clear to the seamstresses, however, just what their priorities should be. Looking back afterward, some remembered that the feminists seemed to be urging the women workers to organize a union; political concerns were at the top of their agenda. But should this be the seamstresses' most pressing demand? If they did immediately form a union, especially one not affiliated to the PRI federation, maybe they would risk government reprisal and so alienate their bosses that they would never receive the cash they so desperately needed. Women workers also had to figure out how to respond to the offers of support from suddenly attentive left-wing parties. And what about their *compañeros*, their male partners: would they feel threatened if women began to take their working conditions so seriously? How could they be persuaded that a woman who stayed out in the evening was being political not unfaithful?

In the months that followed the earthquake garment workers gradually made a number of decisions that matched their own needs and resources. They kept up their road-block and vigil outside the factories until the government pushed the owners to pay compensation for lost wages. They did this in part by embarrassing the president and then leader of the PRI by publicizing the army's role in removing the sewing machines before rescuing trapped women workers. In their public-relations campaign, middle-class feminists proved valuable allies; they had more contacts with the press and helped to raise funds to buy typewriters. Feminists also knew lawyers who could help the seamstresses find their way through the bureaucratic labyrinths of the Ministry of Labor. But women workers remained skeptical of the middle-class women. Too often in the past well-meaning feminists had tried to speak on their behalf, to run meetings and rallies. So they took steps to ensure that whatever organization grew out of the earthquake's aftermath was run by seamstresses on terms that seamstresses themselves found most comfortable and practical.

21 Mexican garment worker sewing a banner that reads 'We Demand the
Right to Unionize'. (photo: Marco A. Cruz/Imagenlatina, 1985)

The union that they created in the autumn of 1985 is the September 19th Garment Workers Union. By 1987 it had gained workers' support and official recognition in twelve factories. It has been difficult, however, to give assistance to women in factories as far away as Juarez or the Yucatan. Bus fares are expensive. The union has remained independent of all political parties and of the PRI federation. Debate over exactly what this independence meant during Mexico's first ever competitive presidential election campaign in 1988 strained bonds of unity inside the union. But such unity was essential given the continuing pressures from outside. The union had managed to gain Ministry of Labor certification in its early days largely because the PRI was running to catch up with the grassroots organizing that spread like wildfire through the neighborhoods in the wake of the earthquake. But once the foreign reporters went home and public attention flagged, the government joined with the garment companies to withdraw official certification. Teenage male thugs were sent to the factories to throw stones at women activists. Some *compañeros* prohibited their wives and companions from taking part in activities that carried such physical risks.

In reaction to this danger women active in the September 19th Union have worked with middle-class feminists to create links with garment workers, union activists and feminists in the United States. If they could mount letter writing campaigns to the Mexican government, officials might stop their efforts to discredit them to avoid international embarrassment. Making a film and organizing speaking tours to Los Angeles, New York, Chicago and Boston helped the Mexican women trade experiences and lessons with Latina and Chinese-American women garment workers. These trips also enabled September 19th union activists to track down those who were making the decisions in their factories. For instance, the Roberts company, a maker of men's suits, had taken the lead among factory owners in Mexico City in trying to persuade the Ministry of Labor that the union was not operating legally. But who owned Roberts? It is difficult to sit at a machine on the shop floor in San Antonio Abad and figure out who your boss reports to across the border. Women in the United States were able to help union organizers locate the Roberts Company's headquarters in Maine. American women were also able to put pressure on the company's US outlets.

The September 19th women spent hours at their newly acquired headquarters in a cement-covered vacant lot across from the ruined factories. They discussed ways to lessen their partners' and their families' resistance to their spending so much time away from home. The union became an all-women organization precisely so that garment workers could bring these questions to their meetings without anyone charging them with

173

being trivial or divisive. There are men in Mexico's garment factories – pressers and cutters – but from the start the seamstresses saw theirs as a women's organization addressing women's needs and remaining accessible to women. At first women felt as though they had to choose either to end their participation in the new union or to leave their male partners. A number of women now serving on the union's executive committee have left their *compañeros*. The need for such a choice had to be challenged, or it would have severely restricted the union's potential membership and made it hard to gain an audience in factories not yet organized. So members chose to try to make children and partners feel like participants in union activities. Setting up a child-care center at their headquarters was intended to relieve some of the tensions that were mounting between union work, factory work and family responsibilities. More recently, child care has fulfilled another purpose. Union women have invited women active in neighborhood organizations to use the child-care center too. Cooperation between Mexico City's unions and its neighborhood organizers – the majority of them women – is a new phenomenon in Mexican grassroots politics.

CONCLUSION

A leaner, more competitive world is what leading politicians are prescribing for the 1990s. The prescription goes by several names: restructuring, *perestroika*, the four modernizations. It is providing a new common language for George Bush, Margaret Thatcher, Mikhail Gorbachev, Brian Mulroney, Deng Xiaoping and Sosuke Uno. They and their aides discuss these restructuring policies in terms of high-technology research, managerial flexibility, decentralized productivity. Their discourse has a futuristic ring: traditional national boundaries will mean less as data and capital goods are transferred electronically around the globe; teenagers in their Benetton sweaters will grow up with a global consciousness. But to turn this vision into reality government officials are relying on old-fashioned ideas about women.

This seductive 1990s formula needs women from Leningrad to Tokyo to continue to see themselves as mothers, wives and daughters. It is as mothers that Canadian or Italian women will be grateful for the intro-duction of more and more home-based jobs, jobs that allow managers and government planners to reduce costly overhead expenditures. It is as wives that American and Panamanian women will be willing to take the lower-paid assembly jobs in high- and low-tech light industry, permitting managers and government officials to compete with foreign rivals. It is as daughters that Soviet and Japanese women will accept the increasingly common part-time jobs which enable officials to fine-tune the economy.

Yet this Brave New Old-Fashioned World is being planned without taking account of many women's mounting ambivalence about the meaning of marriage, motherhood and familial responsibility. It ignores the significance of single mothers and women as family breadwinners throughout the world. It dismisses many women's sophisticated organizational skills. Its proponents are remarkably uncurious about the changing dynamics within households.

To say this is not to suggest that all women everywhere are willing to see other women as allies rather than as competitors or strangers. Nor is it to imply that many women's relationships to male supervisors, husbands and fathers are not problematic. But as we enter the next decade, women as consumers and producers are not simply modern versions of Victorian domestic angels and obedient mill girls. And even those mythologized pioneers of the Industrial Revolution were not as passive as they are often made out to be.

The Mexican garment workers' experience suggests several things. First, despite their striking similarities, garment and other light-industry factories use the women who make up the majority of their workers in different ways. There is no Universal Garment Factory. Some factories are in capital cities, while others are far from the seats of power. Being in the capital does not guarantee influence for the women workers, since they may be employed by the smallest, most marginalized subcontracting factories, neglected by political activists, academics and reporters. But the location did help the Mexico City seamstresses to gain the resources to challenge the government directly when other conditions were on their side. Working for a company in an Export Processing Zone also has mixed implications. Local governments courting investment have designed the EPZs so that workers can be easily controlled. But those conditions can give women a sense of their shared interests. And, as women in the Philippines and Sri Lanka have shown, once they begin to organize, the very intensity of the EPZ experience can generate activism.[38] Then there are the thousands of women who don't do their industrial sewing in a factory at all. In the name of post-modern managerial flexibility, they are hired by subcontractors to work in their own homes. For home workers, recognizing unfair practices and organizing to challenge them may be especially difficult.

The September 19th Union's story also warns us not to collapse all women in Third World countries into a single homogeneous category. There is no such thing as '*the* Third World woman'. Third World peasant women may feel they have little in common with women working in foreign-owned urban factories. Middle-class women, even if they are feminists and want to support factory women in Third World societies, often speak a political language that is unfamiliar, even alienating to the very women they wish to help. And of course, as in industrialized countries, there are those Third World women, admittedly a minority, who are so comfortable with their class and racial privileges that they feel quite threatened when garment workers challenge established ideas about respectable feminine behavior *and* their government's scheme to pay off foreign bankers.

Feminization is being publicly rationalized in terms that appeal to a woman's desire to contribute to her nation, and that appear sympathetic to the double-burdened worker-mother. In the process, the politics of micro-chips and information are becoming as dependent on a particular politics of marriage and femininity as the politics of blouses and jeans were before them.[39] For women assembling micro-chips for state-of-the-art computers and lethal weaponry or entering data for publishers and hospitals, the technology has changed, but the ideology on which it rests has not. So, as the Mexican garment workers have demonstrated, any success in altering managerial and political policies will require taking up sensitive questions about home life, issues that male union leaders and nationalist intellectuals have dismissed as divisive or trivial.

What if . . . What if women continue to change their ideas about husbands as breadwinners? What if increasing numbers of women change their ideas about what a good mother does with her evenings? What if women in more and more countries change their ideas about what constitutes a 'skill'? If any of these ideas could be changed permanently, men in their board rooms, government ministries and union halls would have to revise their own ways of confronting the challenges of the next decade.

8

'JUST LIKE ONE
OF THE FAMILY':
DOMESTIC SERVANTS
IN WORLD POLITICS

British/Irish/Scottish/Welsh nanny/governesses childcare trained/ex-
perienced with impeccable references. Worldwide Service. Regency
Nannies International, 50 Hans Crescent, London SW1 (opposite
Harrods). GB licenced.[1]

Every day the *International Herald Tribune*, *The Times*, the *Toronto Star*
and other cosmopolitan newspapers run such advertisements. Agencies are
eager to place nannies and domestic servants; families are eager to obtain
household help. The women seeking work are British, Irish, American,
Portuguese, Mexican, Colombian, Jamaican, Moroccan, Sri Lankan,
Indian, Filipino and Ethiopian. Their potential employers are Canadian,
American, British, French, German, Italian, Australian, Japanese, Hong
Kong Chinese, Singaporean, Saudi and Kuwaiti. The governments of both
domestic workers and their employers have a stake in those relationships.
So does the International Monetary Fund. Domestic work has become an
international business with political implications.

When middle-class women with families began returning to waged
work in the 1970s, they needed more than polyester suits. The double
burden, which factory and farming women had known for generations,
was now becoming part of middle-class women's daily lives. Since the
1920s they had been told by conservatives and reformers alike that

177

being a competent housewife was a respectable, full-time job, albeit unpaid, for middle-class women. They shouldn't rely on servants to care for husbands and children; they should apply their own energies and skills to household tasks. But fifty years later many middle-class women were readjusting their sights. They wanted to pursue their own careers, to have both public identities and incomes of their own. It was an aspiration that helped swell the second wave of Western feminism. Many women with children devoted considerable energy to persuading their male partners to take more responsibility for such mundane tasks as changing diapers, doing laundry, taking time off work to look after sick children. Simultaneously, women lobbied collectively for increased public and corporate child-care facilities. Some progress was made. Some men stopped expecting a hot meal to be waiting for them when they returned home from work. Other men could be seen on weekends carrying infants on their backs in designer papooses. Governments, especially in Europe, began passing legislation to provide for publicly subsidized day care. But women found that, even with these signs of progress, they remained the adult chiefly responsible for maintaining the household. Now they had paid work, some of it challenging and rewarding; still, they were expected to do everything. Superwoman was replacing Angel in the House as the quintessential middle-class woman.

For many women being 'superwoman' was not an ideal; it was a sentence. When their husband or employer or government didn't move to reduce the stresses imposed by the double burden, women began looking for private solutions. Some lowered their work expectations. They took part-time jobs; they accepted the status of 'associate' in law firms even when that meant abandoning hopes of ever being made a partner; they put off having children as long as possible; they sank more and more of their wages into expensive private nurseries. The hopes generated by the feminist movement began to look like cruel delusions.

Some women began to explore an old alternative. They began to hire other women to do their housework and mind their children.

For centuries women had employed other women to perform household tasks. The Industrial Revolution helped create a demand for domestic servants by nurturing the notion of the middle-class woman who would protect her own feminine purity from manual labor and yet still provide a refuge for her hardworking husband. The histories of working-class British women, Irish women, African-American and Japanese-American women have all been shaped by the domestic jobs created by this Victorian ideology.[2] But the second wave of feminism included pointed critiques of feminized housework and the exploitation of working women. Thus turning to hired domestic servants to resolve the 'superwoman' dilemma appeared politically suspect. Wasn't 'feminist domestic employer' a contradiction?

Despite the ideological contradictions and political unease, many middle-class women have hired domestic servants. Some of these women employers are not products of feminism's careerist agenda; they have had private incomes and have simply followed in the footsteps of their own mothers, who were also affluent enough to hire other women to help care for their homes and children. But for more politically self-conscious middle-class women, hiring a maid today is a difficult decision. Their discomfort may be off-set by the realization that cutbacks in welfare-state programs and the political push for 'privatization' have made it even harder to combine paid work with household maintenance. Facing governments' regressive agendas, some women have been able to rationalize away their initial embarrassment: hiring a domestic servant seems like a response to political forces outside one's control.[3] The task then becomes one of being a 'good employer'.

Some professional women feel guilty that some nannies may have to leave their own children overseas with relatives; so they try to hire only nannies without children. Other women try to include domestic workers in their decisions about holidays and moving house. 'I'm completely dependent on her,' a New York public-relations executive admitted, referring to the West Indian woman, mother of five children still in Trinidad, who cares for her young daughter when she's at the office. 'She's in my home more than I am.' Occasionally a woman will deny that she is an employer at all. As a young journalist living in a large London flat explained, hiring another woman to clean for £2.50 an hour cut down on the squabbles she and her doctor husband had been having over who was going to do which household chores. Besides, the relationship between her and the woman who cleaned didn't feel strictly economic. 'I suppose when I was an idealistic socialist student I thought I'd never, never have people to do things for me. But I never look on it as a sort of employee-employer situation.'[4]

The relationships today between employer and employee in domestic work are complicated both by the middle-class woman's own ambivalence and by the complex political conditions with which the domestic worker herself must cope. Thousands of women now working as domestic servants are recent immigrants whose lives are made precarious not only by the poverty back home but by regulations imposed by home and host governments. Each government has its own reasons for controlling – or deliberately overlooking – the international trade in domestic service. Governmental policy thus has made even more complex the already awkward mix of intimacy and power which has always shaped relations between women doing domestic work and their employers.

Women working in middle-class households as domestic servants are not subjected to identical political pressures. A hierarchy of respectability and security has developed. At the top are the professional nannies, usually white, though frequently from abroad; they often have formal qualifications and organizational support. They expect their employers to treat them as independent adults. In the middle are young women, au pairs. They, too, are usually white but they see it as a short-term job, a way to travel and learn another language before moving on to more serious commitments. They are frequently treated as 'daughters' by their employers. Further down this hierarchy of respectability are women who may do child care, but who are assumed by their employers to be available for ordinary household chores as well. They are not thought of as professionals, no matter how great their experience and skill; they are presumed to be 'maids', and their work defines their social status. More often than not, these domestic workers are women of color from less privileged communities within their employers' country or from abroad. Without either the credentials of the professional nanny or the amateur approach of the au pair, and lacking their racial advantage, these women are more susceptible to loneliness, economic exploitation, sexual harassment by men in the household and perhaps even deportation by the host government. They are especially dependent on the sensitivity and fairness of their employers. Thus, paradoxically, these women, the majority of domestic workers, confront the greatest inequities, yet they may also find faith in their employers' paternalism most appealing.

Women working as nannies, au pairs and domestic servants experience many of the same problems. The labyrinth of immigration rules can bewilder even those women with racial confidence and a formal education. Working in the home raises common issues of isolation, intimacy and possible harassment. All three groups have been treated as less than 'serious workers' by men in trade unions. Finally, all of these women are more likely than most workers to have another woman as their employer. Nevertheless, nannies, au pairs and domestic servants have not yet been able to build political bridges between one another. Some of their organizing, indeed, has served to reinforce the status barriers separating them. Some of these barriers have their roots in nineteenth-century feminists' responses to imperialism.

NANNIES, MAIDS AND EMPIRES

The colonies which promote emigration from the United Kingdom by means of their public funds are New South Wales, Victoria, South Australia, Tasmania, *some* of the provinces of New Zealand, the Cape of Good Hope, and Natal . . . in *all*, the persons assisted must belong strictly to the labouring classes.[5]

Nineteenth-century British feminist Maria Rye quoted this passage from Her Majesty's Emigration Commissioners in disgust. How could Britain's unmarried middle-class women hope to take advantage of employment opportunities in the colonies if their government only offered assistance to those women who would go out as domestic servants?

Maria Rye belonged to a circle of activist British women called the Langham Place Group, who sought to open up paid work to middle-class single women. In mid-Victorian Britain women outnumbered men. There weren't enough husbands to allow all eligible women to get married – the conventional patriarchal solution to financial worries. Moreover, as the women of Langham Place had pointed out in articles and parliamentary petitions, women's economic security in marriage had always been more myth than reality. There also weren't enough governess positions to support the thousands of single middle-class 'surplus' women who needed work that was both respectable and economically viable. So in 1861 Maria Rye helped launch the Female Middle Class Emigration Society (FMCES): *respectable* paid work in the homes of white colonial settlers. The reformers would further the government's imperial aims at the same time as the government addressed unmarried women's pressing economic needs.

Maria Rye did not intend middle-class white women to work as mere domestic servants; that would jeopardize their social status and under-use their considerable skills. FMCES activists wanted middle-class women to emigrate as nannies, governesses, shop managers. The empire needed respectable, skilled nannies to elevate the white settler communities in the colonies.

In actual numbers, the FMCES made only a small dent in the economic problems faced by British single women. In 1861, its first year of activity, the FMCES managed to place fourteen women in paid positions in the colonies: twelve in Australia and two in Natal in South Africa. The following year it was a bit more successful: twenty women were sent to Australia, six to Natal, seven to Vancouver Island in Canada, three to New Zealand and one to India. Although Maria Rye herself developed a fondness for Canada after reading Susannah Moody's autobiographical account of being a pioneer on the Canadian frontier, Australia became the favored destination for British governesses, because of the gold rush and growing white settlement. India and Africa were far down on the list of those colonies considered promising for respectable white single working women.[6]

Middle-class single women stood in Manchester or Kent and looked out at an empire of tea plantations, gold fields and trading ports organized to keep women dependent yet make their skills and reproductive capacities useful to the empire. It was a world in which women had as much stake in maintaining differences of class and race among themselves as in maintaining their feminine distinctiveness from men. Thus while women who sought assistance from FMCES knew that they would have to learn how to cook and wash if they were to be acceptable applicants for the colonial emigration schemes, they also recognized that one of the few valued assets a middle-class single woman possessed was her feminine respectability. They would rather have stayed in Britain, where the chances of waged work and marital security were slim, than go out to the colonies as domestic servants, a position which would surely cost them that prized respectability.

Consolidating an empire, none the less, required domestic servants as well as nannies. Scores of Indian, Malaysian, Aborigine, Maori, Native Canadian and African women worked as servants in the homes of white settlers. The paternalistic relationship between the white mistress on a tea or sugar plantation and her local servants was frequently held up as an example of what the colonizing mission was all about. Today Black South African women are developing a theory of internal colonialism – apartheid – out of their analysis of the paternalistic relations between 'Black maids and White "madams" '.[7] Many colonialists, on the other hand, felt more comfortable hiring working-class women of their own racial groups, or the demand for servants just outran the supply of local women willing to work in colonialists' homes. In Canada at the turn of the century the federal government bent its immigration rules to allow local agencies to import young working-class girls from Britain to work as maids. When that pool wasn't sufficient, Canadians turned to young Finnish women. Some feminists advocated that poor British women take up colonial domestic service. A poor young British woman, they reasoned, was better off emigrating than being unwittingly drawn into a life of crime at home. If she emigrated to the colonies under an appropriate chaperone, she could be assured of placement in the sort of household that would nurture her future respectability.[8]

British women ranked the parts of the empire where they could work. Australia, with its growing white settler population and its suppressed and marginalized Aboriginal population, ranked high. New Zealand sounded appealing, though it was a newer colony and its Maori people were still a cause for some anxiety among whites. Canada's colonial administrators were still refining their policies to encourage middle-class women emigrants.[9] Britain's rule in India had just been shaken by the 1857 Mutiny, and the white colonial community in need of governesses remained small. Africa ranked at the bottom of the single middle-class women's list, though for some it still had the attraction of 'adventure'.[10]

Nannies. They seem such a fixture of an earlier time, when half the map was colored imperial pink, when domestic life was private and when at least some children could be protected from the world's harsh realities. But nowadays nannies are being treated by the press as something new, a symbol of yuppie affluence and the working mother. Nannies are easier to report on if they are white. They don't raise the difficult questions of race and inequality between the First World and the Third World.

Today's nannies – and the agencies which create a business out of them – make a point of distinguishing themselves both from the Jane Eyres of old and from the contemporary domestic servant. They are taking on the mantel of professionalism and are organizing. The second annual conference of the International Nanny Association met in Vail, Colorado, in 1988. Ann Recchia, a graduate of one of Britain's most select training schools for nannies, explained during the meeting that she and her fellow nannies refused to do housework; they were trained educators and nutritionists. Several months later, the New Jersey Nanny Society held its first meeting for the approximately 500 – 1,000 women working as nannies in that state alone. Its president, a 24-year-old white woman who had graduated from a mid-western college and moved east to work as a nanny, also made clear that, 'It's not like I'm a housekeeper . . . I'm part of the family.' But despite the estimated 70,000 – 90,000 American families who want to hire nannies, nannies at the meeting said they do not feel they get the respect they deserve. A young Dutch woman working for a New Jersey family added that, besides lack of respect, nannies have to cope with isolation. She hoped the new association would provide some social companionship.[11] Nannies in Britain, many of whom have passed the National Nursery Examination Board's test, complain that living-in subjects them to low pay (£50 per week, plus accommodation) as well as loneliness.[12]

DOMESTIC SERVANTS AND THE IMF

Women seek domestic-servant jobs outside their own countries for many reasons. While those reasons may be the result of distorted development

– élite corruption, dependence on exploitative foreign investors, refusal to implement genuine land reform – the women who emigrate usually speak in more immediate terms. They need to earn money to support landless parents or an unemployed husband. They are the sole supporter of their children. They are afraid that if they don't emigrate they will have no choice but to work as prostitutes. They cannot find jobs in the fields for which they were trained. Civil war has made life at home unbearable. They have sisters and schoolmates who have gone abroad and promise to help find them work. These may be private calculations, but they help governments trying to balance their trade and pay off their international debts.

International debt politics has helped create the incentives for many women to emigrate, while at the same time it has made governments dependent on the money those women send home to their families. The International Monetary Fund, which serves as a vanguard for the commercial banking community by pressuring indebted governments to adopt policies which will maximize a country's ability to repay its outstanding loans with interest, has insisted that governments cut their social-service budgets. Reductions in food-price subsidies are high on the IMF's list of demands for any government that wants its financial assistance. Keeping wages down, cutting back public works, reducing the numbers of government employees, rolling back health and education budgets – these are standard IMF prescriptions for indebted governments. They usually attract support from at least some members of the government itself, especially in the finance ministry.

These policies have different implications for women and men in the indebted country, because women and men usually have such dissimilar relationships to family maintenance, waged employment, public services and public policy-making. If a government does decide to adopt the IMF package, feeding a family and maintaining its members' health will become more taxing. Food will cost more, while income coming into the household is likely to fall. Senior government officials often fear that if they implement the IMF policies, they will lose their popular support. Daily life will become so hard that large sectors of the public will take the risk of openly calling for the regime's removal. Thus policy-makers make their own calculations: they need the IMF loans to maintain international credibility; but if they swallow the IMF pill whole, they may not be around to benefit from that credibility. Crucial to this political calculation, though not acknowledged, is the absorption capacity of individual households: how much financial belt-tightening can each family tolerate?

This question depends on the skill and willingness of women – as wives and single mothers. An indebted government can institute the IMF prescriptive package and not suffer political destabilization if women can figure out ways to stretch the kerosene and cooking oil, if women can find more ways to earn a bit of money in the casual labor sector, if women can provide demoralized men in their families with emotional support, if women are willing to care for a sick child without resorting to the public clinic. Thus the politics of international debt is not simply something that has an *impact* on women in indebted countries. The politics of international debt won't work in their current form *unless* mothers and wives are willing to behave in ways that enable nervous regimes to adopt cost-cutting measures without forfeiting their political legitimacy. It is the recognition of this strategic link between financial policy, regime stability and women's domestic responsibilities that has made women activists in Third World countries the leading theoreticians in developing a distinctly feminist analysis of international debt politics.[13]

The 'debt crisis' is providing many middle-class women in Britain, Italy, Singapore, Canada, Kuwait and the United States with a new generation of domestic servants. When a woman from Mexico, Jamaica or the Philippines decides to emigrate in order to make money as a domestic servant she is designing her own international debt politics. She is trying to cope with the loss of earning power and the rise in the cost of living at home by cleaning bathrooms in the country of the bankers.

In 1986 money sent back home by citizens working abroad – 'remittances' – comprised 78 per cent of the money that Pakistan earned from exports. For Bangladesh, the figure was 56 per cent; Sri Lanka, 27 per cent; India, 25 per cent; Philippines, 18 per cent; Thailand, 10 per cent.[14]

The women and men who send this money home go abroad to do quite different sorts of jobs. The men emigrate to work as seamen and construction workers. Tankers bombed in the Persian Gulf during the recent Iran–Iraq War were owned by Kuwait, Norway, the United States, Japan, Greece; but they were manned by Indian, Pakistani and Filipino crewmen. The women whose home governments rely on them for remittances go abroad to work as nurses, maids, entertainers and prostitutes.

This gendered labor export system is built on the personal relationships between women and the men in their families. For instance, although Pakistan's overseas labor migration is masculinized, in that mostly men go to work abroad, it depends on wives and mothers. Pakistani men, like most men, are reluctant to take construction jobs in Dubai if they suspect that their wives won't be able to care for their children adequately or that they will have affairs with other men. They might be reassured by a study of Filipino women whose husbands worked overseas; it revealed that cases of infidelity among women left behind were rare. Yet women's lack of access to the resources necessary to cope while their husbands are away can make a man's absence impossibly stressful. The problems of a woman whose husband has left home to take a job on a Kuwaiti tanker are not just those of a single adult; she is a woman in a patriarchal society. Government officials who need those men to earn money overseas count on their wives to cope with the burdens. The politics of international debt are in no small measure the politics of these women's coping. Sometimes, however, the strain is too much. At one hospital in Pakistan psychiatrists have treated so many women whose husbands work in the Middle East for symptoms of mental stress that they talk now of women suffering from 'the Dubai syndrome'.[15]

Sri Lanka and the Philippines are the two countries today whose economic stability is most dependent on feminized migrant labor. Sri Lankan and Filipino women who leave home to work abroad have become economically more important than their male counterparts. Some of the Filipino women are recruited to work as nurses, some as entertainers. But the greatest number work as domestic servants. Their governments have relied on feminized labor at home – on plantations, in tourist resorts, in Export Processing Zones – to stay financially afloat. Now they also depend on women's overseas earnings to keep foreign creditors and their financial policeman, the International Monetary Fund, content.

Turin is one of Italy's booming industrial centers. Its economic success has also made it a center for foreign domestic workers, especially women from Ethiopia and the Philippines. Italian families want household help at low wages. Filipino maids – many of whom are college graduates and have worked as teachers or nurses back home – often Italy with tourist visas, which prohibit paid work. But there is an informal network of Filipino women already working in Turin who help the new arrival to make her way through the bureaucratic labyrinths of the Italian immigration department. To convert her tourist visa into a longer-term 'guest' visa, a Filipino woman becomes a 'guest' of her employer, often the adult man in the household. He then becomes her emissary to the Italian government. For a Filipino woman who has been in Italy for only six months and knows little Italian, this arrangement is attractive because it protects her from bureaucratic intimidation.[16]

In the process, however, the domestic worker's place of employment becomes a prison as well as a sanctuary. The Filipino is only a legal resident of Turin so long as her employer will vouch for her as a guest. Though many Italians stereotype Filipinos as docile, and hard-working, with no social life of their own, domestic workers have tried to create, with the help of Catholic nuns, informal networks among friends, sisters and cousins. Here they share news from home and discuss ways of improving their working conditions. If Filipino maids sometimes appear to offer little resistance to long hours, low pay and condescension, the cause may lie less in cultural determinism than in the bureaucratic procedures that make them so dependent on their employers for their legal status. In the past the Italian government seemed willing to overlook the fiction of the 'guest' visas. But in 1989 it began to take a tougher stand against not only Filipinos, but Senegalese, Ethiopians, Tunisians and other Third World immigrants whose growing presence was generating intolerance among Italians. Italians used to pride themselves on being welcoming to immigrants, but today newspapers are carrying articles headlined, 'Are Italians Racist?'[17] In this atmosphere a Filipino working as a domestic servant on a guest visa may feel increasingly beholden to her employer no matter what the working conditions.

Elsa arrived in Italy in 1982 on a tourist visa. Her employer had asked her sister, who already worked in Turin, to find her a domestic servant from the Philippines. Elsa started her job three days after her arrival.

Elsa begins work at 6:45. She makes breakfast for the husband and wife and their two children. After they leave for work and school she makes her own breakfast and begins household chores.

At 11:00 a.m. Elsa goes out to the market to buy fresh food for lunch and supper. This is one of her few opportunities during the day for social contact, but since she knows little Italian, she keeps to herself.

She prepares a standard five-course midday meal for the family, using recipes she has had to learn since arriving in Italy. She serves the meal, but doesn't eat herself until later, when she can cook Filipino food and not be interrupted by requests from her employers or their children.

After an hour's rest, Elsa returns to household chores. She must complete them by 5 or 6 in the evening so she can start preparing the family's evening meal. She eats alone in the kitchen as the family talks leisurely around the supper table. Between 9:30 and 10:00 she finishes the dishes.

It is 10:00 p.m. Elsa is free to go out. Usually she is too tired. She is also afraid of getting lost and not knowing enough Italian to ask directions. Besides, she may be harassed by men at night, who will presume that she is a prostitute. So most nights she chooses to finish any cleaning that must be done and then to go to bed.

Back home, under President Corazon Aquino the Philippines is as dependent on income from domestic servants such as Elsa as was the previous regime of Ferdinand Marcos, but it is more sensitive to the contradictions between national dignity and sexist development. By March 1988 an estimated 175,000 Filipino women were working overseas, 40 per cent of them as contract workers. As many as 89,000 of the 152,000 Filipino nurses were working overseas, leaving the country with a shortage of medical personnel. An estimated 81,000 women were working abroad as domestic workers. The government requires that overseas workers send home a minimum percentage of their pay; if they do not, the government can withdraw their permission to travel abroad. They were sending home between $60 and $100 million in foreign exchange each year, outstripping the contributions made by either sugar or minerals. Each overseas worker is believed to be supporting at least five dependents back home. Remittances from Filipino men and women together amounted to 18 per cent of the country's $5.7 billion in foreign exchange. In Singapore the government requires Filipino domestic servants to take a pregnancy test every six months. If a woman is found to be pregnant, she forfeits her work permit and must return home. Women working in Asia, the Middle East and Europe tell stories of being sexually assaulted by the men of the households they worked for. In Hong Kong, Filipinas and domestic service have become so merged in the popular culture that a doll sold widely in Hong Kong is called simply 'Filipina maid'.[18]

In the name of national pride the Aquino government in 1988 declared a ban on all recruitment of Filipinas outside the country. The ban was total. In the future if a government wanted to resume importing Filipino domestic servants it hereafter would have to prove that it was taking explicit safeguards to ensure their protection. Some observers suspected that the sweeping character of the ban was a smokescreen: Manila officials had become most alarmed at the reports of abuse from women working in Saudi Arabia, but the Philippines is too dependent on Saudi Oil – and on Arab non-involvement in the simmering insurgency in Mindanao, the Philippines' Muslim region – to risk offending Saudi officials by singling their country out for criticism.

The ban came from the top. It was not the consequence of demands made by Filipino domestic servants or by women in support of them. Despite its apparent good intentions, the Aquino government's action was not universally popular among women. It failed to take account of the dilemmas facing Filipinas working abroad. In Hong Kong twenty-two migrant organizations created a coalition, United Filipinos Against the Ban, to press the Aquino government to repeal the ban. They argued that, rather than protecting them, the ban jeopardized Filipinas' ability to gain employment. Bi-lateral agreements between Manila and various recruiting governments, and the guarantee of on-site educational and welfare services for Filipinas, would be more helpful. The ban remained in place, but gradually the Aquino government, lacking the means to make it stick and needing the foreign currency to keep up with its debt payments, exempted one government after another from its requirements. By 1989 twenty-two governments had obtained exemption.[19]

'DOWN BIG YARD': MAIDS AND THE STATE

Primrose is a 35-year-old Jamaican woman working as a domestic worker in Toronto, Canada. She left her six children in the care of her mother and gave up a job as a nurse in a public hospital in order to earn more money and continue her education in Canada. She endured the petty humiliations experienced by many domestic workers she knew who worked in the homes of white families, and sought out the church to break through her daily isolation. After eight years Primrose had come to the conclusion that the white women – and their often demanding children – for whom she kept house were only part of the problem. The Canadian and Jamaican governments were also to blame for the conditions domestic workers had to cope with:

> I tell myself that if God help me and I get through this country, when I go back to Ja [Jamaica], I'm going to go to RJR and JBC radio stations and announce to all the people the true story of Canada and Canadians. I want to somehow get to the government of Jamaica to let them know they are slack, cause if they had done better, we wouldn't be under this pressure.[20]

Primrose, like other Caribbean, Latin American, Asian and British women working in Canada as domestic servants, comes face to face with the Canadian government in the form of the Immigration Department. 'She is a hassle, but Immigration is also a hassle, and you never know when they might decide to send you home.'[21] Pressing an employer for back pay or time off is risky. If the employer is having marital troubles with her husband and isn't getting sufficient household money to pay the salary due, the domestic worker is reluctant to go to the Immigration Office to get help in enforcing her contract.

> I have a girlfriend and every time she has to go down to Immigration she say, 'I'm going for sentence now. Down big yard.' So if I'm going tomorrow, I'll say, 'I'm going for sentence,' and they'll say, 'Good luck!' because any time you going down there is problems. If the government wanted to do something about it, they could.[22]

In the 1950s Toronto's Negro Citizenship Association established a hostel and a meeting place so that Caribbean women working as domestic servants could talk to each other and, if necessary, escape an intolerable household. This was a period in Canadian political history when government immigration laws allowed a large number of Caribbean men and women to enter Canada. However, without her own home, an immigrant woman facing harassment as a live-in domestic worker had only the option of marrying a man, perhaps against her better judgement.

The 1980s was a turning point. The Canadian parliament had tightened its immigration laws during a period of rising unemployment and increasing public debate about racial tensions. For their part, immigrant domestic workers began to develop their own organizations: Domestic Workers United and Intercede, the International Coalition to End Domestics' Exploitation. Intercede, a group of Caribbean and Filipino women, focussed its attention on Canadian immigration law, for as long as domestic workers were made vulnerable by immigration regulations, they would be too weak to effectively bargain with their employers. In other words, a person who hires a woman to clean or mind her children is never in simply a personal relationship with that woman: her discretion is conditioned by the government's immigration regulations and its bureaucracy's way of administering those rulings.

In 1981 Intercede persuaded the Canadian parliament to change the law so that foreign domestic workers on temporary visas would have the same rights under labor law as Canadian citizens. The group's next goals are to win for domestic workers the same rights to overtime pay as other Canadian workers, and to reduce immigration fees. Canadians, who see themselves as a much more open and less racist society than their American neighbors, have politically active domestic workers to thank for pushing the reality a few inches closer to the national myth.[23]

In Britain, France, Saudi Arabia, Japan and the United States immigrant domestic workers' relationships with each other and with their employers are shaped in large part by political debates over immigration. These debates, so indicative of a society's own national identity and what it thinks of its place in the international system, are usually riddled with assumptions about male and female citizenship. Broadly speaking, many governments since World War II have acted as if an 'immigrant worker' was male. An 'immigrant's family' was composed of the wife and children of that male worker. This portrait does not match the facts, for governments have depended on immigrant women to work in hospitals, to clean office buildings, hotels and airports, to mind children and to operate sewing machines during the decades of post-war economic expansion. In 1951 women were 37 per cent of West Indian-born British residents.[24] The facts notwithstanding, this portrait of a masculinized immigrant workforce encouraged policy-makers to see restrictions on women immigrants as a means of preventing male immigrant workers from putting down roots. If a worker's wife and children could be kept in their home countries, the worker himself could be sent home when his economic utility waned.

Immigration politics was also gendered in the ways legislators and civil servants thought about the legal identities of married women. When a woman married did she necessarily take on the nationality of her husband? What was the international politics of marriage that best suited governments? As early as 1914 the then all-male British Parliament engaged in a lively debate over this point. There was little controversy over the new concept of British citizenship extending to all British colonial subjects (a concept that has been rolled back steadily in more recent decades). But Members of Parliament differed strongly over what should be done with a British woman who married a citizen of another country. Women's suffrage groups and other women's organizations lobbied hard to persuade MPs that women should no longer be treated as their husband's appendages: they were full persons with their own political rights, their own national identities. In Parliament the majority voted otherwise. According to the 1914 Immigration Act, a British woman who married a foreign man would surrender her British citizenship. The government argued that this practice was common throughout the civilized world.[25]

Immigration and marriage remain bound together in British policy. Both Labour and Conservative governments have been afraid of women entering Britain with any sort of autonomy. The result has been that thousands of women, many of them from India, Pakistan and Bangladesh, as well as mail-order brides from Southeast Asia, have been trapped in marriages, afraid to leave for fear that they will be deported, perhaps having to leave their children behind in Britain. However, the government's policy to control domestic workers took a rather different form. The ideal immigrant domestic worker was a woman who had no dependents and who would have to rely on her employer to keep a valid work permit. When a Filipino domestic worker unknowingly revealed she had children in the Philippines and was threatened with deportation in 1978, a campaign was mounted to persuade the Home Office to reverse its administrative ruling. Already in 1977, the British government had banned resident permits for domestic workers altogether. Today, the major source of abuse in domestic service is affluent men and women from abroad who enter Britain, some of them on diplomatic visas, bringing women servants whom they falsely declare to be members of their families. Those women have no recourse to social-service agencies and no legal status except that derived from their employers. Being a foreign-born wife and being a foreign-born domestic worker often become strikingly similar under restrictive immigration laws.[26]

CONCLUSION

Padmini Palliyaguruge had been an elementary-school teacher in Sri Lanka. She had also been an activist in local women's organizations. After taking part in a strike to better low-paid teachers' conditions, she found herself locked out of employment. Her husband and two children depended on her wages, and her husband had never been sympathetic to her activism. Desperate for work, Padmini Palliyaguruge decided that she had no choice but to sign up with one of the 450 Sri Lankan agencies recruiting Sri Lankan women to work as domestic servants in Saudi Arabia. A woman working as a domestic servant received thirty times the wages in the Middle East as in Sri Lanka. Even with agency fees of $500–$1,000 and despite the fact that male recruiters have a reputation for abusing women, the opportunity seemed worth taking.[27]

In 1984 an estimated 18,000 Sri Lankan women migrated to take paid jobs overseas, most on short-term contracts. This was the first time that Sri Lankan women outnumbered Sri Lankan men in foreign employment. Of the 200,000 Sri Lankans working on contract in the Middle East in 1987, 70 per cent were women working as maids. Most of them were married. Most came from the country's Singhalese ethnic community, whose men dominate government offices. The repatriated earnings of women working abroad made foreign remittances Sri Lanka's second largest foreign-exchange earner, after tea.[28]

Once in Saudi Arabia, Padmini, like other Sri Lankan maids, had to provide her employer with around-the-clock service. She worked seven days a week, often for more than eighteen hours a day. She describes the conditions:

> Women have no access to leisure or recreation. Uprooted from their cultural environment and left for themselves in an unknown world under very trying working-conditions, they experience psychological traumas. Medical facilities are almost absent. The woman can be compelled to do any kind of work, and many of the women are severely abused physically and sexually.[29]

For some maids the price of the isolation has been excruciatingly high. Padmini shows photographs of women who have returned from their jobs in the Middle East catatonic or in wheel chairs. They are victims of abuse or physical assault by irate employers impatient with their inability to operate electrical appliances, their unwillingness to work long hours or their resistance to sexual advances. Despite these experiences, some women, faced with family bankruptcy, return to the recruiting agency, pay the fee and sign up for another tour of cleaning and cooking abroad. And thus the flow of remittances to Sri Lanka continues, allowing the government to continue paying the interest on its outstanding foreign loans.[30]

Padmini Palliyaguruge was speaking at the 1985 United Nations Decade for Women conference in Nairobi. She spoke not as a victim but as an organizer. She was one of the participants in a non-governmental panel intended to make the special problems of migrant women workers visible. The panel's organizers recalled how difficult it has been, even among internationally conscious feminists, to keep migrant women's political issues on the agenda. They seemed to slip out of sight so easily. Thus organizing a separate panel at Nairobi was a deliberate effort to make their conditions visible to other women and to governments. It was also designed to give women organizers a chance to exchange analyses and strategies with each other.

Pamini Palliyaguruge was in Nairobi representing Sri Lanka's Progressive Women's Front. She was exchanging ideas with women from Peru, Mexico, the Philippines, Japan and Algeria, all of whom had been migrant workers themselves or were helping to organize women working abroad. It had been almost impossible to get local trade unions to take their issues seriously. Many trade-union men didn't see domestic workers as genuine workers. Their work looked too much like what their own wives did every day without pay. Furthermore, these domestic servants' employers were themselves women, hardly challenging adversaries for male union bargainers!

The experiences of domestic workers discussed at Nairobi served to underscore how simplistic the First World/Third World split is, and how inadequate it is to make sense of today's international politics. Literally hundreds of thousands of women from Third World countries are cleaning the homes and minding the children of *other*, more affluent Third World women. In China today the government and the Communist Party's own Women's Federation are officially encouraging urban households to hire maids as a way of reducing the housework responsibilities of other women. As in Britain and the United States, maids are being seen as the solution to the career woman's 'double burden'. In Latin America 'domestic worker' is the single largest job category for women. Most of those women are working for other women. Furthermore, most Sri Lankan women working in the Gulf States and Filipino women in Singapore and Hong Kong are employed in what we still refer to as 'Third World' societies.

The creation of networks and institutions to empower women working as domestic servants has called for activists to rethink how changing power relations both within and between countries depend on ideas about 'home', 'motherhood' and 'job'.

Politically active maids have not always found feminists in the host countries to be reliable allies. Too often local feminist groups in countries importing maids either from overseas or from the poor regions of their own countries were led by women of precisely the social class that hired domestic workers. Combined with the differences of language and race that often accompany the domestic politics of paid housework, the barriers proved hard to surmount. Finally, some politically active women seemed to have trouble even seeing a domestic servant as a 'worker'. She didn't capture activists' imagination the way a garment worker or a prostitute did. The dangers and struggles involved in washing another woman's kitchen floor were less apparent than those in sewing blue jeans in a hot and dusty factory. As the Nairobi panel organizers explained, 'In most cases the employer is a woman. The domestic is her possession, her object, her diminutive pet, or all these things.'[31] Mary Castro, a leader of a domestic workers' association in Brazil, described some of the pitfalls she had encountered in trying to forge alliances:

> The feminists impose their own priorities; of course, sex, problems with men or with the family are also our problems. After all, who dies from illegal abortions? We do, the poor domestic workers, but they [the feminists] should pay more attention to us, they should understand that when someone has no family, or when she has to live with a domineering, hostile employer, her only friend may be her boyfriend. Anyway, how can we trust the feminists when, as employers, they treat us so badly?[32]

One of the conclusions domestic workers have drawn from these experiences is that they need to build their own organizations. Their principal alliances may be with working women back home, not with either host-country trade unions or host-country feminists. In making these connections, domestic workers throw into sharp relief the connections between their governments' policies of feminizing low-paid factory work, relying on women as mothers and wives to carry the burden of cutbacks in public service imposed by the IMF, and women's own internalized notions of familial duty.[33]

9

CONCLUSION: THE PERSONAL IS INTERNATIONAL

One of the simplest and most disturbing feminist insights is that 'the personal is political'. Disturbing, because it means that relationships we once imagined were private or merely social are in fact infused with power, usually unequal power backed up by public authority. Rape, therefore, is about power more than it is about sex, and not only the rapist but the state is culpable. Likewise interior design and doctors' attitudes toward patients are at least as much about publicly wielded power as they are about personal taste or professional behavior.

But the assertion that 'the personal is political' is like a palindrome, one of those phrases that can be read backwards as well as forwards. Read as 'the political is personal', it suggests that politics is not shaped merely by what happens in legislative debates, voting booths or war rooms. While men, who dominate public life, have told women to stay in the kitchen, they have used their public power to construct private relationships in ways that bolstered their masculinized political control. Without these maneuvers, men's hold over political life might be far less secure. Thus to explain why any country has the kind of politics it does, we have to be curious about how public life is constructed out of struggles to define masculinity and femininity. Accepting that the political is personal prompts one to investigate the politics of marriage, venereal disease and homosexuality – not as marginal issues, but as matters central to the state. Doing this kind of research becomes just as serious as studying military weaponry or taxation policy. In fact, insofar as the political *is* personal, the latter cannot be fully understood without taking into account the former.

To make sense of international politics we also have to read power backwards and forwards. Power relations between countries and their governments involve more than gunboat maneuvers and diplomatic telegrams. Read forward, 'the personal is international' insofar as ideas about what it means to be a 'respectable' woman or an 'honorable' man have been shaped by colonizing policies, trading strategies and military doctrines. On the eve of the 1990s, it has almost become a cliché to say that the world is shrinking, that state boundaries are porous. We persist, none the less, in discussing personal power relationships as if they were contained by sovereign states. We treat ideas about violence against women without trying to figure out how the global trade in pornographic videos operates, or how companies offering sex tours and mail-order brides conduct their businesses across national borders. Similarly, we try to explain how women learn to be 'feminine' without unravelling the legacies of colonial officials who used Victorian ideals of feminine domesticity to sustain their empires; or we trace what shapes children's ideas about femininity or masculinity without looking at governments' foreign investment policies that encourage the world-wide advertising strategies of such giants as McCann Erickson or Saatchi and Saatchi.

Becoming aware that personal relationships have been internationalized, however, may make one only feel guilty for not having paid enough attention to international affairs. Start watching what is going on in Brussels. Don't turn off the TV when the conversation moves to trade deficits. Listen to politicians more carefully when they outline their foreign-policy position. While useful, this new international attentiveness by itself isn't sufficient. It leaves untouched our presumptions about just what 'international politics' is. Accepting that the personal is international multiplies the spectators, it especially adds women to the audience, but it fails to transform what is going on on stage.

The implications of a feminist understanding of international politics are thrown into sharper relief when one reads 'the personal is international' the other way round: *the international is personal*. This calls for a radical new imagining of what it takes for governments to ally with each other, compete with and wage war against each other.

'The international is personal' implies that governments depend upon certain kinds of allegedly private relationships in order to conduct their foreign affairs. Governments need more than secrecy and intelligence agencies; they need wives who are willing to provide their diplomatic husbands with unpaid services so those men can develop trusting relationships with other diplomatic husbands. They need not only military hardware, but a steady supply of women's sexual services to convince their soldiers that they are manly. To operate in the international arena, governments seek other governments' recognition of their sovereignty; but they also depend on ideas about masculinized dignity and feminized sacrifice to sustain that sense of autonomous nationhood.

Thus international politics of debt, investment, colonization, decolonization, national security, diplomacy and trade are far more complicated than most experts would have us believe. This may appear paradoxical. Many people, and especially women, are taught that international politics are too complex, too remote and too tough for the feminine mind to comprehend. If a Margaret Thatcher or a Jeanne Kirkpatrick slips through the cracks, it is presumably because she has learned to 'think like a man'. But investigations of how international politics rely on manipulations of masculinity and femininity suggest that the conventional approaches to making sense of inter-state relations are superficial. Conventional analyses stop short of investigating an entire area of international relations, an area that women have pioneered in exploring: how states depend on particular constructions of the domestic and private spheres. If we take seriously the politics of domestic servants or the politics of marketing fashions and global corporate logos, we discover that international politics is more complicated than non-feminist analysts would have us believe. We especially have to take culture – including commercialized culture – far more seriously. The consumer and the marketing executive have a relationship that is mediated through their respective understandings of national identity and masculinity and femininity. That consumer–marketer relationship not only mirrors changing global power dynamics, it is helping to shape those dynamics.

Women tend to be in a better position than men to conduct such a realistic investigation of international politics simply because so many women have learned to ask about gender when making sense of how public and private power operate. This approach also exposes how much power it takes to make the current international political system work. Conventional analyses of inter-state relations talk a lot about power. In fact, because they put power at the center of their understandings, they are presumed to be most naturally comprehended by men; women allegedly do not have an innate taste for either wielding or understanding power. However, an exploration of agribusiness prostitution, foreign-service sexism and attempts to tame outspoken nationalist women with homophobic taunts all reveal that in reality it takes much *more* power to construct and perpetuate international political relations than we have been led to believe. Conventional international-politics commentators have put power at the center of their analyses – often to the exclusion of culture and ideas – but they have under-estimated the amount and varieties of power at work. It has taken power to deprive women of land titles and leave them little choice but to sexually service soldiers and banana workers. It has taken power to keep women out of their countries' diplomatic corps and out of the upper reaches of the World Bank. It has taken power to keep questions of inequity between local men and women off the agendas of many nationalist movements in industrialized as well as agrarian societies. It has taken power to construct popular culture – films, advertisements, books, fairs, fashion – which reinforces, not subverts, global hierarchies.

'The international is personal' is a guide to making sense of NATO, the EEC and the IMF that insists on making women visible. If it is true that friendly as well as hostile relations between governments presuppose constructions of women as symbols, as providers of emotional support, as paid and unpaid workers, then it doesn't make sense to continue analyzing international politics as if they were either gender-neutral or carried on only by men. International policy-making circles may look like men's clubs, but international politics as a whole has required women to behave in certain ways. When they haven't, relations between governments have had to change.

Women need to be made visible in order to understand how and why international power takes the forms it does. But women are not just the objects of that power, not merely passive puppets or victims. As we have seen, women of different classes and different ethnic groups have made their own calculations in order to cope with or benefit from the current struggles between states. These calculations result in whole countries becoming related to one another, often in hierarchical terms.

In search of adventure, that physical and intellectual excitement typically reserved for men, some affluent women have helped turn other women into exotic landscapes. In pursuit of meaningful paid careers, some women have settled in colonies or hired women from former colonies. Out of a desire to appear fashionable and bolster their sometimes shaky self-confidence, many women have become the prime consumers of products made by women working for low wages in other countries. And in an effort to measure the progress they have made towards emancipation in their own societies, women have often helped legitimize international global pyramids of 'civilization'.

All too often, the only women who are made visible on the international stage are 'Third World women', especially those who are underpaid factory workers or entertainment workers around foreign military bases. There are two dangers here. First, the multiple relationships that women in industrialized countries have to international politics are camouflaged. For instance, we do not see the British Asian woman who is organizing anti-deportation campaigns, which can reshape governments' use of marriage to control international flows of people. The American woman on holiday who is helping to 'open up' Grenada to tourism is made invisible, as is the Canadian woman who is insisting on pursuing her career rather than following her diplomat husband overseas. The Italian woman sewing for Benetton at home is hidden. In the process, the international system is made to look less complicated, less infused with power, less gendered than it really is.

The second danger in this tendency to see only 'Third World women' when thinking about women on the international stage is that the important differences between women in less industrialized countries will be ignored. By portraying all women in Third World societies as sewing jeans, not buying jeans, as prostitutes, not as social workers and activists, we again under-estimate the complex relationships it takes to sustain the current international political system. Middle-class women in countries such as Mexico and Sri Lanka have different kinds of stakes in the present system than do working-class and peasant women. This is compounded by societies' ethnic and racial barriers – between Hispanicized and Indian Mexican women, and between Tamil and Singhalese Sri Lankan women, for instance. International debt may affect all women in Mexico, but not to the same degree or in the same ways. National dignity may be appealing to all Sri Lankan women, but *which* nation one feels part of may be problematic. Sexuality may also divide women in a Third World country. Heterosexual women, for instance, may feel ashamed or contemptuous of lesbian women and thus not be able to confront nationalist men who use homophobic innuendos to delegitimize arguments for women's rights.

The international establishment has needed many women in Third World countries to feel more at ease with women from Europe or North America than with women living in a shanty town a mile from their front door. Therefore, efforts to transcend internationally and locally devised barriers between women of Third World countries have had the most significant impact on foreign military bases, multinational corporations and investment bankers.

While women have not been mere pawns in global politics, governments and companies with government backing have made explicit attempts to try to control and channel women's actions in order to achieve their own ends. Male officials who make foreign policy might prefer to think of themselves as dealing with high finance or military strategy, but in reality they have self-consciously designed immigration, labor, civil service, propaganda and military bases policies so as to control women. They have acted as though their government's place in world affairs has hinged on how women behaved.

Uncovering these efforts has exposed men *as men*. International politics has relied not only on the manipulation of femininity's meanings but on the manipulation of masculinity. Ideas about 'adventure', 'civilization', 'progress', 'risk', 'trust' and 'security' are all legitimized by certain kinds of masculine values and behavior, which makes them so potent in relations between governments. Frequently the reason behind government officials – usually men – trying to control women has been their need to optimize the control of men: men as migrant workers, soldiers, diplomats, intelligence operatives, overseas plantation and factory managers, men as bankers. Thus understanding the international workings of masculinity is important to making feminist sense of international politics. Men's sense of their own manhood has derived from their perceptions both of other men's masculinity and of the femininity of women of different races and social classes. Much of what we have uncovered about the problematic character of masculinity in the armed forces can be applied to other spheres of international politics.

There is much discussion today about fundamental changes occurring in international politics. Japan has become the world's largest aid donor and its largest creditor. The United States no longer has the resources or the status to play global policeman, even if its leaders still try. The twelve countries of the European Community are moving steadily toward not only economic, but also social and political integration. If Mikhail Gorbachev survives, the Soviet Union's international priorities are likely to undergo radical change, with military demands being subordinated to economic needs. At the same time, the 'Third World' is becoming more internally unequal each year, as countries such as South Korea, Brazil, Taiwan and Chile start to produce not only steel and automobiles, but also weapons, while countries such as Vietnam and Ethiopia struggle simply to feed their peoples. All the while, capital, drugs and AIDS are becoming globalized; debt stubbornly spirals; and governments persist in sharing coercive formulas for suppressing dissidents in the name of national security.

It is all too easy to plunge into the discussion of any or all of these contemporary trends without asking, 'Where are the women?' What these chapters suggest is that these seemingly new trends are likely to be gendered, just as past international patterns were. The international trends of the 1990s are as likely to depend on particular relations between women and men, relations fostered by the deliberate use of political power. One of the best ways to start making sense of those gendered politics is to take seriously the analyses of women already engaged in international campaigns to influence these trends. Some of the most cogent international analysis is being generated by women meeting in Japan to discuss migrant workers and proxy brides, women meeting in New York to trace the patterns of the global prostitution industry, women meeting in Finland to discuss militarization, women meeting in Mexico City to discuss labor unions, women meeting in Brussels to discuss 1992. Making feminist sense of international politics, therefore, may compel us to dismantle the wall that often separates theory from practice. We don't need to wait for a 'feminist Henry Kissinger' before we can start articulating a fresh, more realistic approach to international politics. Every time a woman explains how her government is trying to control her fears, her hopes and her labor such a theory is being made.

NOTES

1 GENDER MAKES THE WORLD GO ROUND

1 Cynthia Cockburn, quoted by Melissa Benn, 'In and Against the European Left: Socialist Feminists Get Organized', *Feminist Review*, No. 26, July, 1987, p. 89.

2 Some notable exceptions are: Swasti Mitter, *Common Fate, Common Bond*, London, Pluto Press, 1987; Gita Sen and Caren Grown, *Development, Crises and Alternative Visions: Third World Women's Perspectives*, New York, Monthly Review Press, 1987; Eva Isaksson, editor, *Women and the Military System*, Brighton, Wheatsheaf Books, and New York, St Martin's Press, 1988; Wendy Chapkis and Cynthia Enloe, editors, *Of Common Cloth: Women in the Global Textile Industry*, Amsterdam and Washington, Transnational Institute and Institute for Policy Studies, 1983; Wendy Chapkis, editor, *Loaded Questions: Women in the Military*, Amsterdam and Washington, Transnational Institute and Institute for Policy Studies, 1981; Kathleen Barry, Charlotte Bunch and Shirley Castley, editors, *International Feminism: Networking Against Female Sexual Slavery*, New York, International Tribune Center, 1984; *Millennium: Journal of International Studies* special issue on 'Women and International Relations,' London School of Economics, vol. 17, no. 3, Winter, 1988.

3 *New York Times*/CBS poll, reported in the *New York Times*, July 18, 1987. Only 25 per cent of the American women sampled said that they approved of the US government giving aid to the anti-Sandinista Contra forces; 37 per cent of the American men polled approved of US aid to the Contras, though proportionately fewer Black men approved than did white men.

4 For an interesting exploration of the contradictions behind women as television-news reporters, see Patricia Holland, 'When a Woman Reads the News', in Helen Baehr and Gillian Dyers, editors, *Boxed

In: Women and Television, London and Winchester, MA, Pandora Press, 1988, pp. 133–50.

5 For more on the politics of beauty, see Wendy Chapkis, *Beauty Secrets*, Boston, South End Press, 1986, London, Women's Press, 1987.

6 *Boston Globe*, August 10, 1987.

7 Barbara Gamarekian, 'Consequences of Fawn Hall', *New York Times*, February 28, 1987. For Fawn Hall's own views on a secretary's professional relationships, see Mary Sit, 'Hall Tells Secretaries: "Stand by Your Boss" ', *Boston Globe*, September 30, 1988. See also Beatrix Campbell's analysis of the Sara Keayes–Cecil Parkinson scandal in Britain in her *Iron Ladies*, London, Virago Press, 1987, pp. 274–5.

8 For a suggestive report on the changing images of male bankers in the era of internationalized and deregularized banking, see 'City of London, Survey', *The Economist*, June 25, 1988, pp. 25–9; Sebastian Kinsman, 'Confessions of a Commodity Broker', *New Statesman*, 19 February 1988, pp. 10–11; Steve Lohr, 'London's Resurgent Markets', *New York Times*, September 22, 1986; 'The Risk Game: A Survey of International Banking', *The Economist*, March 21, 1987; 'A Survey of Wall Street', *The Economist*, July 11, 1987; Barbara Rogers, *Men Only*, London and Winchester, MA, Pandora Press, 1988.

9 Cynthia Enloe, 'Beyond Rambo', in Eva Isaksson, op. cit.; a somewhat different version appears as 'Beyond Rambo and Steve Canyon', in John Gillis, editor, *The Militarization of the World*, New Brunswick, NJ, Rutgers University Press, 1989.

10 Sylvia Van Kirk, *Many Tender Ties: Women in Fur-Trade Society 1670–1870*, Winnipeg, Watson & Dwyer, 1980, Norman, OK, University of Oklahoma Press, 1983; Jennifer H. Brown, *Strangers in Blood: Fur Trade Companies' Families in Indian Countries*, Vancouver, University of British Columbia Press, 1980.

11 Cynthia Enloe, *Does Khaki Become You? The Militarization of Women's Lives*, London and Winchester, MA, Pandora Press, 1988.

12 See, for instance, 'Western Women and Imperialism', special issue of *Women's Studies International Forum*, edited by Margaret Strobel and Nupur Chaudhuri, vol. 13, no. 2, 1990.

2 ON THE BEACH: SEXISM AND TOURISM

1 Paul Fussell, 'The Modern Age of Tourism', excerpted from Fussell's *Abroad: British Literary Travelling Between the Wars* in *Utne Reader*, July/August, 1987, p. 105.

2 Shelly Attix, 'Socially Responsible Travel: How to Prevent the Social and Ecological Damage of Tourism', excerpted from *Building Economic Alternatives*, Spring, 1986, in *Utne Reader*, July/August, 1987, p. 109.

3 Among the sharpest critiques of tourism's effects on local cultures is Afro-Caribbean writer Jamaica Kincaid's description of post-colonial Antigua: Jamaica Kincaid, *A Small Place*, London, Virago, 1988; New York, Farrar, Straus & Giroux, 1988. Cultural Survival, an organization devoted to research related to the rights of indigenous peoples, has published a special issue of its journal *Cultural Survival Quarterly*: 'The Tourist Trap: Who's Getting Caught', vol. 6, no. 3, Summer, 1982. A publication monitoring tourism's impact on Third World societies is *Contours: Concern for Tourism*, published by the Ecumenical Coalition on Third World Tourism, 55 m/ 173–4 Saranom 2 Village, Thanon Nuanchan, Sukhapibanl Road, Klong-gum, Bangkapi, Bangkok 10230, Thailand. In Britain the address for *Contours* is c/o Roger Millman, 70 Dry Hill Road, Park Road, Tonbridge, Kent.

4 From Richard Montague's *The Life and Adventures of Mrs. Christian Davies*, 1740, quoted in Julie Wheelwright,'Amazons and Military Maids', *Women's Studies International Forum*, vol. 10, no. 5, 1987, p. 491. See also Julie Wheelwright, *Amazons and Military Maids*, London and Winchester, MA, Pandora Press, 1989.

5 Vita Sackville-West, October 5, 1920, quoted in Nigel Nicolson, *Portrait of a Marriage*, New York, Atheneum, 1973, pp. 109–11. Some Muslim women at this time dressed as men in order to escape the confines of class and gender. On the eve of World War I, Turkish women in the Organization for the Rights of Women launched a campaign to gain for women the right to travel without male consent. One stunt to make their point was a flight in 1913 by Belkis Sekvet, the first Turkish woman to pilot an airplane; she wore men's clothes and meant to demonstrate that women were as brave, and thus as able to travel, as their male counterparts. See Sarah Graham-Brown, *Images of Women: The Portrayal of Women in Photography of the Middle East, 1860–1950*, New York, Columbia University Press, 1988, pp. 142–3.

6 Lisa Wenner with Peggy Perri, 'Pack Up Your Sorrows: The Oral History of an Army Nurse in Vietnam', typescript, Smith College, Northampton, MA, 1986, pp. 15–16. A revised version of this oral history will be published in a volume edited by Peggy Perri and Julia Perez, University of Illinois Press, forthcoming.

7 Mary Seacole, a Black Caribbean woman, is an important exception to the otherwise white Victorian lady travellers. For an account of her adventures in the Crimea and Europe, see Ziggi Alexander and Audrey Dewjee, editors, *Wonderful Adventures of Mrs Seacole in Many Lands*, Bristol, Falling Wall Press, 1984. Two useful guides to the abundant literature written by lady travellers, much of it now in new editions, are: Jane Robinson, editor, *A Bibliography of Women Travellers*, Oxford, Oxford University Press, 1989; Marion Tinling, editor, *Woman into the Unknown: A Source Book on Women Explorers and Travelers*, Westport, CT, Greenwood Press, 1989.

8 Katherine Frank, *A Voyager Out*, New York, Houghton Mifflin, 1986. For a more critical assessment of Mary Kingsley, see Deborah Birkett, 'The Invalid at Home, the Samson Abroad', *Women's Review*, London, no. 6, 1987, pp. 18–19. Also Deborah Birkett, 'West Africa's Mary Kingsley', *History Today*, May, 1987. Deborah Birkett's biography of Mary Kingsley is forthcoming from Macmillan.

9 'Ladies in the Field: The Museum's Unsung Explorers', exhibition at the American Museum of Natural History, New York, December, 1986. The papers and diaries of Delia Akeley, Dina Brodsky, Sally Clark, Mrs Bogoras and Yvette Borup Andrew are available in the museum's Rare Book Department.

10 Robert W. Rydell, *All the World's a Fair: Visions of Empire at the World Expositions 1876–1916*, Chicago, University of Chicago Press, 1984, p. 2.

11 Ibid., p. 118.

12 Jeanne Madeline Weimann, *The Fair Women*, Chicago, Academy Press, 1981. On the 1876 Centennial Exhibition, see William D. Andrews and Deborah C. Andrews, 'Technology and the Housewife in Nineteenth Century America', *Women's Studies*, vol. 2, 1974, pp. 323–4.

13 Louis Turner and John Ash, *The Golden Hordes: International Tourism and the Pleasure Periphery*, New York, St Martin's Press, 1976, pp. 20–21.

14 Maxine Feifer, *Tourism in History: From Imperial Rome to the Present*, New York, Stern & Day, 1986, pp. 10–11. For more on later European travel, especially by male aristocrats in the seventeenth and eighteenth centuries, see John Tower, 'The Grand Tour: A Key Phase in the History of Tourism', *Annals of Tourism Research*, vol. 12, 1985, pp. 297–333; Judith Adler, 'Youth on The Road: Reflections on the History of Tramping', *Annals of Tourism Research*, vol. 12, 1985, pp. 337–50; Susan L. Blake, 'A Woman's Trek: What Difference Does Gender Make?' in Margaret Strobel and Nupur Chaudhuri,

editors, 'Western Women and Imperialism', special issue of *Woman's Studies International Forum*' forthcoming.

15 The principal source of information on Thomas Cook Tours is the Thomas Cook Archives: Edmund Swinglehurst, archivist, 45 Berkeley Street, London W1. The archives hold the collections of Cook's *Excursionist*, launched in 1855, and *Travellers' Gazette*, which made its debut in 1905.

16 Thomas Cook's editorial in the first issue of his *Cook's Exhibition Herald and Excursion Advertiser*, May 31, 1851.

17 Edmund Swinglehurst, 'Miss Matilda Lincolne's Trip to Paris', *Time Traveller*, newsletter of the Thomas Cook Archives, no. 5, January, 1988, p. 2.

18 'How Four Ladies Visited the Rhine', *Cook's Excursionist and Cheap Trip Advertiser*, August 20, 1855, p. 2. In Boston, abolitionist and anti-war campaigner Julia Ward Howe helped launch the Women's Rest Tour Association in 1891. Its upper-class members, eager to travel abroad without male companions, created a file of practical information about places to stay in Europe suitable for respectable women. Today the association and its files exist as the Travel International Exchange; see William A. Davis, 'Travel Exchange is Still Marching On', *Boston Globe*, November 15, 1987.

19 'Across the Class Divide', *The Economist*, January 16, 1988, pp. 47–8; 'Europe's Charter Airlines Love the Summer Weather', *The Economist*, August 1, 1987, p. 57.

20 'Japanese Tourism: Broadening the Mind', *The Economist*, May 7, 1988, p. 64; Susan Chira, 'It's Official! Vacations Really Aren't UnJapanese', *New York Times*, August 6, 1988.

21 Peter Stalker, 'Going Places: Westerners Invade Paradise', *The New Internationalist*, December 1984, excerpted in *Utne Reader*, July/August, 1987, p. 104.

22 Joseph Treaster, 'Caribbean Savors Tourism Boom', *New York Times*, November 7, 1988. On Gulf and Western's sale of its Dominican Republic sugar lands to Florida's Franjui development company, see Joseph Treaster, 'Is There Life After Gulf and Western?', *New York Times*, May 26, 1985. On Japanese tourism earnings, see *New York Times*, September 12, 1987. On Hawaii's sugar-tourism connection, see Walter Cohen, 'Hawaii Faces the Pacific', *Pacific Research*, vol. 6, no. 2, January–February, 1975; Noel Kent, *Islands Under the Influence*, New York, Monthly Review Press, 1979; Jan H. Mejer, 'Capitalist Stages, State Formation and Ethnicity in Hawaii', *National Journal of Sociology*, vol. 1, no. 2, Fall, 1987, pp. 173–207.

23 *New York Times*, June 5, 1988; Erlet A. Carter, 'Tourism in the Least Developed Countries', *Annals of Tourism Research*, vol. 14, 1987; Linda Richter, *The Politics of Tourism in Asia*, Honolulu, University of Hawaii Press, 1988.

24 In 1988 Fidel Castro announced that Cuba would put into effect policies meant to attract 600,000 foreign tourists by 1992. Although he led a revolution which sought to end the tourist industry's corruption of Cuban society, the fall in the international price of sugar, the country's chief export, left the government with no choice but to pursue the tourism strategy: *New York Times*, September 1, 1988. On Vietnam's tourism policies, see Murray Hiebert, 'Enterprise Encouraged to Invigorate the Economy', *Far Eastern Economic Review*, July 23, 1987, p. 31; Barbara Crossette, 'Vietnam for Visitors', *New York Times*, September 13, 1987; Melanie Beresford, 'Revolution in the Countryside: Report on a Visit to Vietnam', *Journal of Contemporary Asia*, vol. 16, no. 3, 1986, p. 399. On North Korean tourist policy, see Derek Hall, 'North Korea Opens to Tourism: A Last Resort', *Inside Asia*, July–August, 1986, pp. 21–2; Nicholas D. Kristof, 'North Korea Tourism Signals New Openness', *New York Times*, September 20, 1987. On Nicaragua's still tentative moves to develop tourism, see Stephen Kinzer, 'Nicaragua's Ideology of Sun and Surf', *New York Times*, November 23, 1988.

25 Air Lanka advertisement, *Far Eastern Economic Review*, May 1, 1986. See also Jane Clarke and Amanda Hood, 'Hostess with the Mostest', *Spare Rib*, October, 1986, pp. 15–17.

26 Jo Stanley, 'Women at Sea', *Spare Rib*, September, 1987, pp. 26–7. See also Henriette Louise, *Sailors in Skirts*, London, Regency Press, 1980; John Maxtone Graham, *Liners to the Sun*, London and New York, Macmillan, 1985. For reports on the now booming cruise-ship industry, see *New York Times*, September 28, 1987 and August 28, 1988. I am indebted to David G. Enloe for his research on ocean-liner crews.

27 Tom Barry, Beth Wood and Deb Preusch, *The Other Side of Paradise*, New York, Grove Press, 1984, p. 85. See also E. Philip English, *The Great Escape: An Examination of North–South Tourism*, Ottawa, North–South Institute, 1986.

28 Jan H. Mejer, op. cit., p. 199; Phyllis Andors, 'Women and Work in Shenshen', *Bulletin of Concerned Asian Scholars*, vol. 20, no. 3, 1988, p. 27.

29 Veronica M. Fenix, 'Beyond 8 to 5: Women Workers Speak Out', in Pennie S. Azarcon, editor, *Kamalayaan: Feminist Writings in the Philippines*, Quezon City, Philippines, Pilipina, 1987, p. 37. Pilipina's

address is: 12 Pasaje de la Paz, Project 4, Quezon City, Philippines. For more on the effects of tourism on women's economic status, see Janice Monk and Charles Alexander, 'Free Port Fallout: Gender, Employment and Migration on Margarita Island', *Annals of Tourism Research*, vol. 13, 1986, pp. 393–413; Shireen Samarasuriya, *Who Needs Tourism? Employment for Women in the Holiday Industry of Sudugama, Sri Lanka*, research project, Women and Development, Colombo, Sri Lanka, 1982.

30 'Britain: Making History Pay', *The Economist*, August 1, 1987, p. 48; Steve Lohr, 'British Find the Past Enriching', *New York Times*, March 29, 1988; *The Independent*, July 4, 1987; Harriet Lamb, 'The Hamburger Economy', *Spare Rib*, October, 1987, p. 27.

31 The population figures come from a Malaysian journalist, Halinah Todd, in her article 'Military Prostitution: Assault on Women', *The Mobilizer*, Mobilization for Survival, Summer, 1987, p. 8. The figures on business establishments come from Pasuk Phongpaichit, 'Bangkok Masseuses: Tourism – Selling Southeast Asia', *Southeast Asian Chronicle*, no. 78, April, 1981, pp. 15–16.

32 According to South Korean feminist Mi Kyung Lee, the South Korean military government made the service industry, and within it the sexualized entertainment industry, one of the major props of its entire development program. The low pay that women in the industry receive compels them to enter the prostitution subsidiary of that industry: Mi Kyung Lee, speaking at the International Trafficking in Women Conference, New York City, October 22, 1988. For a report of the entire conference, see 'The First US Conference on Trafficking in Women Internationally', *Off Our Backs*, December, 1988, pp. 1–5. To contact the conference follow-up committee: The Coalition on Trafficking in Women, Times Square Station, PO Box 2166, New York, NY 10108. An earlier conference to organize women against prostitution is described in Kathleen Barry, Charlotte Bunch and Shirley Castley, editors, *International Feminism: Networking Against Female Sexual Slavery*, New York, International Women's Tribune Center, 777 UN Plaza, New York, NY 10017, 1984. (A Spanish edition translated by Ximena Bunster is also available.)

33 For a graphic account of international sex tourism, see Joni Seager and Ann Olson, *Women in the World: An International Atlas*, London, Pan Books, New York, Simon & Schuster, 1986, map 36. On Goan women organizing to reverse the Indian government's plans for sex tourism development, see Paola Bacchetta, 'Indian

Women Fight Sex Tourism', *Off Our Backs*, January, 1988, p. 12.

34 Quoted in Pasuk Phongpaichit, op. cit. For more on the evolution of the sex-tourism industry in Thailand, see Khin Thitsa, *Providence and Prostitution*, London, Change, International Reports: Women and Society, 1982.

35 'Thailand Stupefied', *The Economist*, August 1, 1987, p. 82; 'Survey – Thailand', *The Economist*, October 31, 1987.

36 *The Economist*, October 8, 1987, p. 8; Barbara Crossette, 'Fear of AIDS Surfaces in Permissive Bangkok', *New York Times*, November 8, 1987. See also Susanne Thorbek, *Voices From the City: Women of Bangkok*, London and Highland, NJ Zed Books, 1987. I am also indebted to Kari Hartwig for sharing with me her unpublished manuscript, 'The Spread of AIDS in Southeast Asia', International Development Program, Clark University, Worcester, MA, 1988.

37 Niramon Prudtotorn, 'Women in Thailand', in *WRI Women*, vol. 2, no. 1, 1988, p. 9: newsletter of the Women's Working Group of War Resisters International, 55 Dawes Street, London SE17 1EL.

38 Quoted from Deborah Dover, *Prostitution in the Philippines: Political Dependency and Sexual Exploitation*, undergraduate thesis, Department of Political Science, Indiana University, Bloomington, IN, 1987. For a complex analysis of prostitution's causes and effects by Filipino commentators, see *Cast the First Stone*, National Council of Churches in the Philippines, 879 Epifmo de los Santos Ave., Quezon City, Philippines, 1987. See also Linda Richter, *Land Reform and Tourism: Policy Making in the Philippines*, Boston, Schenkman Publishers, 1982.

39 A critique of the raids on Ermita's dance-halls is included in Liza Maza and Cath Jackson, 'When the Revolution Came', *Trouble and Strife*, no. 14, Autumn, 1988, pp. 19–22. For more information on anti-prostitution activism, contact Gabriela, PO Box 4386, Manila 2800, Philippines.

40 Liza Maza and Cath Jackson, op. cit.

41 For a report on the First National Consultations on Japayuki held in May 1988 in Japan, see *Flights*, vol. 1, no. 4, June, 1988, pp. 5–6. *Flights* is the newsletter of the Women's Resource and Research Center, Maryknoll College, Quezon City, Philippines. For more on Asian migrant women in Japan, see Ohshima Shizuko, 'Gathering the Fires of Help', and Yamazaki Hiromi, 'Japan Imports Brides: Can Isolated Farmers Buy Consolation?', and Nakamura Hisashi, 'Japan Imports Brides: From a New Poverty Discovered', all in *AMPO*,

vol. 19, no.4. *AMPO* is a critical Japanese political journal written in English.

3 NATIONALISM AND MASCULINITY

1 The North African postcards are displayed and analyzed in Malek Alloula, *The Colonial Harem*, Minneapolis, University of Minnesota Press, 1986, with a helpful introduction by Barbara Harlow.

2 Rana Kabbani, *Europe's Myths of the Orient*, Bloomington, IN, Indiana University Press, 1986, London, Pandora Press, 1988. See also Sarah Graham-Brown, *Images of Women in Photography of the Middle East 1860–1950*, New York, Columbia University Press, 1988; Edward Said, 'Orientalism Reconsidered', *Race and Class*, vol. 27, no. 2, 1985.

3 Sylvia Van Kirk, *Many Tender Ties: Women in Fur-Trade Society, 1670–1870*, Winnipeg, Watson & Dwyer, 1980 Norman, OK, University of Oklahoma Press, 1983; Jennifer S. H. Brown, *Strangers in Blood: Fur Trade Company Families in Indai Country*, Vancouver, University of British Columbia Press, 1980.

4 Mona Etiene and Eleanor Leacock, editors, *Women and Colonization*, New York, Praeger, 1980; Esther Boserup, *Women's Role in Economic Development*, New York, St Martin's Press, 1970; E. Frances White, *Sierra Leone's Settler Women Traders: Women on the Afro-European Frontier*, Ann Arbor, University of Michigan Press, 1987; Beverly Grier, 'Pawns, Porters and Petty Traders: Women in the Transition to Export Agriculture in Ghana', *Signs*, special issue on African women, forthcoming.

5 Marie-Aimée Hélie-Lucas, 'The Role of Women During the Algerian Struggle and After: Nationalism as a Concept and a Practice towards Both the Power of the Army and the Militarization of the People', in Eva Isaksson, editor, *Women and the Military System*, London, Wheatsheaf, New York, St Martin's Press, 1988, p. 186. See also Marie-Aimée Hélie-Lucas, 'Against Nationalism: The Betrayal of Algerian Women', *Trouble and Strife*, no. 11, Summer, 1987, pp. 27–31. See also a contemporary novel by Algerian feminist Fettouma Touati, *Desperate Spring*, London, The Women's Press, 1987; Peter R. Knauss, *The Persistence of Patriarchy: Class, Gender and Ideology in Twentieth Century Algeria*, New York, Praeger, 1987.

6 Hélie-Lucas in Isaksson, op. cit., p. 176. Marie-Aimée Hélie-Lucas has organized an international network to address these issues: Women Living Under Muslim Laws, Combaillaux 34980, France.

7 Cynthia H. Enloe, *Ethnic Conflict and Political Development*, Lanham, MD, University Press of America, 1986; Cynthia H. Enloe, *Ethnic Soldiers: State Security in Divided Societies*, London, Penguin, 1980.

8 The excerpts are from an undated typescript by Pattie (Paxton) Hewitt, held by the Schlesinger Library, Radcliff College, Cambridge, MA.

9 Kathleen Barry, *Susan B. Anthony: A Biography of a Singular Feminist*, New York, New York University Press, 1988, pp. 327–8. Anne Summers's history of British women military nurses suggests some of the contradictions among feminist suffragists on the subject of British imperialism, since proving women's value to the empire was a tempting strategy to use in persuading anti-suffrage male officials: Anne Summers, *Angels and Citizens: British Women as Military Nurses 1854–1914*, London and New York, Routledge & Kegan Paul, 1988, pp. 182–3.

10 American and European women's varied and complex roles in their government's colonizing efforts are analyzed in Margaret Strobel and Nupur Chaudhuri, editors, 'Westren Women and Imperialism', special issue of *Women's Studies International Forum*, vol. 13, no. 2, 1990; Helen Callaway, *Gender, Culture and Empire: European Women in Colonial Nigeria*, London, Macmillan, Chicago, University of Illinois Press, 1987; Jane Hunter, *The Gospel of Gentility: American Women Missionaries in Turn of the Century China*, New Haven, Yale University Press, 1984; Elisabeth Croll, *Wise Daughters from Foreign Lands: The Writings of European Women on China*, London, Pandora Press, 1989; Claudia Knapman, *White Women in Fiji*, London and Winchester, MA, Unwin Hyman, 1989; Margaret Strobel, 'Gender and Race in the Nineteenth and Twentieth Century British Empire', in Renate Bridenthal and Claudia Koonz, editors, *Becoming Visible: Women in European History*, Boston, Houghton Mifflin, revised edition, 1987; Margaret Strobel, *European Women in British Africa and Asia*, Bloomington, IN, Indiana University Press, forthcoming; Patricia R. Hill, *The World Their Household: The American Women's Foreign Mission Movement and Cultural Transformation, 1870–1920*, Ann Arbor, University of Michigan Press, 1988; Helen M. Bannan, 'Womanhood on the Reservation: Field Matrons in the United States Indian Service', Paper no. 18, Southwest Institute for Research on Women, University of Arizona, Tucson, AZ, 1984; Luis Martin, *Daughters of the Conquistadors: Women of the Viceroy of Peru*, Albuquerque, NM, University of New Mexico Press, 1983; Susan Bailey, *Women and the British Empire: An Annotated Guide to Sources*, New York, Garland Publishing Company, 1987; Margaret

Macmillan, *Women of the Raj*, London and New York, Thames & Hudson, 1988; Joanna Trollope, *Britannia's Daughters: Women of the British Empire*, London, Hutchinson, 1983.

11 James Mills, *History of India*, quoted by Mrinalini Sinha, 'Gender and Imperialism: Colonial Policy and the Ideology of Moral Imperialism in Late Nineteenth Century Bengal', in Michael S. Kimmel, editor, *Changing Men: New Directions in Research on Men and Masculinity*, Newbury Park, CA, Sage, 1987, p. 218.

12 Ibid., pp. 218–19.

13 Joanna Liddle and Rama Joshi, 'Gender and Imperialism in British India', *Economic and Political Weekly*, New Delhi, vol. 20, no. 43, October 26, 1985, special supplement on Women's Studies in India, pp. W S72–W S78. See also Joanna Liddle and Rama Joshi, *Daughters of Independence: Gender, Caste and Class in India*, New Delhi, Kali for Women, London, Zed Books, Totowa, NJ, Biblio Distributors, 1986; Kumkum Sangari and Sudesh Vaid, editors, *Recasting Women: Essays in Colonial History*, New Delhi, Kali for Women, 1988; Dagmar Engles, 'The Limits of Gender Ideology: Bengali Women, the Colonial State and the Private Sphere, 1890–1930', *Women's Studies International Forum*, vol. 12, no. 4, 1989.

14 Robert Baden-Powell, *Rovering to Success*, London, Herbert Jenkins, 1922, p. 120.

15 Ibid., pp. 109–10. See also Michael Rosenthal, *The Character Factory: Baden-Powell's Boy Scouts and the Imperatives of Empire*, New York, Pantheon Books, 1986; Raphael Samuel, 'Patriotic Fantasy', *The New Statesman*, July 18, 1986, pp. 20–22; Simon Schama, *The Embarrassment of Riches: An Interpretation of Dutch Culture*, New York, Knopf, 1987. I am indebted to Patrick Miller for his insights into the American debates at the turn of the century over masculinity and imperialism; his dissertation is 'College Sports and American Culture', Department of History, Rutgers University, New Brunswick, NJ, 1988. For new critical thinking on masculinity and the state, see Robert W. Connell, *Gender and Power*, Stanford, Stanford University Press, 1988.

16 Jane Kramer, 'The Eighth Gothic Tale', *New York Review of Books*, July 17, 1986, p. 25. See also Beryl Markham's best-selling autobiography *West with the Night*, San Francisco, North Point Press, 1987; it has been turned into a film. For a biography of Markham, see Mary S. Lovell, *Straight On Till Morning*, New York, St Martin's Press, 1987.

17 Doris Lessing, *The Grass is Singing*, New York, New American Library, 1976; *A Proper Marriage* and *Martha Quest*, New York,

New American Library, 1970. A memoir of another British white woman living on a poor farm in colonial Kenya is Hilda Richards *Next Year Will Be Better*, Lincoln, NE, and London, University of Nebraska Press, 1985.

18 The quote is from the book on which the film is based: James Fox, *White Mischief*, New York, Vintage, 1988, p. 5. The film's director, Michael Radford, justifies the absence of African characters by arguing, 'The people who should make films about Africa are Africans. This I would call a European film set in Africa. In fact, Africa is there by its absence. Where this movie took place is the cradle of mankind. These people [the white characters in *White Mischief*] chose to ignore that, and in the end it destroyed them.' Quoted in Pat Aufderheide, 'Radford's White-Out of Africa', *In These Times*, April 13, 1988, p. 20.

19 Marie-Aimée Hélie-Lucas in Isaksson, op. cit. Cynthia Nelson and Akram Khater, 'al-Harakah al-Nisa'eyya: the Women's Movement and Political Participation in Modern Egypt', *Women's Studies International Forum*, vol. 11, no. 5, 1988; Selma Botman, 'The Experience of Women in the Egyptian Communist Movement, 1939–1954', *Women's Studies International Forum*, vol. 11, no. 2, 1988; Sarah Graham-Brown, op. cit.; Margot Bardon, 'Dual Liberation: Feminism and Nationalism in Egypt, 1870–1925', *Feminist Issues*, vol. 8, no. 1, Spring, 1988; Huda Shaarawi, *Harem Years: The Memories of an Egyptian Feminist*, London, Virago, 1986; Mervat Hatem, 'The Politics of Sexuality and Gender in Segregated Patriarchal Systems: the Case of Eighteenth and Nineteenth Century Egypt', *Feminist Studies*, vol. 12, no. 2, Summer, 1986; Elizabeth Sanasarian, *The Women's Rights Movement in Iran*, New York, Praeger, 1983.

20 Mervat Hatem, 'Through Each Other's Eyes: Egyptian, Levantine-Egyptian and European Women's Images of Themselves and of Each Other, 1862–1920', *Women's Studies International Forum*, forthcoming.

21 Ibid.

22 For further discussion of these tensions, see Nira Yuval-Davis and Floya Anthias, editors, *Woman–Nation–State*, London, Macmillan, 1989; Floya Anthias, Nira Yuval-Davis and Harriet Cain, *Resistance and Control: Racism and 'The Community'*, London and New York, Routledge, 1989.

23 Linda K. Kerber, *Women of the Republic: Intellect and Ideology in Revolutionary America*, Chapel Hill, NC, University of North Carolina Press, 1980; Mary G. Dietz, 'Context is All: Feminism and Theories of Citizenship', *Daedalus*, Fall, 1987, pp. 1–24; Sian

Reynolds, 'Marianne's Citizens? Women, the Republic and Universal Suffrage in France', in Sian Reynolds, editor, *Women, the State and Revolution*, Amherst, MA, University of Massachusetts Press, 1987.

24 'A Letter from the Women's Study Circle of Jaffna', *Women's Studies International Forum*, vol. 12, no. 1, 1989. This point was confirmed by Anita Nesiah, a Sri Lankan feminist, in her lecture, Clark University, Worcester, MA, November 7, 1988.

25 'Philippine Women Say Repression is Worsening', *Listen Real Loud*, American Friends Service Committee, Philadelphia, vol. 9, no. 1, 1988, p. 7.

26 For instance, Sylvia, 'Nicaragua: Working Women in a Women's Brigade', *Off Our Backs*, June, 1988, pp. 12–13; Ailbhe Smyth, guest editor, special issue on 'Feminism in Ireland', *Women's Studies International Forum*, vol. 11, no. 4, 1988; Eileen Fairweather, Roissin McDonough and Melanie McFaryean, *Only the Rivers Run Free – Northern Ireland: The Women's War*, London, Pluto Press, 1984; Ailbhe Smyth, Pauline Jackson, Caroline McCamley, Ann Speed, 'States of Emergence', *Trouble and Strife*, no. 14, Autumn, 1988, pp. 46–52; The Clio Collective, *Quebec Women: A History*, Toronto, Women's Press, 1987; Stephanie Urdang, *And Still They Dance: Women, War and the Struggle for Change in Mozambique*, New York, Monthly Review Press, 1989.

27 Henry Kamm, 'Afghan Peace Could Herald War of Sexes', *New York Times*, December 12, 1988.

28 Henry Kamm, 'Afghanistan Refugee Women Suffering from Isolation Under Islamic Custom', *New York Times*, March 27, 1988; Donatella Lorch, 'An Afghan Exile, Her School and Hopes for the Future', *New York Times*, June 12, 1988; Doris Lessing, *The Wind Blows Away Our Words*, New York, Vintage Books, 1987, pp. 77–80.

29 Laura Cumming, 'Forgotten Struggle for the Western Sahara', *New Statesman*, May 20, 1988, pp. 14–15.

30 Curtis Wilkie, 'Roles Change for Palestinian Women', *Boston Globe*, May 17, 1988.

31 Ellen Cantarow, 'Palestinian Women Resisting Occupation', *Sojourner*, April, 1988, p. 19. See also Beata Lipman, *Israel – The Embattled Land: Jewish and Palestinian Women Talk about Their Lives*, London and Winchester, MA, Pandora Press, 1988; Hamida Kazi, 'Palestinian Women and the National Liberation Movement', in Mageda Salman, et al., *Women in the Middle East*, London, Zed Books, 1987.

32 Hue-Tam Ho-Tai, lecture, Clark University, Worcester, MA, October 25, 1987.

33 David Marr, *Vietnamese Tradition on Trial, 1920–1945*, Berkeley, University of California Press, 1981; Kumari Jayawardena, *Feminism and Nationalism in the Third World*, London, Zed Books, New Delhi, Kali for Women, Totowa, NJ, Biblio Distribution, 1986, pp. 196–212.

34 I am grateful to Christine White of Cornell University for introducing me to two accounts of Vietnamese women who fought as guerrillas in the nationalist movement: Nguyen Thi Dinh, *No Other Road to Take*, translated by Mai V. Elliott, data paper no. 102, Southeast Asia Program, Cornell University, Ithaca, NY, June, 1976; Phan Thi Nhu Bang, *Ta Thi Kieu: An Heroic Girl of Bentre*, South Vietnam, Liberation Editions, 1966.

35 Sophie Quinn Judge, 'Vietnamese Women: Neglected Promises', *Indochinese Issues*, no. 42, December, 1983. See also Christine White, 'On Promissory Notes', and 'Vietnamese Socialism and the Politics of Gender Relations', both in Sonia Kruks, Rayna Rapp, Marilyn Young, editors, *Promissory Notes: Women in the Transition to Socialism*, New York, Monthly Review Press, 1989.

36 Jayawardena, op., cit. p. 1.

37 Conversations with Anita Nesiah and Kumari Jayawadena, Cambridge, MA, March, 1988. South Asian lesbians in the United States publish a newsletter that grapples with some of these same issues: *Anamika*, Brooklyn, NY. In *Anamika*, vol. 1, no. 2, March, 1986, a Sri Lankan lesbian describes Sri Lankan society as tolerant and/or ambivalent towards homosexuality, permitting a substantial degree of intimacy between women. But the pressure for a woman to marry is great, and the only women living as lesbians that this author knew were upper-class women living in the capital, Colombo. Jamaican feminists were taunted with charges of 'lesbian' too: Sistren, with Honor Ford Smith, *Lionheart Gal*, London, The Women's Press, 1986, p. xxvi. Irish lesbians' relationships to nationalism are discussed in *Out for Ourselves: The Lives of Irish Lesbians and Gay Men*, Dublin, Dublin Lesbian and Gay Men's Collective and Women's Community Press, 1986. Also helpful: Carmen, Shaila, Pratibha, 'Becoming Visible: Black Lesbians Discuss Feminism', in *Feminist Review*, special issue on Black women in Britain, no. 17, Autumn, 1984.

38 E. Frances White, 'Africa on my Mind', lecture, Clark University, Worcester, MA, March 31, 1988, part of a larger project on Black feminism for Pandora Press, forthcoming. See also: Ayesha Mei-Tje Imam, 'The Presentation of African Women in Historical Writing', in S. Jay Kleinberg, editor, *Retrieving Women's History*, Oxford and New York, Berg, 1988.

39 Sistren, with Honor Ford Smith, op. cit., p. xxiii.

40 Delia Aguilar, 'On the Women's Movement Today', *Midweek*, Manila, November 9, 1988.

4 BASE WOMEN

1 E. P. Thompson, 'Introduction', in E. P. Thompson, Mary Kaldor et al., *Mad Dogs: The US Raids on Libya*, London, Pluto Press, 1987, p. 6.
2 Michael Kidron and Dan Smith, *The War Atlas*, London, Pan Books, New York, Simon & Schuster, 1983, map 17. See also 'Pulling Back', a report on US bases policies by the American Friends Service Committee, Philadelphia; *New York Times*, December 23 and December 25, 1988.
3 Duncan Campbell, *The Unsinkable Aircraft Carrier: American Military Power in Britain*, London, Paladin Books, 1986.
4 Ibid., p. 16.
5 The following account draws on Graham Smith, *When Jim Crow Met John Bull: Black American Soldiers in World War II Britain*, London, I. B. Travis, 1987; New York, St Martin's Press, 1988. Also, Mary Penick Motley, editor, *The Invincible Soldier: The Experience of the Black Soldier, World War II*, Detroit, Wayne State University Press, 1987.
6 On racial policies in the armed forces, see Cynthia H. Enloe, *Ethnic Soldiers: State Security in Divided Societies*, London, Penguin, 1980.
7 Graham Smith, op. cit., p. 188.
8 Ibid., pp. 192–3. An oral history of Black American women in military service during the World Wars is being compiled by Julia Perez, William Joiner Center, University of Massachusetts, Boston.
9 Graham Smith, op. cit., p. 186.
10 Ibid., p. 200.
11 John Costello, *Virtue Under Fire: How World War II Changed Our Social and Sexual Attitudes*, Boston, Little, Brown & Company, 1985, p. 254. On British women who married Canadian soldiers, see Joyce Hibbert, *War Brides*, Toronto, New American Library of Canada, 1980.
12 Graham Smith, op. cit., p. 206.
13 Norman Lewis, 'Essex', *Granta*, no. 23, London and New York, Penguin, Spring, 1988, p. 112.
14 On military wives, see Myna Trustram, *Women of the Regiment: Marriage and the Victorian Army*, Cambridge and New York, Cambridge University Press, 1984; Cynthia Enloe, *Does Khaki Become You? The Militarization of Women's Lives*, London and Winchester, MA, Pandora Press, 1988; Mona Macmillan, 'Campfollower: A

Note on Wives in the Armed Forces', in Hilary Callan and Shirley Ardener, editors, *The Incorporated Wife*, London, Croom Helm, 1984; Rosemary McKechnie, 'Living with Images of a Fighting Elite: Women and the Foreign Legion', in Sharon Macdonald, Pat Holden and Shirley Ardener, editors, *Images of Women in Peace and War*, London, Macmillan, 1987, Madison, WI, University of Wisconsin Press, 1988, pp. 122–47; a play depicting British army wives' lives, Gillian Richmond, *The Last Waltz*, available from Valerie Hoskins, Eagle House, 109 Jermyn Street, London, SW1; research in progress by Helena Terry, Women's Studies, York University, Toronto, Canada; on Canadian military wives' organizing, Lucie Richardson Laliberté, Law School, Queens University, Kingston, Ontario, Canada; Ximena Bunster, 'Watch Out for the Little Nazi Man That All of Us Have Inside: The Mobilization and Demobilization of Women in Militarized Chile', *Women's Studies International Forum*, vol. 11, no. 5, 1988.

15 On American military daughters' reactions to living on military bases, Mary Wertsch, *Military Brats: Legacies of Childhood Inside the Fortress*, New York, Crown, forthcoming. On the social networks created by British officers out of their enclosed worlds, Barbara Rogers, *Men Only*, London and Winchester, MA, Pandora Press, 1988.

16 Quoted in the *New York Times*, March 20, 1988. See also 'The Flip Side of Volunteering', *Washington Report*, October/November, 1987, p. 3: published by Women's Equity Action League, 1250 I Street NW, Washington, D C 20005.

17 *New York Times*, December 18, 1988.

18 Correspondence with Janice Hill, Women and the Military Project, Military Counseling Network, Rottenburg, West Germany, July, 1988.

19 Quoted by Joan Smith, 'Ghost Riders in the Sky', *New Statesman and Society*, June 10, 1988, p. 16.

20 Ibid., p. 17.

21 Norman Lewis, op. cit., p. 115.

22 Ibid., p. 116.

23 Lynchcombe, *At Least Cruise is Clean*, UK, Niccolo Press, 1984.

24 Ibid.

25 Alice Cook and Gwyn Kirk, *Greenham Women Everywhere*, London, Pluto, Boston, South End Press, 1983.

26 Lynne Jones, 'Perceptions of Peace Women at Greenham Common 1981–1985', in Sharon Macdonald, et al., op. cit., pp. 179–204.

27 Beatrix Campbell, *The Iron Ladies: Why Do Women Vote Tory?*, London, Virago, 1987, p. 126.

28 For a map of women's peace camps: Joni Seager and Ann Olson, *Women in the World: An International Atlas*, London, Pan Books, New York, Simon & Schuster, 1987, map 39.

29 Members of the Faslane peace camp, *Faslane: Diary of a Peace Camp*, Edinburgh, Polygon Books, 1984, p. 78. For debates within all-women and mixed peace camps, see *We Are Ordinary Women: A Chronicle of the Puget Sound Women's Peace Camp*, Seattle, Seal Press, 1985; Jane Held, 'The British Peace Movement: A Critical Examination of Attitudes to Male Violence within the British Peace Movement, as Expressed with Regard to the "Molesworth Rapes" ', *Women's Studies International Forum*, vol. 11, no. 3, 1988, pp. 211–21.

30 Rebecca Johnson, quoted in Cook and Kirk, op. cit,. p. 68.

31 Yarrow Cleaves, 'Greenham Common: One World, Many Women', in *Greenham Women Against Cruise Missiles*, a newsletter edited by Gwyn Kirk, 339 Lafayette Street, New York, NY 10012, December, 1988.

32 Rebecca Green, 'Greenham to Aldermaston', *Everywoman*, February, 1988. *We Are Ordinary Women*, op, cit., also describes a peace camp outside a weapons factory.

33 Mariano Aguirre, 'Spain's Nuclear Allergy', *The Nation*, December 26, 1988, pp. 722–3. John Gilbert, 'F-16s Find a New Home After Spain Evicts Them', *The Guardian* (US), February 24, 1988, pp. 16–17. Elisabetta Addis, an editor of the Italian peace journal *Giano*, suggests that Italian feminists and peace activists did not mount a campaign against acceptance of the new US base in part because they were preoccupied with the issue of the Palestinian uprising on the West Bank and in part because it was difficult to galvanize local opposition given the economic depression in the region selected for the base: conversation, Cambridge, MA, December 10, 1988.

34 James Markham, 'Over the Screeching Jets, Germans Cry Enough', *New York Times*, August 10, 1988. I am indebted to Peter Armitage and Wendy Mishkin of Labrador for sharing information about the impact assessments and local debates surrounding the proposed expansion of the Goose Bay air force base.

35 Alexander Alexiev, *Inside the Soviet Army in Afghanistan*, Santa Monica, CA, Rand Corporation, 1988.

36 Joanna Liddle and Rama Joshi, 'Gender and Imperialism in British India', *Economic and Political Weekly*, New Delhi, vol. 20, no. 43, October 26, 1985, special supplement on Women's Studies in India, p. WS–74. See also Kenneth Ballhatchet, *Race and Sex and Class under the Raj*, London, Weidenfeld & Nicolson, 1980.

37   *The Dawn*, no. 1, May, 1888, p. 5. The collected volumes of *The Dawn* are available at the Fawcett Library, City of London Polytechnic, London. For a feminist interpretation of Josephine Butler's attitudes toward imperialism, see Antoinette Burton, 'The White Woman's Burden: British Feminists and 'The Indian Woman', 1865–1915'', in Margaret Strobel and Nupur Chaudhuri, guest editors, 'European Women and Imperialism', special issue of *Women's Studies International Forum*, vol. 13, no. 2, 1990.

38   *The Dawn*, no. 27, May, 1895, pp. 1–2.

39   On military prostitution debates in the US see Allan Brandt, *No Magic Bullet*, Oxford and New York, Oxford University Press, 1987; Katherine Bushnell, 'Plain Words to Plain People', a World War I pamphlet, undated, Schlesinger Library, Radcliffe College, Cambridge, MA; Cynthia Enloe, *Does Khaki Become You?* op. cit. The Canadian debate about soldiers' sexuality during World War II is discussed in Ruth Roach Pierson, *'They're Still Women Afterall': The Second World War and Canadian Womanhood*, Toronto, McClelland & Stewart, 1986.

40   Jessie Anglum, unpublished diary, 1901–1902, Schlesinger Library, Radcliffe College, Cambridge, MA.

41   Alexander R. Magno, 'Cornucopia or Curse: The Internal Debate on the US Bases in the Philippines', *Kasarinlan*, Third World Studies Program, University of the Philippines, Quezon City, vol. 3, no. 3, 1988, pp. 9–12; Pilar Ramos-Jimenez and Elena Chiong-Javier, 'Social Benefits and Costs: People's Perceptions of the US Bases in the Philippines', Research Center, De La Salle University, Manila, 1987, pp. 9–10; *Philippine Resource Center Monitor*, no. 3, August 12, 1988, available from PO Box 40090, Berkeley, CA 94704.

42   Ramos-Jimenez and Chiong-Javier, op. cit., p. 16.

43   Ibid., p. 17.

44   Sr. Mary John Mananzan, editor, *Essays on Women*, Manila, St Scholastica's College, 1987; Pennie S. Azarcon, editor, *Kamalayan: Feminist Writings in the Philippines*, 12 Pasaje de la Paz, Quezon City, Pilipina, 1987; Sergy Floro and Nana Luz, editors, *Sourcebook on Philippine Women in Struggle*, Berkeley, CA, Philippine Resource Center, 1985.

45   Jacquelyn K. Davis, 'Summary of Findings of 1987 DACOWITS WestPac Trip', memo to the Secretary of Defense Casper Weinberger, August 26, 1987, p. 6.

46   Ibid.; Nonna Cheatham, 'Report of DACOWITS Spring, 1988 Meeting', *Minerva*, vol. 6, no. 2, Summer, 1988, pp. 1–42; testimony

of Carolyn Becraft, Women's Equity Action League, House of Representatives Armed Services Committee, Subcommittee on Personnel, October 1, 1987.
47 'AIDS is Here! Fight AIDS!', *Women's World*, ISIS, no. 14, 1987, p. 37.
48 Ibid., p. 38.
49 *Christian Science Monitor*, February 18, 1988.
50 Jacqui Alexander, an Afro-Caribbean feminist and sociologist, has reported that Belizean women activists believe that British authorities are bringing Guatemalan women into Belize to provide sexual services for British soldiers stationed there; this has caused some tension between Belizean and Guatemalan women. Jacqui Alexander, in conversation, Cambridge, MA, December 1988.
51 Sister Soledad Perpinan, one of the founders of CAMP, Third World Movement Against the Exploitation of Women, Manila, Philippines; lecture at Clark University, Worcester, MA, April, 1987; Leopoldo Moselina, 'Prostitution and Militarization', in *Cast the First Stone*, Quezon City, World Council of Churches in the Philippines, 1987, pp. 49–65; Saundra Sturdevant, 'The Bargirls of Subic Bay', *The Nation*, April 3, 1989, pp. 444–6.
52 For more on the impact of military bases on Pacific women and women's anti-nuclear activism in the Pacific, see Jane Dibblin, *Day of Two Suns: US Nuclear Testing and the Pacific Islands*, London, Virago, 1988. Also, Women Working for a Nuclear Free and Independent Pacific, c/o Beech Range, Levenshulme, Manchester, M19 2EO.

5 DIPLOMATIC WIVES

1 Governor Sir George Simpson, quoted by Sylvia Van Kirk, *Many Tender Ties: Women in Fur-Trade Society, 1670–1870*, Winnipeg, Watson & Dwyer, 1980, Norman, OK, University of Oklahoma Press, 1983, p. 93.
2 Ibid., pp. 75–84.
3 Julie Wheelwright, *Amazons and Military Maids: Women Who Dressed as Men in Pursuit of Life, Liberty and Happiness*, London and Winchester, MA, Pandora Press, 1989.
4 Van Kirk, op. cit., pp. 192–4. Also: Clio Collective, *Quebec Women: A History*, Toronto, Women's Press, 1987, pp. 40–46.
5 Cynthia Enloe, *Does Khaki Become You? The Militarization of Women's Lives*, London and Winchester, MA, Pandora Press, 1988.
6 Beryl Smedley, *Partners in Diplomacy*, fothcoming.
7 Ibid.

8 Victoria Glendinning, *Vita: A Biography of Vita Sackville-West*, New York, Quill, 1983, p. 157.

9 Beryl Smedley, interview with the author, Byfleet, England, February 2, 1987.

10 Sue Pilkington, 'Lady in Waiting', *The Guardian*, September 14, 1988. See also Jane Ewart-Biggs, *Pay, Pack and Follow*, London, Weidenfeld & Nicolson, 1984; Jane Ewart-Biggs, *Lady in the Lords*, London, Weidenfeld & Nicolson, 1988.

11 Statements by Sir John Nicholas, Britain's ambassador to Sri Lanka, and David Gore-Booth, Britain's ambassador to the United Nations, quoted in Simon Jenkins and Ann Sloman, *With Respect, Ambassador: An Inquiry into the Foreign Office*, London, BBC, 1985, p. 63.

12 Lady Wade-Gery, quoted in ibid., pp. 64–5.

13 Sir Oliver Wright, quoted in ibid., p. 79.

14 Ibid.

15 Victoria McKee, 'National Velvet, Patriotic Silk', *Sunday Times*, December 12, 1988, p. 39.

16 Much of the following information is derived from an interview with Gay Murphy, then chair of the Diplomatic Service Wives Association, London, January 30, 1987. Additional information comes from the DWSA's periodical publication.

17 DWSA publication, Autumn, 1986, p. 28.

18 Ibid., p. 20.

19 Ibid., p. 28.

20 Gay Murphy, interview.

21 Gay Murphy, interview.

22 Interview by the author with a Washington-based advocate for women in the military and military wives, April 3, 1987.

23 Interviews by the author with Washington-based activists working on issues relating to the rights of women married to government employees, Washington, April 3, 1987, and May 6, 1987.

24 Barbara Gamarekian, 'Foreign Service Wives' Goal: Pay', *New York Times*, April 10, 1984.

25 Ibid.

26 Susan Parsons, Family Liaison Officer, US State Department, interview with the author, Washington, May 4, 1987.

27 Ibid. See the Association of American Foreign Service Women, *Report on the Foreign Service Families in Situations of International Crisis*, Washington, DC , July 1, 1983; Forum of the Association of American Foreign Service Women, 'The Role of the Spouse in the Foreign Service', Washington, DC, February, 1985. I am indebted

to Pamela Moffat, AAFSW President, for sharing these reports with me.

28 'One Wife's Story', *New York Times*, April 10, 1984.

29 Interviews with US Foreign Service wives, Washington, May 4, 1987, and May 6, 1987.

30 Interview by the author with Mary Ann White, whose husband Robert White resigned from his post as US ambassador to El Salvador in protest over the Reagan administration's military policies in Central America, Washington, May 5, 1987.

31 A four-part series on 'America's Fading Foreign Service', by John Goshko, *Washington Post*, April 26, 27, 28, 29, 1987. Also see Elaine Sciolino, 'Austerity is Said to Gain on Diplomacy at State', *New York Times*, November 15, 1987.

32 Interview by the author with Pamela Moffat, President, Association of American Foreign Service Women, Washington, May 6, 1987.

33 For more on institutionalized wives, see Hilary Callan and Shirley Ardener, editors, *The Incorporated Wife*, London, Croom Helm, 1984; Janet Finch, *Married to the Job: Wives in Corporations in Men's Work*, London and Boston, George Allen & Unwin, 1983.

34 From interviews in Britain, January 22, 1987.

35 Interviews by the author with Nien Ling Lieu, a Chinese writer and feminist now living in the United States: Cambridge, MA, March 30, 1987, and May 9, 1987.

36 Nien Ling Lieu, interview.

37 Interview by the author with a former teacher in China, Cambridge, MA, May, 1987.

38 Jenkins and Sloman, op. cit., p. 25.

39 Sir Oliver Wright quoted in ibid., p. 31.

40 *The Guardian*, November 25, 1986.

41 Ibid.

42 *The Independent*, January 28, 1987.

43 Jean Joyce, interviewed by Valerie Kreutzer, Women's Action Organization Oral History Project, typescript, n. d., p. 10, Schlesinger Library, Radcliffe College, Cambridge, MA.

44 Ibid., p. 14.

45 Interviews by Barbara Good and Nira Long in ibid.

46 Ibid.

47 Elizabeth Cotton, 'Morning Edition', National Public Radio, April 22 1987.

48 Phyllis Oakley, quoted by John Goshko, 'Tackling a White Male Bastion', *Washington Post*, April 29, 1987.

49 Elizabeth Cotton, op. cit.

50 Ibid. A year later President Reagan appointed Robert Oakley, Phyllis Oakley's husband, acting ambassador to Pakistan, on the understanding that 'a job would be found in Pakistan for Mrs Oakley'. *New York Times*, August 22, 1988.
51 Mary S. Olmstead, Bernice Baer, Jean Joyce and Georgina M. Prince, *Women at State: An Inquiry into the Status of Women in the United States Department of State*, Washington, DC, Women's Research and Education Institute, 1987, p. 11.
52 Figures for September 1987, derived from data supplied to the author by the Equal Opportunities Office of the US Department of State in June, 1988. See also: Equal Opportunities Office, US Department of State, '1987 Annual Report to Congress', Washington, DC, September 1987.
53 'Military Policy: Subject of WEAL Panel at 18th Women and Law Conference', *Minerva*, Fall, 1987, p. 42. See also Barbara Ann Scott, 'Help Wanted: Women Defense Experts and Decision-Makers', *Minerva*, vol. 6, no. 4, Winter, 1988. Scott's survey of all US civil departments and agencies responsible for national security policy revealed that women occupied only forty-four out of 1,015 policy-making posts, that is, 4.3 per cent.
54 Olmstead, et al., op. cit., pp. 22, 29. See also Joan Hoff-Wilson, 'Conclusion: Of Mice and Men', in Edward P. Crapol, editor, *Women and American Foreign Policy*, Westport, CT, and London, Greenwood Press, 1987, pp. 173–88. An organization recently formed to increase American women's influence in foreign policy making is the Women's Foreign Policy Council, 1133 Broadway, New York, NY 10010.
55 'Under Pressure, State Department Moves to End its Sex Discrimination', *New York Times*, April 21, 1989.
56 Goshko, op. cit.
57 Judith Hippler Bello and Marian Barell, quoted by Clyde H. Farnsworth, 'A Difference in Societies that Can Give US Edge in Talks', *New York Times*, July 4, 1988.
58 *New York Times*, December 6, 1984.
59 Catherine Watson, 'Appendix: Working at the Bank', in Teresa Hayter and Catherine Watson, *Aid: Rhetoric and Reality*, London, Pluto Press, 1985, pp. 271–2.
60 Ibid.
61 Susan Mendaro, quoted in *New York Times*, December 6, 1984.
62 'UN Women Unhappy', *Off Our Backs*, April, 1984, p. 6.
63 Yolanda Samayoa, quoted in ibid.
64 *New York Times*, April 19, 1987.

65 Mercedes Pulido de Briceno, quoted by Elaine Sciolino, 'Equality Remains an Elusive Goal for UN Women', *New York Times*, September 11, 1985.

66 Ibid.

67 General Assembly, 'Personnel Questions: Other Personnel Questions – Improvement of the Status of Women in the Secretariat, Report of the Secretary General', New York, United Nations, November 3, 1987, p. 7.

68 Ibid.

6 CARMEN MIRANDA ON MY MIND: INTERNATIONAL POLITICS OF THE BANANA

1 James Robert Parish, *The Fox Girls*, New Rochell, NY, Arlington House, 1972, pp. 499–528.

2 Ibid., p. 504.

3 George Black, *The Good Neighbor: How the United States Wrote the History of Central America and the Caribbean*, New York, Pantheon, 1988, pp. 68–71. See also Neal Gabler, *An Empire of their Own: How the Jews Invented Hollywood*, New York, Crown, 1988.

4 Eduardo Galeano, *Century of the Wind*, New York, Pantheon, 1988, p. 131. For Galeano's description of Hollywood's Latin American male stereotype in the 1940s, see p. 122.

5 Claire Shaver Houghton, *Green Immigrants: The Plants that Transformed America*, New York and London, Harcourt Brace Jovanovich, 1978, pp. 30–5. Also, *People Like Bananas*, Boston, United Fruit Company, 1968.

6 *People Like Bananas*, op. cit. Chiquita Brands, a subsidiary of United Brands (formerly United Fruit), publishes a newsletter, *Chiquita Quarterly*, which makes regular mention of the company's shipping fleet, the world's largest refrigerated shipping fleet, 12 per cent of the world's total.

7 Black, op. cit., pp. 77–8. For a critical assessment of American banana companies' political role in Central America, see Stephen Schlesinger, *Bitter Fruit: The Untold Story of the American Coup in Guatemala*, New York, Doubleday, 1982.

8 I am grateful to Beth C. Schwartz of United Brands for providing the original lyrics of the Chiquita Banana song.

9 Advertisement, *The Economist*, December 5, 1987.

10 For a detailed investigation of the Japanese banana industry, see 'AMPO', *Japan and Asia Quarterly Review*, vol. 13, no. 3, 1981.

11 Books and articles analyzing the gendered character of plantation agriculture include Angela Davis, 'Reflections on the Black Women's Role in the Community of Slaves', *The Black Scholar*, no. 3, December,1971; Rhoda Reddock, 'Women and the Slave Plantation Economy in the Caribbean', in S. Jay Kleinberg, editor, *Retrieving Women's History*, Oxford and New York, Berg, 1988, pp. 105–32. Jacqueline Jones, *Labor of Love, Labor of Sorrow: Black Women, Work and the Family from Slavery to the Present*, New York, Vintage, 1986; Elizabeth Fox-Genovese, *Within the Plantation Household: Black and White Women of the Old South*, Chapel Hill, NC, University of North Carolina, 1988; Ronald Takaki, *Pau Hana: Plantation Life and Labor in Hawaii*, Honolulu, University of Hawaii Press, 1983; Belinda Coote, *The Hunger Crop: Poverty and the Sugar Industry*, Oxford, Oxfam, 1987; Shaista Shameen, 'Gender, Class and Race Dynamics: Indian Women in Sugar Production in Fiji', *The Journal of Pacific Studies*, special issue, 'Women and Work in the Pacific', vol. 13, 1987, pp. 10–35; Sidney Mintz, *Worker in the Cane: A Puerto Rican Life History*, New Haven, Yale University Press, 1960; Laurel Herbener Bossen, *The Redivision of Labor: Women and Economic Choice in Four Guatemalan Communities*, Albany, SUNY Press, 1984; Noeleen Heyzer, *Working Women in South-East Asia*, Milton Keynes and Philadelphia, Open University Press, 1986; Ravinda K. Jain, *South Indians on the Plantation Frontier in Malaya*, New Haven, Yale University Press, 1970; Ann Laura Stoler, *Capitalism and Confrontation in Sumatra's Plantation Belt, 1870–1979*, New Haven, Yale University Press, 1985; Rachel Kurian, *Women Workers in the Sri Lanka Plantation Belt*, Geneva, International Labor Organization, 1982; Rachel Kurian, 'Ethnicity, Patriarchy and Labor Control: Tamil Women in Plantation Production', Institute of Social Sciences, The Hague, 1986; Dan Jones, *Tea and Justice: British Tea Companies and the Tea Workers of Bangladesh*, London, Bangladesh International Action Group, 1986; Maitrayee Mukhopadhyay, *Silver Shackles: Women and Development in India*, Oxford, Oxfam, 1984; Stella Hillier and Lynne Gerlach, *Whose Paradise? Tea and the Plantation Tamils in Sri Lanka*, London, Minority Rights Group, 1987.

12 Philippe Bourgois, *Ethnic Diversity on a Corporate Plantation*, Cambridge, MA, Cultural Survival, 1986.

13 Ibid., pp. 10–11.

14 'The Banana Man', song written by Jamaican writer Evan Jones in 1952, reproduced in *Whose Gold? Geest and the Banana Trade*, London, Latin America Bureau, 1987, p. 12.

15   On the feminization of agriculture and its developmental conse-
     quences, see Esther Boserup, *Women's Roles in Economic Development*,
     London, George Allen & Unwin, 1970; Barbara Rogers, *The Domes-
     tication of Women: Discrimination in Developing Societies*, London,
     Kogan Page, 1980. For a perceptive examination of the gender and
     ethnic hierarchies that support a multinational mining company's
     operations in Indonesia, see Kathryn M. Robinson, *Stepchildren of
     Progress*, Albany, State University of New York Press, 1986.
16   Philippe Bourgois, Department of Anthropology, Washington Uni-
     versity, St Louis, in correspondence with the author, October 2,
     1986.
17   See Susan Bridger, *Women in the Soviet Countryside*, Cambridge and
     New York, Cambridge University Press, 1987; Sharon L. Wolchik
     and Alfred G. Meyer, editors, *Women, State and Party in Eastern
     Europe*, Durham, Duke University Press, 1988.
18   Elizabeth U. Eviota, 'The Articulation of Gender and Class in the
     Philippines', in Eleanor Leacock and Helen I. Safa and contributors,
     Women's Work, South Hadley, MA, Bergin & Garvey, 1986, p.
     199. Also correspondence with Philippe Bourgois, October 2 1986.
     On women working in the food-processing business, see Lourdes
     Arizpe and Josephina Aranda, 'Women Workers in the Strawberry
     Agribusiness in Mexico', in Leacock and Safa, op. cit., pp. 174–93;
     Vicki Ruiz, *Cannery Women, Cannery Lives*, Albuquerque, NM,
     University of New Mexico Press, 1987; Patricia Zavella, *Women's
     Work and Chicano Families*, Ithaca, NY, Cornell University Press,
     1987.
19   Sr. Mary Soledad Perpinan, 'Women and Transnational Corpora-
     tions: The Philippines Experience', reprinted in Daniel Schirmer
     and Stephen R. Shalom, editors, *The Philippines Reader*, Boston,
     South End Press, 1987, p. 243.
20   Quoted in the slide-show, 'Bananas', produced by a progressive
     Filipino organization in the early 1980s. For a description of women
     workers' lives on Dole's pineapple plantations in the Philippines,
     see 'Women of Dole', originally published in *Womenews*, vol. 3,
     no. 1, January–March, 1986, reprinted in *Philippine Women*,
     NY, Women's International Resources Exchange, 1987. On Castle
     and Cook's banana and pineapple operations in the Philippines,
     see Dorothy Friesen, *Critical Choices: A Journey with the Filipino
     People*, Grand Rapids, MI, William B. Eerdmans Publishing Co.,
     1988. For an assessment of policies needed to ensure redistribution
     of plantation land – much of it leased from large Filipino landowners,
     not owned outright by the foreign companies – see Yujio Hayami,

Lourdes S. Adriano and Agnes R. Quisumbing, *Agribusiness and Agrarian Reform: A View from the Banana and Pineapple Plantations*, Quezon City, Center for Policy and Development Studies, University of the Philippines, 1988.

21   Eduardo Galeano, op. cit., p. 73.
22   Clive Thomas, *Plantations, Peasants and the State*, Los Angeles, Center for Afro-American Studies, UCLA, 1984.
23   Ann Laura Stoler, op. cit., pp. 30–34.
24   Correspondence with Philippe Bourgois, October 2, 1986.
25   Information on Geest comes from: *Geest Gold: Bananas and Dependency in the Eastern Caribbean*, London, Latin American Bureau, and New York, Monthly Review Press, 1987; *Whose Gold*, op. cit. For information on women's and men's relationships in Zaïre's banana farming, see Catherine Newbury, 'From Bananas to Cassava', typescript, Department of Political Science, University of North Carolina, Chapel Hill, NC, 1985.
26   'Britain's Rich', *Sunday Times* colour supplement, April 2, 1989 p. 41.
27   *Geest Gold*, op. cit., pp. 45–6. See also Pat Ellis, editor, *Women of the Caribbean*, London, Zed Books, and Atlantic Highlands, NJ, Humanities Press, 1986; *Daughters of the Nightmare: Women in the Caribbean*, London, Change, International Reports on Women, 1983.
28   Gita Sen and Caren Grown, *Development, Crises and Alternative Visions: Third World Women's Perspectives*, New York, Monthly Review Press, 1987; Troth Wells and Foo Gaik Sim, *Till They Have Faces: Women as Consumers*, Penang and Rome, International Organization of Consumers' Unions, Regional Office for Asia and ISIS International, 1987; Ng Sock Nye, 'Status of Rural Women', in Evelyn Hong, editor, *Malaysian Women: Problems and Issues*, Penang, Consumers' Association of Penang, 1983, pp. 38–48; Lucy E. Creevey, editor, *Women Farmers in Africa*, Syracuse, Syracuse University Press, 1986; Barbara Rogers, op. cit.; Georgina Ashworth, *Of Conjuring and Caring: Women in Development*, London, Change, International Reports on Women, 1984; Peggy Antrobus, 'Feminist Issues in Development', *Reports*, World Education, Boston, Fall, 1987, pp. 5–8; Bina Agarwal, *Structures of Patriarchy, the State, the Community and the Household*, New Delhi, Kali for Women, London, Zed Books, 1988.
29   Elizabeth Odour, a Kenyan environmental expert, has noted the problems of plantation expansion for her country's environment, making the connection between women's concerns and environmental issues: conversation with the author, Clark University, Worcester, MA, December, 1988.

30 Elvia Alvarado, with Medea Benjamin, *Don't Be Afraid, Gringo*, San Francisco, Food First, 1987.

31 'Bananas, Broomsticks and Bookshelves', *Pueblo to People*, holiday issue, 1988, pp. 22–3.

32 'Organizing Malaysian Women Workers', *Voices Rising: A Bulletin about Women and Popular Education*, International Council for Adult Education, Toronto, May/June, 1987, p. 19.

33 Sistren, with Honor Ford Smith, *Lionheart Gal: Life Stories of Jamaican Women*, London, The Women's Press, 1986.

34 Chuck Klein Hans and Julia Lesage, editors, 'Life and Work at El Crucero: Interviews with Nicaraguan Coffee Workers', *Radical America*, vol. 9, no. 5, 1985, pp. 48–9.

35 Maria Rogers, 'Filipina Peasants Fight Repression', *Sojourner*, March, 1988, p. 14.

36 'Banana Ban: Colombia Killings', *New Internationalist*, special issue on international debt, November 1988, p. 27. The plantations companies involved are Del Monte, United Brands and Standard Fruit (owned by Castle and Cook, which also owns Dole).

37 Judith Sutphen, ' "Low Intensity Conflict" in the Philippines,' *Sojourner*, November, 1988, p. 22. I have tried to develop a feminist approach to Low Intensity Conflict doctrine in the new edition of *Does Khaki Become You?*, London and Winchester, MA, Pandora Press, 1988. For more on Filipino feminist thinking about Low Intensity Conflict and agrarian reform, contact the Women's Resource and Research Center, Maryknoll College Foundation, Quezon City, Philippines.

38 Denise Stanley, 'Banana Workers End Walkout over Company-sponsored Union', *Guardian* (US), December 2, 1988; 'Del Monte: Fresh Fruit Sales Climbing', *Boston Globe*, June 26, 1988. On Brooke Bond's flower business in Kenya, see John Clark, *For Richer or Poorer*, Oxford, Oxfam, 1986.

39 I am grateful to Ximena Bunster for information on Chile's fruit industry; to Shari Geistfeld for information on Unilever's oil-palm operations in Zaîre; to Jennifer Schirmer and Mimi Stephens for information on Guatemalan military thinking about broccoli cultivation; Mimi Stephens, *The Impact of Militarized Development on Indigenous Culture in Guatemala and USAID 's Role in It*, master's thesis, International Development Program, Clark University, Worcester, MA, 1988. For more on Unilever, see *New Internationalist*, special issue on Unilever, issue no. 172, June, 1987; *Unilever's World*, a report by the Counter-Information Service, London, 1975. On Coca Cola's Belize plantations, see *Rainforest Action Network*, San Francisco, February, 1987 and May, 1987.

40 For an insightful analysis of Latin American market women, see Ximena Bunster and Elsa Chaney, *Sellers and Servants: Working Women in Lima, Peru*, South Hadley, MA, Bergin & Garvey, 1988.

41 'Women in Agriculture', special issue of *Women in Europe*, Women's Information Service, Commission of the European Community, Brussels, October, 1988. In 1988 there were an estimated 62,000 women running farms in the EEC, 8.2 per cent of the total. There were 566,000 women farmers working full-time on EEC farms; another 322,000 worked part-time on farms. Still, European women farmers lack training, tax benefits and pensions.

7 BLUE JEANS AND BANKERS

1 Quoted in James Lardner, 'Annals of Business – The Sweater Trade', Part II, *New Yorker Magazine*, January 18, 1988, p. 64.

2 Editorial, *New York Times*, June 19, 1988.

3 Lardner, op. cit., p. 64.

4 Ibid.

5 Alexander Reid, 'In Hard Times, Garment Union Places Hopes in New Leadership', *New York Times*, June 3, 1986.

6 Swasti Mitter, *Common Fate, Common Bond*, London, Pluto Press, Winchester, MA, Unwin Hyman, 1986, p. 127.

7 An Asian British woman interviewed by Swasti Mitter, ibid., p. 130. Feminist studies of immigrant factory women in Britain include Sallie Westwood, *All the Live Long Day*, London, Pluto Press, 1984; Barbro Hoel, 'Company Clothing Sweatshops, Asian Female Labor and Collective Organization', in Jackie West, editor, *Women, Work and the Labor Market*, London and Boston, Routledge & Kegan Paul, 1982; Sally Westwood and Parminder Bhachu, editors, *Enterprising Women: Ethnicity, Economy and Gender*, London and New York, Routledge, 1988; Annie Phizacklea, *One Way Ticket: Migration and Female Labor*, New York and London, Routledge & Kegan Paul, 1983. Descriptions of the home-work system are included in Wendy Chapkis and Cynthia Enloe, *Of Common Cloth: Women in the Global Textile Industry*, Amsterdam and Washington, Transnational Institute, 1983; Liz Bisset and Ursula Hews, *Sweated Labour: Homeworking in Britain Today*, London, Low Pay Unit, 1984; Amy Gamerman, 'Homeworkers: Bottom of the Rag Trade Heap', *New Statesman*, May 3, 1988, pp. 18–19. Home workers in Mexico are described subtly in Lourdes Beneria and Martha Roldan, *The Crossroads of Class and Gender: Industrial Homework, Subcontracting and Household Dynamics in Mexico City*, Chicago and London, University

of Chicago Press, 1987. See also Alison Lever, 'Capital, Gender and Skill: Women Homeworkers in Rural Spain', *Feminist Review*, no. 30, Autumn, 1988, pp. 3–24; Laura C. Johnson, *The Seam Allowance: Industrial Home Sewing in Canada*, Toronto, Women's Press, 1982; Joan McGrath, 'Home is Where the Work Is', *In These Times*, October 14, 1987, pp. 12–13.

8   I'm grateful to Sandra Suarez for providing insight into Puerto Rican textile politics.

9   In 1987, as the impact of the stringent new US immigration law began to be felt, Los Angeles companies lobbied the US Naturalization and Immigration Agency to allow them to import workers from China under special 'H2B' visas to make up for the illegal Latino workers they were losing under the new law: Celeste Wesson, 'All Things Considered', National Public Radio, December 27, 1987.

10   *Global Electronics*, a newsletter edited by Lenny Segal, has persistently monitored the gender and race hierarchies within the electronics industry in California's Silicon Valley. See, for instance, 'Race and Gender in High Tech', *Global Electronics*, March, 1988, p. 2. The newsletter is available from Pacific Studies Center, 222B View Street, Mountain View, CA 94041.

11   Andrea Lee, 'Profiles: Being Everywhere', *New Yorker Magazine*, November 10 1986, p. 53. I was first alerted to the 'Benetton model' by Swasti Mitter, op. cit.

12   Lee, op. cit, p. 68.

13   *New York Times*, August 1 1988.

14   The Irish government's promotion of flexibility and its dependence on women is outlined in Patricia O'Donovan, 'Low Pay and Women', *Council News*, Council for the Status of Women, Dublin, no. 6, 1987, p. 4. See also Jean Larson Pyle, *Women, the State and Development: Lessons for Sex Discrimination in the Republic of Ireland, 1961–1981*, Albany, State University of New York Press, 1989. For the impact of the 'Benetton model' on women in the European Community, see Diane Elson, 'Women's Employment and Multinationals in the EEC Textiles and Clothing Industry', typescript, Department of Economics, University of Manchester, Manchester, 1985.

15   Hank Gilman, 'More Apparel Makers Turn Abroad', *Wall Street Journal*, May 9, 1985.

16   Harvey D. Nadel, President of Capital Fashions Corporation, San Diego, quoted in ibid.

17   James Lardner, 'Annals of Business: The Sweater Trade', Part I, *New Yorker Magazine*, January 11, 1988; Lindsey Gruson, 'Against

Odds, Panama Economy Stays Afloat', *New York Times*, February 11, 1989.

18 I am indebted to Ann Seidman, an expert on foreign investment in South Africa, for this information: Clark University, Worcester, MA, April, 1988.

19 Murray Hiebert, 'Hanoi Courts Capitalist Investment', *Indochina Issues*, no. 67, July, 1986, pp. 3–4.

20 Anthony B. Van Fossen, 'Two Military Coups in Fiji', *Bulletin of Concerned Asian Scholars*, vol. 19, November 4, 1988, p. 29; *Far Eastern Economic Review*, March 3, 1988, p. 49.

21 Lynn Ashburner, 'Women Inside the Counting House: Women in Finance', in Angela Coyle and Jane Skinner, editors, *Women and Work*, London, Macmillan, and New York, New York University Press, 1988, pp. 130–51. Also Penny Fox, 'Sisters in the City', *Observer*, May 24, 1987. On women as American stockbrokers, see Nancy Nichols, 'Up Against the Wall Street', *Ms.*, November, 1988, pp. 66–9. For a provocative analysis of the relationships between technological change and the sexual division of labor, see Cynthia Cockburn, *Machinery of Dominance: Women, Men and Technical Know How*, London, Pluto Press, 1985, Boston, Northeastern University Press, 1988.

22 For a detailed account of patriarchy and women's lives in a nineteenth-century English textile mill, see Judy Lown, *Women and Industrialization in Nineteenth-Century England*, Cambridge, Polity Press, forthcoming. Workforce figures presented here also appear in briefer form in a book based on Judy Lown's research: Carol Adams, Paula Bartley, Judy Lown, Cathy Laxton, *Under Control: Life in a Nineteenth-Century Silk Factory*, London and New York, Cambridge University Press, 1983. For descriptions of Japanese and Russian gendered industrial revolutions, see Mikiso Hane, *Peasants, Rebels and Outcasts: The Underside of Modern Japan*, New York, Pantheon, 1982, pp. 172–205; Sharon Sievers, *Flowers in Salt: The Beginning of Feminist Consciousness in Modern Japan*, Stanford, Stanford University Press, 1983; Rose Glickman, *Russian Factory Women, Workplace and Society, 1880–1914*, Berkeley, University of California Press, 1984.

23 Maggie McAndrew and Jo Peer, *The New Soviet Woman: Model or Myth?* London, Change, International Reports on Women, 1981, p. 26. Women also comprised 99 per cent of Soviet typists and secretaries and 98 per cent of nurses.

24 Lown, op. cit.

25 Advertisement contributed by Joni Seager to Chapkis and Enloe, op. cit., p. 68.

26 Karen Offen, '"Powered by a Woman's Foot" – A Documentary Introduction to the Sexual Politics of the Sewing Machine in Nineteenth Century France,' *Women's Studies International Forum*, vol. 11, no. 2, 1988, p. 93.

27 Ibid.

28 Interview by the author with a Levis factory manager, Manila, March, 1980. See also *Daughters in Industry: Work Skills and Consciousness of Women Workers in Asia*, Women's Program, 1988, Asia and Pacific Development Centre, Periaran Duta, PO Box 12224, 50770 Kuala Lumpur, Malaysia.

29 For feminist critiques of this practice see Barbara Rogers, *The Domestication of Women: Discrimination in Developing Societies*, London, Kogan Page, 1980; Joni Seager and Ann Olson, *Women in the World: An International Atlas*, London, Pan Books, New York, Simon and Schuster, 1987.

30 From 'White Light', by Chris Llewellyn, part of her book of poems retelling the story of the fire at the Triangle Shirtwaste Company in New York City, March 25, 1911, in which 146 garment workers, most of them young Jewish, Irish and Italian women, died: Chris Llewellyn, *Fragments from the Fire*, London, Penguin, 1987, pp. 48–9. Attitudes of early twentieth-century American women garment workers toward marriage and unionization are described in Sarah Eisenstein, *Give Us Bread, But Give Us Roses*, London and Boston, Routledge & Kegan Paul, 1983.

31 The survey of women workers in the Sri Lankan Export Processing Zone was reported in *Women Workers in the Free Trade Zone of Sri Lanka: A Survey*, Voice of Women Publication Series, no. 1, 1983, p. 10, available from Voice of Women, 18/9 Chitra Lane, Colombo 5, Sri Lanka. The organizing experience is detailed in 'Experiences of Women Workers Organizing', *Asian Women Workers Newsletter*, vol. 7, nos. 3 and 4 December, 1988, pp. 1–2, published by the Committee for Asian Women, 57 Peking Road, 5/F Kowloon, Hong Kong. On Malaysian women's attitudes toward marriage and resistance to factory life, see Evelyn Hong, editor, *Malaysian Women: Problems and Issues*, Penang Consumers' Association of Penang, Penang, Malaysia, 1983; Aiwah Ong, *Spirits of Resistance and Capitalist Discipline: Factory Women in Malaysia*, Albany, State University of New York Press, 1987.

32 Seager and Olson, op. cit., map 28.

33 For instance, Tono Haruhi, 'Japan's Industrialization and Women Workers', in *Women's Journal: Industrial Women Workers in Asia*, vol. 4, September, 1985, coedited by ISIS International and Committee

for Asian Women, available from the Committee for Asian Women, 57 Peking Road, 5/F Kowloon, Hong Kong.

34 Susan Chira, 'Anyang Journal: Near Seoul, A Dream Turns to Ashes', *New York Times*, April 6, 1988.

35 Ibid. For more on South Korean women workers, see Bernard Stephens, 'Defiant Tiger', *New Statesman and Society*, September 11, 1988, p. 18; Jim Woodward, 'Korean Workers Consolidating Unions', *Labor Notes*, November, 1988, pp. 8–9.

36 This account was based on the following sources: talks by September 19th Garment Workers Union representatives Alicia Cervantes and Gloria Juandiego, Clark University, Worcester, MA, April 18, 1988; discussions by union representatives with a group of visiting American feminists at the union's headquarters, Mexico City, September 5, 1986; Marta Lamas, 'The Women Garment Workers' Movement: Notes for a Feminist Reflection', *Fem*, Mexico City, March, 1986 (translated by Elaine Burns); Rachel Kamel, 'September 19th Garment Workers Fight Government, Owners', *Listen Real Loud*, newsletter of the Women's Project, American Friends Service Committee, Philadelphia, vol. 9, no. 1, 1988; Rebecca Ratcliffe, 'Women United Across Borders', *Sojourner*, 1987; *Correspondencia*, 1987 and 1988 issues: newsletter of Mujer a Mujer, AP 24–553, Colonia Roma, 06701 Mexico DF, Mexico.

37 David Brooks, 'The Future: Who Will Manage It?', *NACLA: Report on the Americas*, special issue on Mexico, vol. 21, nos. 5 and 6, September–December, 1987, pp. 23–4. Two excellent studies of working women in the US–Mexican border factories, *maquiladoras*: Vicki L. Ruiz and Susan Tiano, editors, *Women on the US–Mexican Border: Responses to Change*, Boston and London, George Allen & Unwin, 1987; Patricia Fernandez-Kelly, *For We Are Sold, I and My People: Women and Industry on Mexico's Frontier*, Albany, State University of New York Press, 1983.

38 Other books dealing with Third World garment workers' organizing include: Committee for Asian Women, *Beyond Labor Issues: Women Workers in Asia*, Hong Kong, 1988; Dennis Shoesmith, editor, *Export Processing Zones in Five Countries, the Economic and Human Consequences*, Hong Kong, Asia Partnership for Human Development, 1986; *The Global Factory: An Organizing Guide for a New Economic Era*, Philadelphia, the Women's Project of the American Friends Service Committee, 1989; 'Feminizing Unions', special issue of *Labor Research Review*, Chicago, no. 11, Spring, 1988.

39 For a ground-breaking analysis of women and men in the rapidly changing electronics industry, see June Nash, 'Segmentation of the

Work Process in the International Division of Labor', in Steven Sunderson, editor, *The Americans in the New International Division of Labor*, New York, Holmes & Meier, 1985; Karen Hossfield, *Divisions of Labor, Divisions of Lives: Immigrant Women Workers in Silicon Valley*, dissertation, Department of Sociology, University of California, Santa Cruz, CA, June 1988. A summary of Hossfield's findings appears in *Global Electronics*, no. 84, July, 1988, pp. 1–2; *Connecta: International Information Bulletin for Philips Workers*, published by SOBE, Demer 38, 5611 AS Eindhoven, The Netherlands. For information on the internationalization of clerical work, see Ann Posthuma, 'The Automated Office: A New Global Assembly Line', *Listen Real Loud*, newsletter of the Women's Project, American Friends Service Committee, Philadelphia, vol. 5, 1984, pp. A4–A5; Steve Lohr, 'The Growth of the Global Office', *New York Times*, October 18, 1988.

8 'JUST LIKE ONE OF THE FAMILY': DOMESTIC SERV- ANTS IN WORLD POLITICS

1 Advertisement, *International Herald Tribune*, December 10–11, 1988.
2 For histories of nineteenth- and early twentieth-century domestic workers, see Mary Lennon, Marie McAdam and Jane O'Brien, *Across the Water: Irish Women's Lives in Britain*, London, Virago, 1987; Hasia R. Diner, *Erin's Daughters in America*, Baltimore and London, Johns Hopkins University Press, 1983; Joy Rudd, 'Invisible Exports: The Emigration of Irish Women This Century', *Women's Studies International Forum*, special issue on 'Feminism in Ireland', edited by Ailbhe Smyth, vol. 11, no. 4, 1988; Evelyn Nakano Glenn, *Issei, Nisei, Warbride: Three Generations of Japanese American Women in Domestic Service*, Philadelphia, PA, Temple University Press, 1986; Trudier Harris, *From Mammies to Militants: Domestics in Black American Literature*, Philadelphia, PA, Temple University Press, 1982; Judith Rollins, *Between Women: Domestics and Their Employers*, Philadelphia, PA, Temple University Press, 1985; David M. Katzman, *Seven Days a Week: Women and Domestic Service in Industrializing America*, Urbana and London, University of Illinois Press, 1981; Joni Seager, *'Father's Chair': Domestic Reform and Housing Change in the Progressive Era*, Ph.D. dissertation, School of Geography, Clark University, Worcester, MA, 1988; Donna L. van Raaphorst, *Union Maids Not Wanted: Organizing Domestic Workers, 1870–1940*, Westport, CT, Greenwood Press, 1988.

3   See for instance, Ursula Huws, *Working Women: A Woman's Guide to Rights at Work*, London, Channel 4 Television, 1988, p. 20; 'The Mommy Track', *Businessweek*, March 20, 1989; editorial, *New York Times*, March 11, 1989.

4   John Rentoul, ' "It's So Difficult to Get Servants These Days" ' *New Statesman*, November 7, 1986, p. 20; Sara Rimer, 'Childcare at Home: Two Women, Complex Roles', *New York Times*, December 26, 1988.

5   Quoted by Maria Susan Rye, in 'On Assisted Emigration', reprinted in Candida Ann Lacey, editor, *Barbara Leigh Smith Bodichon and the Langham Place Group*, Women's Source Library, London and New York, Routledge & Kegan Paul, 1987, pp. 337–8.

6   I am indebted to British researcher Sally Davis for sharing her findings on the FMCES with me: correspondence, March 17, 1985.

7   See for instance, Claudia Knapman, *White Women in Fiji, 1835–1850: Ruin of the Empire?*, Sydney, London and Winchester, MA, Unwin Hyman, 1989 Suzanne Gordon, *A Talent for Tomorrow: Life Stories of South African Servants*, Bramfontein, South Africa, 1985; Beata Lipman, *We Make Freedom: Women in South Africa*, London and Winchester, MA, Pandora Press, 1984; Jacklyn Cock, *Maids and Madams*, London, The Women's Press, 1989.

8   Isa Craig, 'Emigration as a Preventative Agency', reprinted in Lacey, op. cit., p. 297. For information on Canadian recruitment of British and Finnish women as domestic servants, see Varpu Lindstrom–Best, ' "I Won't Be a Slave!" Finnish Domestics in Canada', in Jean Burnet, *Looking into My Sister's Eyes*, Toronto, Multicultural Historical Society of Ontario, 1986, pp. 31–53.

9   For more on British and French emigration to Canada, see Susan Jackel, editor, *A Flannel Shirt and Liberty: British Emigrant Gentlewomen in the Canadian West, 1880–1914*, Vancouver, University of British Columbia Press, 1983; The Clio Collective, *Quebec Women: A History*, Toronto, Women's Press, 1987.

10 Correspondence with Sally Davis, March 17, 1988.

11 'Jersey Nannies Organize for Status and Friendship', *New York Times*, October 30, 1988.

12 Rentoul, op. cit.

13 A. Lynn Bolles, 'IMF Destabilization: The Impact on Working Class Jamaican Women', *Transafrica Forum*, vol. 2, no. 1, Summer, 1983, pp. 63–76; Gita Sen and Caren Grown, *Development Crises and Alternative Visions: Third World Women's Perspectives*, New York, Monthly Review Press, pp. 59–66; *Women's World*, published by

ISIS, special issue on the 'Debt Crisis', no. 17, March, 1988; Maria de los Angeles Crummett, 'Women in Crisis: Paying the Costs of "Adjustment" in Rural Mexico', typescript, Department of Economics, Barnard College, Columbia University, NY, 1988; conversations with Peggy Antrobus, Women and Development Program, University of the West Indies, Barbados, in Cambridge, MA, spring, 1987. Peggy Antrobus is developing a detailed analysis of the gendered implications of the global economic crisis.

14 Figures supplied by the International Monetary Fund, in 'Asian Migrant Workers', *The Economist*, September 10, 1988, p. 24.

15 'Asian Migrant Workers', op. cit. Arati Rao, an Indian feminist scholar, also describes how the strains experienced by women of Kerala whose husbands have left to work abroad sometimes are so acute as to produce mental breakdown: conversation, Wellesley College, Wellesley, MA, February 23, 1989.

16 This account is drawn from the interview-based research in Turin, Italy of South African scholar Elaine Salo: *Obscure Lives: Filipino Women in an Italian City*, Master's Thesis, International Development Program, Clark University, Worcester, MA, 1986.

17 Clyde Haberman, 'Africans Find Italy's Doors Swinging Shut', *New York Times*, December 14, 1988.

18 Walden Bello, 'Lucky Plaza, Singapore', *Monitor*, Philippine Resource Center, Berkeley, CA, no. 4, February 1989, pp. 2–4; Seth Mydens, 'Manila Frets Over Export of Its Women', *New York Times*, March 12, 1988; James Clad, 'A Domestic Problem', *Far Eastern Economic Review*, March 17, 1988, pp. 18–19; lecture by Sr. Soledad Perpinan, Conference on Women and Military Systems, Helsinki, January 1987.

19 'Ban on the Employment of Filipino Women as Domestic Workers Abroad', *Migration Today*, no. 40, 1988, p. 17; *Monitor*, Philippines Resource Center, no. 4, February, 1989, p. 2.

20 This quote and material surrounding it is drawn from Makeda Silvera, *Silenced*, Toronto, Williams-Wallace Publishers, 1983; the quote appears on p. 100.

21 Ibid., p. 107.

22 Ibid.

23 Celia Mather, 'Good Enough to Stay', *International Labor Reports*, no. 17, September–October, 1986, p. 17. See also Silvera, op., cit., for a list of groups active in lobbying for Canadian domestic workers' rights. Also Pat Bradshaw-Campbell and Rena Cohen, 'Feminists: Explorers or Exploiters?' *Women and Environments*, Toronto, Fall 1988, pp. 8–10.

24 Elyse Dodgson, *Motherland: West Indian Women to Britain in the 1950s*, London, Heinemann Educational Books, 1974, p. 8.

25 Women, Immigration and Nationality Group (WING), *Worlds Apart: Women Under Immigration and Nationality Law*, London, Pluto Press, 1985, pp. 12–14. According to Amrit Wilson, a combination of social racism and institutional racism towards Asians changed the pattern of immigration to Britain: in the 1950s Asian immigrants were mostly men; in the following two decades increasingly male *and* female Asians came to Britain: Amrit Wilson, *Finding a Voice: Asian Women in Britain*, London, Virago, 1984. Other sources on women and immigration include: Rita James Simon and Caroline B. Brettel, editors, *International Migration: The Female Experience*, Totowa, NJ, Rowman and Allenheld, 1986; *International Migration Review*, special issue on 'Women in Migration', vol. 18, Winter, 1984; Annie Phizacklea, *One Way Ticket: Migration and Female Labor*, London and New York, Routledge & Kegan Paul, 1983; Jean Guyot, et al., *Migrant Women Speak*, London, Search Press, 1978; Nancy Foner, *New Immigrants in New York*, New York, Columbia University Press, 1987.

26 WING, op. cit., pp. 137–9; Yasmin Alibhai, 'For Better or for Worse', *New Statesman and Society*, January 6, 1989, pp. 22–3. For a feminist analysis of the 1988 US Immigration Reform Act, see Annette Fuentes, 'Immigration "Reform;" Heaviest Burdens on Women', *Listen Real Loud*, American Friends Service Committee, 1988.

27 Padmini Palliyaguruge, 'Sri Lanka House Maids and Free Trade Zone Workers', in *Migrant Women Claim Their Rights: Nairobi and After*, Geneva, World Council of Churches, Dossier no. 15, July, 1986, pp. 21–4.

28 Centre for Society and Religion, 'Alone in a Strange Land', *Asian Migrant*, vol.1, no. 1, January–February, 1988, p. 16. *Asian Migrant* is published by the Catholic Scalabrini Centrum, Quezon City, Philippines. See also, Asoka Bandarage, 'Women and Capitalist Development in Sri Lanka, 1977–1987', *Bulletin of Concerned Asian Scholars*, vol. 20, no. 2, 1988, pp. 69–71.

29 Palliyaguruge, op. cit.

30 Ibid. Also, Prema Embuldeniya, 'Their Suffering is Beyond Human Endurance: From the Report of the Committee on Migrant Workers, Sri Lanka', *Migration Today*, no. 40, 1988, pp. 12–13.

31 Linda Basch and Gail Lerner, Introduction to *Migrant Women Claim Their Rights: Nairobi and After*, op. cit. p., 11.

32 Ibid. For more on the relationships between women working as maids and their middle-class Latin American employers, see Ximena

Bunster and Elsa Chaney, *Sellers and Servants: Working Women in Lima, Peru*, South Hadley, MA, Bergin Publishers, 1988; Elsa Chaney and Marcey Garcia Castro, editors, *Muchachas No More: Household Workers in Latin America and the Caribbean*, Philadelphia, Temple University Press, 1989. A novel that graphically describes a West Indian woman's impressions of her US domestic employers is Paula Fox, *A Servant's Tale*, London and New York, Penguin, 1984.

33 On the return of maids to Chinese cities as unemployment has increased in the wake of the government's modernization policies, see Elizabeth Croll, 'Grannies, Maids and Housekeepers', *China Now*, no. 118, 1986; pp. 21–3.

INDEX

AIDS, 37–9, 84–92, 140
Ad Hoc Group on Equal Rights for Women
   in the United Nations, 121–2
advertising, 1–2, 32–3, 127–30, 149, 198
Afghanistan, 56–7, 82
Africa, 23–5, 123, 127, 143; see also specific
   countries
African-Americans, 26, 61, 66–71, 177–99;
   see also Black women
agribusiness, 2, 62, 133, 147–9, 197; see also
   bananas, plantations, farmers
airlines, 33; see also flight attendants
Akeley, Delia, 24–5
Alaska, 25
alcoholism, 111
Algeria, 18, 42–6, 63, 193
Alloula, Malek, 42–4
American Museum of Natural History, 24–5
Anglum, Jessie, 84–5
Angola, 66
Anthony, Susan B., 47
anti–Semitism, 125
Antrobus, Peggy, xii
Aquino, Corazon, 39, 85, 187–9; see also
   Philippines
Argentina, 121
Armenia, 63
Asian–American women, 154, 173, 178
Asian British women: see Black women
Association of American Foreign Service
   Women, 105–9
Australia, 39, 157, 177, 181–3

Baden-Powell, Robert, 49–51
Bahamas, 31
Baker, James, 119
banana industry, 2, 16, 31, 124–50,
   197–8; see also plantations
'banana republics', 133–6
Bangladesh, 157
bankers, 12, 14, 55, 148, 150, 156–60, 170,
   184; see also international debt
Barbados, 166
beauty, 8

Belau, 85, 92
Belize, 2, 66, 84, 91, 148
Bello, Judith Hippler, 120
Benetton, 153–6, 174
Black women: African-American women,
   68–9; 117–19, 154, 178; Afro-Caribbean
   women in Britain, 153, 190–1; Asian
   women in Britain, 153–4, 198; see also
   African-Americans; Asian-American
   women; Latinas; Racism
Boer War, 49
Boggs, Paula, 118
Boy Scouts, 49–51
Brazil, 124–6, 132, 168, 194, 200
Britain: colonialism, 14, 23–4, 45, 48–54,
   82–4, 94–5, 124, 160, 181–3; diplomatic
   wives, 96–105; domestic
   servants in, 177–9, 190–2; food imports,
   132, 142; mail-order brides in, 39–40,
   191; military, 2, 13, 21–2, 49, 66, 73;
   nannies in; 177–81; racism in 154, 190–2;
   tourism, 19–21, 28–30, 35; US military
   in, 65–81; women diplomats, 114–15,
   120; world's fairs in, 26–8; see also Black
   women, bankers
British Museum, 23
broccoli, 147–9
Brodsky, Dina, 24
Brooke Bond, 148
bureaucracy, 8–9, 17, 28, 32, 37–8, 101,
   104, 186–7
Butler, Josephine, 82–4

Cameroon, 148
Campaign Against Military Prostitution
   (CAMP), 91–2
Canada, 14, 31, 45–6, 56, 66, 73–4, 78, 81,
   84, 95, 153–4, 156, 174, 177, 181–2,
   189–90; Native Canadian women, 14, 81,
   94–5, 182
Cantonment Acts, 82–4
capitalism, 17, 137; see also bankers, export
   processing zones, garment industry,
   international debt, plantations

239